INDIAN PALEOGRAPHY

INDIAN PALEOGRAPHY

G. BUHLER

GYAN

Published by

GYAN

Gyan Publishing House
5, Ansari Road
Daryaganj, New Delhi-110002
Phone: 011-47034999, 9811692060
E-mail: books@gyanbooks.com

Distribution Network
gyanbooks.com
India, USA, Canada, UK, Australia

ISBN: 978-93-7097-713-6 (HB)

First Published, 1889

2nd Impression 2025

Printed at: Gyan Press, Delhi.

INDIAN PALEOGRAPHY
Author: G. BUHLER

School of Archaeology.

INDIAN PALEOGRAPHY

G. BÜHLER

Published by
Indian Studies : Past & Present
3, Sambhunath Pundit Street, Calcutta 20

Printed at **Mudrani** by Kartik Chandra Panda, 71 Kailas Bose Street, Calcutta 6 and Published by Ramakrishna Maitra from 3 Shambhunath Pundit Street, Calcutta 20.

INDIAN PALEOGRAPHY

EDITOR'S NOTE

With all the later researches in the subject, Bühler's **Indian Paleography** retains and will always retain the value of a classic. It has, however, been a misfortune of the students and scholars that the English version of the text, which Bühler himself took such care to prepare, has not so far been available in book-form along with the portfolio of the plates and transliteration tables, so much indispensable for the text. The only occasion on which this English version had previously been printed was in the form of an **Appendix** to **Indian Antiquary**, 1904. But it was only the text without the plates and tables. Besides, the copies of the **Indian Antiquary** have become quite rare.

We have recently started a quarterly journal, called **Indian Studies : Past & Present**, with the primary object of reprinting those monumental contributions to Indian studies the copies of which have become extremely rare. We considered it fit to reprint Bühler's **Indian Paleography** in the first issue of our journal. Unfortunately, however, the plates and the tables could not be reproduced there because of the obvious financial considerations : the selling price of the journal had to be kept within the purchasing power of our students. But we went on working on the production of the portfolio and we have at last succeeded in bringing out the book in its proper book-form. And we have the satisfaction of publishing for the first time the complete English version of Bühler's **Indian Paleography** along with the reproduction of the plates and tables. A limited number of extra-copies of the plates and tables are also printed so that the purchasers of the journal can buy these separately.

We are grateful to the authorities of the Asiatic Society, Bengal, who provided us with a copy of the text and lent us the original portfolio of the German edition for the purpose of reproducing the plates and tables.

Sri Haridas Sinharay and Srimati Alaka Chattopadhyaya have helped us labouriously in the matter of proof-reading. We are also grateful to Sri S. Chaudhury, librarian of the Asiatic Society, for helping us in various ways.

Calcutta
19. 11. 59.

Debiprasad Chattopadhyaya
for **Indian Studies : Past & Present**

CONTENTS

V—THE SOUTHERN ALPHABETS—80

VI—NUMERAL NOTATION—96

VII—THE EXTERNAL ARRANGEMENT OF INSCRIPTIONS AND MANUSCRIPTS—107

Georg Bühler

1837—1898

GEORG BÜHLER,—1837-98.

F. MAX-MÜLLER

It is not often that the death of a scholar startles and grieves his fellow-workers as the death of my old friend, Dr. Bühler, has startled and grieved us all, whether in Germany, England, France, or India. Sanskrit scholarship has indeed been unfortunate: it has often lost young and most promising scholars in the very midst of their career; and though Dr. Bühler was sixty-one years of age when he died, he was still so young and vigorous in body and mind that he made us forget his age, holding his place valiantly among the πρόμαχοι of the small army of genuine Indian students, and confidently looking forward to many victories and conquests that were still in store for him. By many of us he was considered almost indispensable for the successful progress of Sanskrit scholarship—but who is indispensable in this world?—and great hopes were centred on him as likely to spread new light on some of the darkest corners in the history of Sanskrit literature.

On the 8th of April last, while enjoying alone in a small boat a beautiful evening on the Lake of Constance, he seems to have lost an oar, and in trying to recover it, to have overbalanced himself. As we think of the cold waves closing over our dear friend, we feel stunned and speechless before so great and cruel a calamity. It seems to disturb the regular and harmonious working of the world in which we live, and which each man arranges for himself and interprets in his own way. It makes us feel the littleness and uncertainty of all our earthly plans, however important and safe they may seem in our own eyes. He who for so many years was the very life of Sanskrit scholarship, who helped us, guided us, corrected us in our different researches, is gone; and yet we must go on as well as we can, and try to honour his memory in the best way in which it may be honoured—not by idle tears, but by honest work.

Non hoc praecipuum amicorum munus est, prosequi defunctum ignavo questu, sed quae voluerit meminisse, quae mandaverit exsequi.

A scholar's life is best written in his own books; and though I have promised to write a biographical notice for the *Journal of the Royal Asiatic Society*, in which he took so warm and active an interest, I have to confess that of the personal circumstances of my old friend, Dr. Bühler, I have but little to say. What I know of him are his books and pamphlets as they came out in rapid succession, and were always sent to me by their author. Our long and never-interrupted friendship was chiefly literary, and for many years had to be carried on by correspondence only. He was a man who, when once one knew him, was always the same. He had his heart in the right place, and there was no mistaking his words. He never spoke differently to different people, for, like a brave and honest man, he had the courage of his opinions. He thought what he said, he never thought what he ought to say. He belonged to no clique, he did not even try to found what is called a school. He had many pupils, followers, and admirers, but they knew but too well that though he praised them and helped them on whenever he could, he detested nothing more than to be praised by his pupils in return. It was another charming feature of his character that he never forgot any kindness, however small, which one had rendered him. He was kṛtajña in the real sense of the word. I had been able, at the very beginning of his career, to render him a small service by obtaining for him an appointment in India. He never forgot it, and whenever there was an opportunity he proved his sincere attachment to me by ever so many small, but not therefore less valuable, acts of kindness. We always exchanged our books and our views on every subject that occupied our interest in Sanskrit scholarship, and though we sometimes differed, we always kept in touch. We agreed thoroughly on one point—that it did not matter who was right, but only what was right. Most of the work that had to be done by Sanskrit scholars in the past, and will have to be done for some time to come, is necessarily pioneer work, and pioneers must hold together even though they are separated at times while reconnoitring in different directions. Bühler could hold his own with great pertinacity; but he never forgot that in the progress of knowledge the left foot is as essential as the right. No one, however, was more willing to confess a mistake than he was when he saw that he had been in the wrong. He was, in fact, one of the few scholars with whom it was a real pleasure to differ, because he was always straightforward, and because there was nothing mean or selfish in him, whether he defended the Pūrva-pakṣa, the Uttara-pakṣa, or the Siddhānta.

Of the circumstances of his life, all I know is that he was the son of a clergyman, that he was born at Borstel, 19th July, 1837, near Nienburg in the then kingdom of Hanover, that he frequented the public school at Hanover, and in 1855 went to the University of Göttingen. The professors who chiefly taught and influenced him there were Sauppe, E. Curtius, Ewald, and Benfey. For the last he felt a well-deserved and almost enthusiastic admiration. He was no doubt Benfey's greatest pupil, and we can best understand his own work if we remember in what school he was brought up. After taking his degree in 1858 he went to Paris, London, and Oxford, in order to copy and collate Sanskrit and chiefly Vedic MSS. It was in London and Oxford that our acquaintance, and very soon our friendship, began. I quickly recognised in him the worthy pupil of Benfey. He had learnt how to distinguish between what was truly important in Sanskrit literature and what was not, and from an early time had fixed his attention chiefly on its historical aspects. It was the fashion for a time to imagine that if one had learnt Sanskrit grammar, and was able to construe a few texts that had been published and translated before, one was a Sanskrit scholar. Bühler looked upon this kind of scholarship as good enough for the vulgus profanum, but no one was a real scholar in his eyes who could not stand on his own feet, and fight his own way through new texts and commentaries, who could not publish what had not been published before, who could not translate what had not been translated before. Mistakes were, of course, unavoidable in this kind of pioneering work, or what is called original research, but such mistakes are no disgrace to a scholar, but rather an honour. Where should we be but for the mistakes of Bopp and Burnouf, of Champollion and Talbot?

Though Bühler had learnt from Benfy the importance of Vedic studies as the true foundation of Sanskrit scholarship, and had devoted much time to this branch of learning, he did not publish much of the results of his own Vedic researches. His paper on Parjanya, however, published in 1862 in Benfey's *Orient und Occident*, vol. I, p. 214, showed that he could not only decipher the old Vedic texts, but that he had thoroughly mastered the principles of Comparative Mythology, a new science which owed its very existence to the discovery of the Vedic Hymns, and was not very popular at the time with those who disliked the trouble of studying a new language. He wished to prove what Grimm had suspected, that Parjanya, Lith.—Perkunas, Celt—Perkons, Slav—Perun, was one of the deities worshipped by the ancestors of the whole Aryan race, and in spite of the usual frays and bickerings, the main point of his argument has never been shaken. I saw much of him at that time, we often worked together, and the index to my *History of Ancient Sanskrit Literature* was chiefly his work. The most important lesson which he had learnt from Benfey showed itself in the quickness with which he always seized on whatever was really important in the history of the literature of India. He did not write simply in order to show what he could do, but always in order to forward our knowledge of ancient India. This explains why, like Benfey's books, Bühler's own publications, even his smallest essays, are as useful today as they were when first published. Benfey's edition of the Indian fables of the Pañcatantra produced a real revolution at the time of its publications. It opened our eyes to a fact hardly suspected before, how important a part in Sanskrit literature had been acted by Buddhist writers. We learnt in fact that the distinction between the works of Brahmanic and Buddhist authors had been far too sharply drawn, and that in their literary pursuits their relation had been for a long time that of friendly rivalry rather than of hostile opposition. Benfey showed that these Sanskrit fables of India had come to us through Buddhist hands, and had travelled from India step by step, station by station, through Pahlavi, Persian, Arabic, Hebrew, Latin, and the modern languages of Europe, till they supplied even Lafontaine with some of his most charming Fabliaux. Benfey was in many respects the true successor of Lassen in calling the attention of Sanskrit scholars to what are called in German the Realia of Sanskrit scholarship. He was bold enough to publish the text and translation of the Sāmaveda, and the glossary appended to this edition marked the first determined advance into the dark regions of Vedic thought. Though some of his interpretations may now be antiquated he did as much as was possible at the time, and nothing is more painful than to see scholars of a later generation speak slightingly of a man who was a giant before they were born. Benfey's various Sanskrit grammars, founded as they are on the great classical grammar of Pāṇini, hold their own to the present day, and are indispensable to every careful student of Pāṇini, while his *History of Sanskrit Philology* is a real masterpiece, and remains still the only work in which that important chapter of modern scholarship can be safely studied.

Bühler was imbued with the same spirit that had guided Benfey, and everyone of his early contributions to Benfey's *Orient und Occident* touched upon some really important question, even though he may not always have settled it. In his article on θεός, for instance ("O. u. O," vol. I, p. 508), which was evidently written under the influence of Curtius' recent warning that θεός could not be equated with *deus* and Skt. *deva* without admitting a phonetic anomaly, he suggested that θεός as well as the Old Norse *diar*, 'gods', might be derived from a root *dhī*, 'to think, to be wise.' Often as we discussed their etymology together—and it was more than a mere etymology, because on it depended the question whether the oldest Aryan name of the gods in general was derived from the bright powers of nature or from the abstract idea of divine wisdom—he could never persuade me that these two branches of the Aryan race, the Greek and the Scandinavian, should have derived the general name for their gods from a root different from that which the other branches had used, viz., *div*, 'to be brilliant', and from which they had formed the most important cluster of mythological names, such as Zeus, Jovis, Diespiter, Dia, Diana, etc. I preferred to admit a phonetic rather than a mythological anomaly. If I could not persuade him he could not persuade me, et adhuc sub judice lis est !

Several more etymologies from his pen followed in the same Journal, all connected with some points of general interest, all ingenious, even if not always convincing. In all these discussions he showed himself free from all prejudices, and much as he admired his teacher, professor Benfey, he freely expressed his divergence from him when necessary, though always in that respectful tone which a *śiṣya* would have observed in ancient India when differing from his *guru*.

While he was in Oxford, he frequently expressed to me his great wish to get an appointment in India. I wrote at his desire to the late Mr. Howard, who was then Director of Public Instruction in Bombay, and to my great joy got the promise of an appointment for Bühler. But, unfortunately, when he arrived at Bombay, there was no vacancy, Mr. Howard was absent, and for a time Bühler's position was extremely painful. But he was not to be disheartened. He soon made the acquaintance of another friend of mine at Bombay, Sir Alexander Grant, and obtained through him the very position for which he had been longing. In 1865 he began his lectures at the Elphinstone College, and proved himself most successful as a lecturer and a teacher. His power of work was great, even in the enervating climate of India, and there always is work to do in India for people who are willing to do work. He soon made the acquaintance of influential men, and he was chosen by Mr. (now Sir) Raymond West to co-operate with him in producing their famous *Digest of Hindu Laws*. He supplied the Sanskrit, Sir Raymond West the legal materials, and the work, first published in 1867, is still considered the highest authority on the subjects of the Hindu Laws of Inheritance and Partition. But Bühler's interest went deeper. He agreed with me that the matrical Law-books of Ancient India were preceded by legal Sūtras belonging to what I called the Sūtra-period. These Sūtras may really be ascribed to the end of the Vedic period, and in their earliest form may have been anterior to the Indo-Scythian conquest of the country, though the fixing of real dates at that period is well-nigh an impossibility. When at a much later time I conferred with him on the plan of publishing series of translations of the *Sacred Books of the East*, he was ready and prepared to undertake the translation of these Sūtras, so far as they had been preserved in in MSS. Some of these MSS., the importance of which I had pointed out as early as 1859 in my *History of Ancient Sanskrit Literature*, I handed over to him; others he had collected himself while in India. The two volumes in which his translation of the legal

Sūtras of Āpastamba, Gautama, Vasiṣṭha, and Baudhāyana are contained, have been amongst the most popular of the series, and I hope I shall be able to publish a new edition of them with notes prepared by him for that purpose. In 1886 followed his translation of the Laws of Manu, which, if he had followed the example of others, he might well have called his own, but which he gave as founded on that of Sir William Jones, carefully revised and corrected with the help of seven native commentaries. These were substantial works, sufficient to establish the reputation of any scholar, but with him they were by-work only, undertaken in order to oblige a friend and fellow-worker. These translations kept us in frequent correspondence, in which more than one important question came to be discussed. One of them was the question of what caused the gap between the Vedic period, of which these Sūtras may be considered as the latest outcome, and the period of that ornate metrical literature which, in my lectures on India delivered at Cambridge in 1884, I had ventured to treat as the period of the Renaissance of Sanskrit literature, subsequent to the invasion and occupation of India by Indo-Scythian or Turanian tribes.

It was necessary to prove this once for all, for there were scholars who went on claiming for the author of the Laws of Manu, nay, for Kālidāsa and his contemporaries, a date before the beginning of our era. What I wanted to prove was, that nothing of what we actually possessed of that ornate (alaṃkāra) metrical literature, nor anything written in the continuous śloka, could possibly be assigned to a time previous to the Indo-Scythian invasion. The chronological limits which I suggested for this interregnum were from 100 B C. to 300 A.D These limits may seem too narrow on either side to some scholars, but I believe I am not overstating my case if I say that at present it is generally admitted that what we call the Laws of Manu are subsequent tot he Sāmayā-Kārika or Dharma-sūtra, and that Kālidāsa's poetical activity belong to the sixth, nay, if Professor Kielhorn is right, even to the end of the fifth century A. D., and that all other Sanskrit poems which we possess are still later. Bühler's brilliant discovery consisted in proving, not that any of the literary works which we possess could be referred to a pre-Gupta date, but that specimens of ornate poetry occurred again and again in pre-Gupta inscriptions, and, what is even more important, that the peculiar character of those monumental poems presupposed on the part of their poets, provincial or otherwise, an acquaintance, if not with the Alaṃkāra sūtras which we possess, at all events with some of their prominent rules. In this way the absence or non-preservation of all greater literary compositions that could be claimed for the period from B. C. 100 to 300 A. D. became even more strongly accentuated by Bühler's discoveries. It might be said, of course, that India is a large country, and that literature might have been absent in one part of the Indian Peninsula and yet flourishing in another; just as even in the small Peninsula of Greece, literary culture had its heyday at Athens while it was withering away in Lacedaemon. But literature, particularly poetry, can never be quite annihilated. Nor is this the question. The question is, why was it preserved, after the rise of the national Gupta dynasty, in the only ways in which at that time it could be preserved in India, either by memory or by the multiplication of copies, chiefly in Royal libraries under the patronage of Rājās, whether of Indian or alien origin—and why is there at present, as far as manuscripts are concerned, an almost complete literary blank from the end of the Vedic literature to the beginning of the fourth century A. D. ?

The important fact which is admitted by Bühler, as well as by myself, is this—that whatever literary compositions may have existed before 300 A. D., in poetry or even in prose, nothing remains of them at present, and that there must surely be a reason for it. Here it was Bühler who, in the *Transactions of the Vienna Academy*, 1890, came to my help, drawing our attention to the important fact that among certain recently published ancient inscriptions, eighteen of which are dateable, two only can with any probability be proved to be anterior to what I called the four blank centuries between 100 B.C. to 300 A.D. (See *India*, p. 353.) There occur verses which prove quite clearly that the ornate style of Sanskrit poetry was by no means unknown in earlier times. The as yet undeveloped germs of that ornate poetry may even go back much further, and may be traced in portions of the Brāhmaṇas and in some Buddhistic writings ; but their full development at the time of these Sanskrit inscriptions was clearly established for the first time by Bühler's valuable remarks. So far we were quite agreed, nor do I know of any arguments that have been advanced against Bühler's historical views. There may be difference of opinion as to the exact dates of the Sanskrit Girnār inscription of Rudradāman and the Prakṛt Nāsik inscription of Pulumāyi, but they contain sufficient indications that an ornate, though perhaps less elaborate style of poetry, not far removed from the epic style, prevailed in India during the second century A. D. All the evidence accessible on that point has been carefully collected by my friend, and reflects the greatest honour on his familiarity with the Sanskrit Alaṃkāra poetry. But the fact remains all the same that nothing was preserved of that poetry before 300 A. D. ; and that of what we possess of Sanskrit Kāvya literature, nothing can for the present be traced back much beyond 500 A. D. We must hope that the time may soon come when the original component parts of the ancient epic poetry, nay, even the philosophical Darśanas, may be traced back with certainty to times before the Indo-Scythian Invasion. It is well known that the Mahābhārata and the Purāṇas are mentioned by name during the Sūtra period, and we cannot be far wrong in supposing that something like what we posses now of these works may have existed then. Bühler was full of hope that it might be possible to fix some of the dates of these popular works at a much earlier time than is assigned to them by most scholars. I was delighted to see him boldly claim for the Veda also a greater antiquity than I had as yet ventured to suggest for it, and it seemed to me that our two theories could stand so well side by side that it was my hope that I should be able to bring out, with his co-operation, a new and much improved edition of my chapter on the Renaissance of Sanskrit Literature. I doubt whether I shall be able to do this now without his help. The solution of many of the historical and chronological questions also, which remain still unanswered, will no doubt be delayed by the sudden death of the scholar who took them most to heart, but it is not likely to be forgotten again among the problems which our younger Sanskrit scholars have to deal with, if they wish truly to honour the memory and follow in the footsteps of one of the greatest and most useful Sanskrit scholars of our days.

These chronological questions were, of course, intimately connected with the date of the Sanskrit alphabets and the introduction of writing into India, which produced a written, in place of the ancient purely mnemonic literature of the century. There, too, we had a common interest, and I gladly handed over to him, for his own purposes, a MS. sent to me from Japan that turned out to be the oldest Sanskrit MS. then known to exist, that of the Prajñāpāramitā-hṛdaya-sūtra. It had been preserved on two palm-leaves in the Monastery of Horiuzi, in Japan, since 609 A. D., and, of course, went back to a much earlier time, as the leaves seem to have travelled from India through China, before they reached Japan. Bühler sent me a long paper of paleographical remarks on this Horiuzi palm-leaf MS. which form a most valuable Appendix to my edition of it. Thus we remained always united by our work and I had the great satisfaction of being able to send him the copy of Aśvaghoṣa's Buddha-carita, which my Japanese pupils had copied for me at Paris, and which, whether Aśvaghoṣa's date is referred to the first or the fifth century A.D., when it was translated into Chinese, represents as yet the only complete specimen of that ornate scholastic work which, as he had proved from numerous inscriptions, must have existed previous to the Renaissance. Thus our common work went on, if not always on the same plan, at all events on the same ground. We never lost touch with each other, and were never brought nearer together than when for a time we differed on certain moot points.

I have here dwelt on the most important works only which are characteristic of the man, and which will for ever mark the place of Bühler in the history of Sanskrit scholarship. But there are many other important services which he rendered to us while in India. Not only was he always to help us in getting MSS. from India, but our knowledge of a large number of Sanskrit works, as yet unknown, was due to his Reports on expeditions undertaken by him for the Indian Government in search for MSS. This idea of cataloguing the literary treasures of India, first started by Mr. Whitley Stokes, has proved a great success, and no one was more successful in these researches than Bühler. And while he looked out everywhere for important MSS. his eyes were always open for ancient inscriptions also. Many of them he published and translated for the first time, and our oldest inscriptions, those of Aśoka, in the third century B.C., owe to him and M. Senart their first scholarlike treatment. This is not meant to detract in any way from the credit due to the first brilliant decipherers of these texts, such as Prinsep, Lassen, Burnouf, and others. Bühler was most anxious to trace the alphabets used in these inscriptions back to a higher antiquity than is generally assigned to them ; for the present, at least, we cannot well go beyond the fact that no dateable inscription has been found in India before the time of Aśoka. It is quite true that such an innovation as the introduction of alphabetic writing does not take place of a sudden, and tentative specimens of it from an earlier time may well be discovered yet, if these researches are carried on as he wished them to be carried on, in a truly systematic manner. In this field of research Bühler will be most missed, for though absent from India he had many friends there, particularly in the Government, who would gladly have listened to his suggestions. One may regret his departure from a country where his services were so valuable and so much appreciated. I have not dwelt at all in this place on the valuable services which he rendered as inspector of schools and examiner, but I may state that I received several times the thanks of the Governor of the Bombay Presidency, the late Sir Bartle Frere, for having sent out such excellent scholars as Bühler and others. Unfortunately his health made it imperative for him to return to his own country, but he was soon so much restored under a German sky that he seemed to begin a new life as Professor at Vienna. If he could not discover new MSS. there, he could digest the materials which he had collected, and he did so with unflagging industry. Nay, in addition to all his own work, he undertook to superintend and edit an Encyclopaedia of Indo-Aryan Philology which was to be a resume up to date of all that was known of the languages, dialects, grammars, dictionaries, and the ancient alphabets of India; which was to give an account of Indian literature, history, geography, ethnography, jurisprudence; and finally, to present a picture of Indian religion, mythology, philosophy, astronomy, mathematics, and music, so far as they are known at present. No one knows what an amount of clerical work and what a loss of time such a superintendence involves for a scholar who has his hands full of his own work, how much reading of manuscripts, how much letter-writing, how much protracted and often disagreeable discussion it entails. But Bühler, with rare self-denial, did not shrink from this drudgery, and his work will certainly prove extremely useful to all future Indo-Aryan students. One thing only one may regret—that the limits of each contribution are so narrow, and that several of the contributors had no time to give us much more of their own original work. But this is a defect inherent in all encyclopaedias or manuals, unless they are to grow into a forest of volumes like the Allgemeine Encyclopaedie der Wissenschaften und Kunste by Ersch, begun in 1831 and as yet far from being finished. Under Bühler's guidance we might have expected the completion of his Encylopaedia within a reasonable time, and I am glad to hear that his arrangements were so far advanced that other hands will now be easily able to finish it, and that it may remain like Lassen's Altertumskunde, 1847-1861, a lasting monument of the lifelong labours of one of the most learned, the most high-minded and large-hearted among the Oriental scholars whom it has been my good fortune to know in the course of my long life.

F. M. M.

Reprinted from the
Journal of the Royal Asiatic Society (London)
1898. 695-707.

INTRODUCTORY NOTE ON BÜHLER'S INDIAN PALEOGRAPHY

By

J. F. FLEET

Professor Bühler's *Indische Palaeographie*, consisting of 96 pages of letter-press, with a portfolio of 9 plates of alphabetical characters and numerals and 8 tables of explanatory transliteration of them, was published in 1896 as part II of Vol. I of Dr. Karl J. Trübner's "Grundriss der Indo-Arischen Philologie und Altertumskunde," or "Encyclopaedia of Indo-Aryan Research," which was planned and started by Professor Bühler himself, and was superintended by him up to the time of his death, in April, 1898.

There was always the intention of issuing the letter-press of the work in English also. The English version was made by Professor Bühler. And his manuscript of it was on its way to the Press, at the time of his death. Steps were taken towards having it printed and published under the direction of Professor Kielhorn, who succeeded to the editorial management of the Grundriss. At that time, however, owing partly to the great interruption of business in India caused by the plague, partly to the manner in which the manuscript was written, and partly to a natural difficulty in the way of doing what had been contemplated, namely, of issuing the English version in such a form as to resemble the German original exactly in type and in arrangement page by page, the preparation for publication could not be taken far, and eventually had to be abandoned.

Feeling, myself, the want of the English version, and knowing that there must be others placed in the same position, in 1902 I made some inquiries and proposals about it. The result, with the consent and help of Professor Kielhorn, was a generous public-spirited response by Dr. Trübner, who, after consultation with Mrs. Bühler, agreed to transfer the copyright of the English version on practically nominal terms, subject to certain conditions as to the method of publication. Dr. Trübner's terms and conditions were accepted in a similar spirit by Colonel Sir Richard Temple, the proprietor of the *Indian Antiquary*. And thus it came to me to take the work through the Press, and to arrange the issue of it in its present form as an Appendix to the *Indian Antiquary* Vol. XXXIII, 1904.

As far as the commencement of the second paragraph of §16, A, on page 33, the English version has been produced from an advanced proof of 1900, prepared in the circumstances indicated in paragraph 2 above, and revised by Professor Kielhorn. From that point onwards, it has been done from Professor Bühler's manuscript, written by himself. In order, however, to set the printers fairly at work, it was necessary, because of the very numerous and sometimes rather perplexing abbreviations to which Professor Bühler had had recourse, to furnish them with a fair copy. The copy was, of course, closely compared by me with the original manuscript. And it is hoped that no mistakes have been introduced, in interpreting any of the abbreviations in passages which are not in the German original.

A perusal of a very few pages of the English work, thus issued, will suffice to show that it is not altogether a literal rendering of the German original. It is, therefore, sent forth as an English version, not as an actual translation. At the same time, the English version does not in any way supersede the German original. In the first place, as the stones were not preserved, it has not been practicable to issue with the English version the plates and tables which form so important a part of the whole work ; however, there is available, for separate purchase, a limited number of copies of the plates and tables, printed off in excess of the number required for issue with the German original. In the second place, in writing his English version, Professor Bühler made here and there certain deviations, sometimes by insertion, sometimes by omission, from the German original. But these deviations, made chiefly in connection with the second edition, published in 1898, of his *Indian Studies* No. III on *The Origin of the Indian Brāhma Alphabet*, are in points of detail, and do not in any way amount to a revised edition of his *Indische Palaeographie*[1]. The German original is still the text-book, as much as is the English version. The latter is for the benefit of those, interested in any way whatsoever in their subject, who are not able to utilise the German text.

This work of Professor Bühler has brought to a climax, for the present, the paleographic line of Indian research. And it would be impossible to speak in too high terms of the manner in which he has handled the subject, and of the value of the results which he has placed before us. In the paleographic line, however, as also in the historical line, on which it is largely dependent, and, in fact, in every line of Indian research, we are steadily accumulating more facts and better materials, and making substantial progress, every year. I venture, therefore, to draw attention to a few details, which already might now be treated, or at least considered, from other points of view.

A notable point, regarding which I differ from the opinions of Professor Bühler as expressed in this work, is that of both the relative order and also the actual dates of the varieties of the Kharoṣṭhī alphabet, indicated on Page 25 under §10, (3) and (4), which are found in the epigraphic records and on the coins of—(following the order in which, in my opinion, they should properly be placed)—Kaniṣka, and Huviṣka, Śuḍasa-Śoḍāsa and Patika, and Gondophernēs. Kaniṣka certainly founded the Mālava-Vikrama era, commencing B. C. 58. And in that era there are certainly dated, in addition to records of the times of him and his direct successors, the dated records of the times of Śuḍasa-Śoḍāsa, Patika, and Gondophernēs, and of Vāsudēva, who was a contemporary of Gondophernēs[2].

A similar remark applies to the order and dates of the varieties of the Brāhma or Brāhmī alphabet, indicated on Page 32, under §15, (8), (9), from records of the times of Kaniṣka, Huviṣka, Śuḍasa-Śoḍāsa, and Vāsudēva.

As regards the nomenclature of those same varieties of the Kharoṣṭhī alphabet, it is now certain that it is erroneous to describe one of them, mentioned there and discussed on Page 27f., as a Śaka variety. Śuḍasa-Śoḍāsa and Patika were not Śakas or Sakas, if that should be the correct expression according to the original form of the name[3]. None of the Sakas, Śakas, ever played a leading historical part in Northern India.

In respect of the Eraṇ coin, mentioned first on Page 8, which presents a reversed Brāhmī legend running from right to left, we must not lose sight of the possibility that the explanation is to be found, as has been suggested by Professor Hultzsch in the *Indian Antiquary*, Vol. XXVI, Page 336, in a mistake of the engraver of the die, who, like the die-sinker in the case of a certain coin of Hoḷkar of the last century, may have forgotten that he ought to reverse the legend on the die itself. We have one instance of such remissness in ancient times in a coin of Rajula-Rājuvula, the reverse of which presents a monogram, formed of the Greek letters E and Y, facing in the wrong direction; See Professor Gardner's Catalogue of the Coins of the Greek and Scythic Kings of Bactria and India, Page 67, No. 5. And we have another in the legend on a bronze stamp for making seals, where the engraver omitted to reverse the syllable *śrī*; JRAS. 1901, 98. plate, No. 9.

On page 67, under §29, B, (2) there is a statement about strongly cursive Kanarese *kh*, which is calculated to be misleading, and on the strength of which some erroneous assertions have already been made[4].

In the plates and tables there are some selections that might have been avoided, and some incorrect details, which are due to two causes[5]: partly to the fact, the explanation of which has been indicated in some remarks made by me in the *Epigraphia Indica*, Vol. VI, Page 80, that, owing to the nature of the only available materials, the plates have sometimes been based upon reproductions of original records which are not actual facsimiles; partly to the fact, which we learn from the Concluding Remarks on page 102, that some of the details of the plates were not selected and filled in by Professor Bühler himself.

And in any revision of the work there would have to be added, in connection with § 20, D, on Page 44, a notice of the more recently discovered peculiar variety of the southern alphabet which is illustrated in the Mayidavolu plates of the Pallava king Śiva-Skandavarman and the Koṇḍamudi plates of Jayavarman, edited by Professor Hultzsch in the *Epigraphia Indica*, Vol. VI, Pages 84ff., 315ff.

It would, however, have been contrary to the spirit of the arrangement with Dr. Trübner to introduce any comments and additions of my own, either in the text or in footnotes. And I do not find it convenient or appropriate to present them here, beyond the extent of the indications given above. Anything of that kind must be left for other occasions.

My editorial functions in the issue of this English version of Professor Bühler's work have thus been confined to details of a formal kind: chiefly in the matter of giving more prominence to the titlings of the sections and the divisions of them; in transferring to a more convenient position, as separated footnotes at the bottom of the pages to which they belong, the notes which in the German original stand massed together at the end of each section[6]: and in marking, by figures in square brackets in thick type, the commencement of each page of the German original, as closely as has been found convenient. Following, however, an example set by Professor Bühler himself in his manuscript, I have gone somewhat further still in breaking up some of the very long paragraphs of the original. Following his lead in another direction also, I have endeavoured to present everywhere the correct spelling, as far as it can be ascertained, of all the place-names which occur in the work; but in conformity with his practice in this work, without discriminating between the long and the short forms of *e* and *o*. And I have corrected a few obvious mistakes; for instance, under 29, A, in line 18 on page 66, I have substituted "Bādāmi" for the "Aihole" (properly Aihoḷe) of the German original and of the manuscript translation.

In §29, Page 65ff., and anywhere else where the word may occur, I have taken the liberty of substituting the word "Kanarese" for the "Kāṇara" of the German original and of the manuscript translation; and similarly, on page 46, line 4, and page 51, lines 21, 27f., I have substituted "the Kanarese country" for the "Kāṇara" of the original and of the manuscript. The form "Kāṇara", with the lingual *ṇ*, is nothing but an imaginative advance upon the official figment "Kānara", with the dental *n*, for which, itself, there is no basis in the Kanarese language, nor any necessity. I had thought at first of using like, the late Rev. Dr. Kittel and some other writers, the original vernacular word "Kannaḍa"—the source of our conventional "Canarā, Kanara," which, however, do not mean the whole of the Kanarse country. And that word, which denotes both the country and its language and also their alphabetical characters, would have been appropriate enough. But I decided eventually on "Kanarese": partly because, though this term, also, is conventional, it is so well-established, familiar, and definitive; and partly because it was practically used, alongside of the word "Kāṇara" by Professor Bühler himself in the "Kanaresische" and "Altkanaresische" of the original German work (e.g. page 66 lines 4, 6) and in the "Canarese" and "Old Canarese" of corresponding passages in his English version.

Except, however, in such details as the above, and in the abolition of the inconvenient abbreviations of which mention has been made on Page 2 above, the English version is simply a reproduction of Professor Bühler's manuscript.

In bringing this somewhat intricate work to a successful issue, I have been greatly indebted to the zeal and ability of Mr. J. S. Foghill, the Head Reader of the Bombay Education Society's Press. But for the extreme care with which he disposed of the first rough proofs before any proof was sent out for revision by me, I should certainly not have been able to take the work through, as has actually been done, on only one proof and a revise of it.

Footnotes to Fleet's Introductory Note

1. A final paragraph on Page 96 of the German work mentions "some recent publications, amongst them Dr. Grierson's Examination of the Gayā alphabet of the stone-masons", which could not be considered then, but were to be noticed in the second edition of *Indian Studies*, No. III. A treatment of them in that way explains the omission of that final paragraph in professor Bühler's English manuscript. And it also, no doubt, accounts for the omission of the Brāhma charater for the guttural nasal, *ṅ*, in line 14 of Col. VI of the table on page 11, as compared with the same table on page 12 of the German text, and for the introduction of an inset illustration of that character in an addi-

tional remark made on Page 35, under § 16, *c*, (12), in connection with which there is to be taken an observation made on Page 14, under §4, B, (4) *e*. In a reference to the Gayā alphabet on Page 29, in line 5 from the bottom, for *ṅa* read *ṅa*.

2. See JRAS. 1905, 232ff Regarding Vāsahka, Vāsuṣka whom it has not been necessary to mention by name above, see *ibid*, 357f. It may be observed here that on page 40, line 7 from the bottom, in the words "or of the fourth century of the Seleucid era," and in the corresponding place on Page 41, line 10, of the German text, there must be a slip of the pen. The alternative proposed initial date of Kaniṣka, which Professor Bühler had in view, is certainly A. D, 89. And in that year there began the Seleucidan year 401 ; that is, the first year of the fifth (not fourth) century of that era.

3. For the real meaning of the inscription P. on the Mathurā lion-capital, which has been supposed to mark them as Sakas, i. e. Śakas, see JRAS 1904, 703ff., and 1905, 154ff.

4. See, for the present, my remarks about them in EI, 6, 77ff.

5. For three instances of incorrect details, see some remarks by Professor Kielhorn, in EI. 8 38, note 1, below the introduction to his edition of the Junāgaḍh inscription or Girnār Praśasti, of Rudradāman. As instances of the other kind, I may mention the following. Col. IV. of plate VIII. is from a reproduction (IA. 13, 186), which is not an actual facsimile, of a record the authenticity of which is open to question. And Col. VII of the same plate is mostly from a lithograph (IA. 6, 138) which was made, at a time when our methods of dealing with the original records were still decidedly primitive, from a plain uninked estampage, made by myself, the ground of which was painted in by my own hand, with results which cannot exactly be taken as furnishing a thoroughly typical illustration of the Western Cālukya alphabet of the eleventh century A. D.

6. In doing this, I have corrected a few wrong references which came to notice, and have added a very few new references which seemed likely to be of use.

Reprinted from
Indian Antiquary
1904, Appendix. 1—6.

J. F. Fleet

INDIAN PALEOGRAPHY

From About B.C. 350 to About A.D. 1300

By

G. BÜHLER.

I.—The Antiquity Of Writing In India And The Origin Of The Oldest Indian Alphabet

§1.—*The Indian tradition.*[1]

The tradition of both the orthodox and the heterodox sects of India ascribes the invention of writing, or at least of the chief script, to the creator Brahmā, and thereby claims it as a national invention of the remotest antiquity. The former view is found in the Nārada-Smṛti,[2] a redaction of the Manusaṃhitā (mentioned by Bāṇa about A. D. 620), and in Bṛhaspati's Vārttika on Manu,[3] as well as in Hiuen Tsiang[4] and in the Jaina Samavāyāṅga-Sūtra (traditional date about B. C. 300), the account of which latter work is repeated in the Paṇṇāvaṇā-Sūtra (traditional date B. C. 168).[5] The story is also indicated in the representations of Brahmā at Bādāmi of about A. D. 580, where the deity holds in one of his hands a bundle of palm-leaves,[6] for which in later representations an inscribed sheet of paper is substituted.[7]

The story, according to which in particular the Indian script running from the left to the right is an invention of Brahmā (*Fan*), is told in full in the Chinese Buddhistic Fawanshulin.[8] The two Jaina works mentioned above, and the Lalitavistara,[9] indicate its existence by naming the most important script *bambhī* or *brāhmī*. These traditional statements make it advisable to adopt the designation *Brāhmī* for the characters in which the majority of the Aśoka edicts are written, and for their later developments.

Berūnī[10] mentions a slightly different story. He says that the Hindus once had forgotten the art of writing, and that through a divine inspiration it was rediscovered by Vyāsa, the son of Parāśara. Accordingly, the history of the Indian alphabets would begin with the Kaliyuga, in B. C. 3101.

While these myths tend to show that the Hindus had forgotten the origin of their alphabet in early times,—perhaps already about B. C. 300, but certainly before the beginning of our era,—there are some other portions of their traditions which possess a greater and a positive value. The two Jaina Sūtras referred to above, contain a list of 18 separate alphabets ; and the Lalitavistara[11] enumerates 64 scripts which are said to have existed in the time of Buddha. Several among the names of the two lists agree, and there are in particular four which, as may have been already recognised, have a claim to be considered authentic and historical. Besides the *brāhmī* or *bambhī*, which is the parent of all the still existing alphabets of India, two more can be identified with known scripts. The *Kharoṣṭhī* or *kharoṭṭhī* is, as the Fawanshulin states,[12] the writing running from the right to the left, invented by one Kharoṣṭha, "Ass-lip,"[13] and is the same character which European scholars formerly used to call Bactrian, Indo-Bactrian, Bactro-Pali, Ariano-Pali, &c. The *drāviḍī* or *ḍāmilī* of the lists is very [2] probably the partly independent variety of the Brāhmī, which recently has become known through the relic vessels from the Stūpa of Bhaṭṭiprolu in the Kistna district.[14] Besides, the name *puṣkarasārī* or *pukkharasāriyā* is certainly historical, as it is evidently connected with the *nomen gentile Puṣkarasādi* or *Pauṣkarasādi* (with the Northern Buddhist's *Puṣkarasāri*) by which one or several ancient teachers of law and grammar are mentioned in Pāṇini's grammar, Āpastamba's Dharmasūtra, and other works. It appears not incredible that a member of the family of *Puṣkarasad* may have invented a new alphabet or modified an existing one. The list of the Jainas includes also the name *yavaṇāliyā* or *yavaṇāṇiyā*, which is identical with *yavanānī*, "the writing of the Yavanas or Greeks," of Pāṇini (traditional date about B. C. 350).[15] An early acquaintance of the Hindus with the Greek alphabet may have been brought about by the expedition of Skylax to North-Western India in B. C. 509, or by the fact that Indian and Gandharian troops took part in Xerxes' war against Greece,[16] and even by an ancient commercial intercourse. At all events, finds of Indian imitations of Attic drachmes with Greek inscriptions tend to prove the use of the Greek alphabet in North-Western India before the time of Alexander.[17]

As some names of the Jaina list are thus shown to be ancient by the results of epigraphic researches and by Pāṇini, as well as by the agreement of the independent tradition of the Northern Buddhists, the list is not without historical value. And it may be considered at least highly probable that a fairly large number of alphabets was known or used in India about B. C. 300. The exact number, 18, which the Jainas mention, must however be taken merely as conventional, as it frequently occurs in traditional statements.

An extract from the lost Dṛṣṭivāda of the Jainas also gives some further account of the ancient Brāhmī[18]. It states that this alphabet contained only 46 radical signs, instead of the usual number of 50 or 51. The letters intended are without a doubt: *A, Ā, I, Ī U, Ū, E, AI, O, AU (10), Aṃ, Aḥ*; *ka, kha, ga, gha, ṅa, ca, cha, ja (20), jha, ña. ṭa, ṭha, ḍa, ḍha, ṇa, ta, tha, da (30), dha, na, pa, pha, ba, bha, ma, ya, ra, la (40), va, śa, ṣa, sa, ha, ḷa*; while the *mātṛkās Ṛ, Ṝ, Ḷ, Ḹ*, and the ligature *kṣa*, which in later times was often erroneously considered a *mātṛkā*, were excluded. The four liquid vowels are wanting also in the alphabet of the Lalitavistara[19] and in that of the modern elementary schools. In the latter the instruction is based on the so-called *Bārākhaḍī* (Skt. *dvādaśākṣarī*), a table of the combinations of the consonants with the twelve vowels mentioned above, *e.g.*, *ka, kā*, to *kaṃ, kaḥ*. The antiquity of the *Bārākhaḍī*, which from its Maṅgala *Oṃ namaḥ siddham* is at present sometimes called *Siddhākṣarasamāmnāya* or *Siddhamātṛkā*, is attested by Hui-lin

(A. D. 788-810)[20], who mentions it as the first of the twelve *fan* or 'cycles' (evidently Hiuen Tsiang's twelve *chang*[21]) with which the Hindu boys began their studies. Further evidence for the omission of the vowels *Ṛ, Ṝ, Ḷ, Ḹ* is furnished by Hiuen Tsiang's remark[22] that the Indian alphabet of his time contained 47 letters (the last one being probably the ligature *kṣa*), and by the fragments of the incomplete alphabet of Aśoka's stone-masons at Gayā[23], which may be restored as follows: *A*, **Ā*, **I*, **Ī*, **U*, **Ū*, **E*, **AI*, **O*, **AU (10)*, **Aṃ* or **Aḥ*, *ka*, **kha*, **ga*, **gha*, *ṅa*, **ca*, *cha*, **ja*, **jha (20)*, **ña*, **ṭa*.

All these various points tend to show that the popular Brāhmī contained, as the Jaina tradition asserts, since the third century B. C. only 46 letters, and that, as the occurrence of the vowels *AI*, *AU*, *Aṃ*, *Aḥ* and the consonant *ṅa* proves, it was adapted to the wants of the Sanskrit language. But it is not [3] improbable that the Brahmans already then used particular signs for the liquid vowels in their works on grammar and phonetics. The method, however, according to which the actually known signs for these sounds have been formed, differs from that adopted for the other vowel-signs. The medial *ṛ*, *ṝ* and *ḷ* were developed first, and the initials later; while in the case of *a*, *ā*, &c., the process was the contrary one (see below, § 4, and § 24, A, 6, 7). The Chinese have also preserved an Indian tradition asserting that *ṛ*, *ṝ* and *ḷ* are later additions to the original alphabet[24].

§ 2.—*Literary evidence for the use of writing.*

A.—*Brahmanical literature*[25].

Among Vedic works, the Vāsiṣṭha Dharmasūtra, which according to Kumārila (about A. D. 750) originally belonged to a school of the Ṛgveda, and which is younger than the lost Mānava Dharmasūtra but older than the existing Manusaṃhitā,[26] offers clear evidence for the widely spread use of writing during the "Vedic" period. Vasiṣṭha in XVI, 10, 14-15, mentions written documents as legal evidence, and the first of these sūtras is a quotation from an older work or from the traditional lore. Further, Pāṇini's grammar, which belongs to the Vedāṅgas, contains, besides the term *yavanānī* mentioned above, the compounds *lipikara* and *libikara*, "writer" (III, 2, 21), which sometimes have been rendered erroneously, against the authority of the Koṣas, by "maker of inscriptions."[27] In addition to these few certain passages, the later Vedic works contain some technical terms such as *akṣara*, *kāṇḍa*, *paṭala*, *grantha*, &c., which some scholars have quoted as evidence for writing. But others have explained them differently, and it is indeed not necessary to consider them as referring to written letters and MSS[28]. Similarly, opinions are much divided with respect to the force of some other general arguments for the early use of written documents and MSS., drawn from the advanced state of Vedic civilisation, especially from the high development of trade and the complicated monetary transactions mentioned in Vedic works, from the use of prose in the Brāhmaṇas from the collection, the methodical arrangement, the numeration, and the analysis of the Vedic texts, and from the grammatical, phonetic, and lexicographic researches in the Vedāṅgas.[29] Though some of these points, especially the first and the last, undeniably possess considerable weight, they have yet not gained general recognition, as will always happen if an *argumentum ex impossibili* is used, even if it should be supported by fuller special enquiries than Sanskrit scholars have hitherto devoted to these subjects.

While this kind of evidence will probably not be generally accepted very soon, it is to be hoped that the *argumentum ex silentio*,—the inference that a Vedic work which does not mention writing must have been composed when writing was unknown in India,—will be dropped. The *argumentum ex silentio* is certainly not conclusive, because the Hindus even at present, in spite of a long continued use of writing, esteem the written word less than the spoken one, because they base their whole literary and scientific intercourse on oral communications, and because, especially in scientific [4] works, writing and MSS. are mentioned very rarely. Though MSS., being *Sarasvatīmukha*, "the face of the goddess of speech," are held sacred and are worshipped, the Veda and the Śāstras exist, even for the modern Hindu, only in the mouth of the teacher, whose word has more weight than a written text, and they can only be learned properly from a teacher, not from MSS. Even in our days, the Hindus esteem only the *mukhasthā vidyā*, the learning which the Pandit has imprinted on his memory. Even in our days, learned discussions are carried on with reference to living speech, and even the modern poets do not wish to be read, but hope that their verses will become "ornaments for the throats of the learned" (*satāṃ kaṇṭhabhūṣaṇa*). As far as our observation reaches, this state of things has been always the same since the earliest times. Its ultimate cause probably is that the beginning of the Hindu Śāstras and poetry goes back to a time when writing was unknown, and that a system of oral teaching, already traceable in the Ṛgveda, was fully developed before the introduction of written characters. The reasons just stated do not permit us to expect many traces for the use of writing in the works of the schools of priests or Pandits, or to look in them for frequent references to letters and written documents. But, on the other hand, there is nothing to bar the conjecture, repeatedly put forward, that, even during the Vedic period, MSS. were used as auxiliaries both in oral instruction and on other occasions. And, as an argument in favour of this conjecture, it is now possible to adduce the indisputable fact that the Brāhmī alphabet has been formed by phonologists or by grammarians and for scientific use[30].

But such Brahmanical works as the Epics, Purāṇas, Kāvyas, dramas, &c., which describe actual life, or the metrical law-books which fully teach not only the sacred but also the civil and criminal law, as well as compositions such as the Nīti-, Nāṭya-, and Kāma-śāstras which exclusively refer to worldly matters, contain numerous references to writing and to written documents of various kinds, and likewise evidence for the occurrence of MSS. of literary works. Unfortunately, however, it is not possible to assert of any of the existing books of these classes,—excepting the two Epics,—that they are older than the period to which the oldest inscriptions belong. And even the evidence of the Epics may be impugned, since we cannot prove that every word of their texts goes back to a high antiquity. Professor Jacobi's examination of the several recensions of the Rāmāyaṇa has shown that the greater part of the verses, now read, did not belong to the original poem.[31] As far as is known at present, the MSS. of the Mahābhārata do not show equally great variations. But the existence of the majority of its chapters can be proved only for the eleventh century A.D.[32] Though the testimony of the Epics can therefore, only be used with due reserve, yet it is undeniable that their terms regarding writing and writers are archaic. Like the canonical works of the Southern Buddhists,[33] they use the ancient expressions *likh*, *lekha*, *lekhaka*, and *lekhana*, not the probably foreign word *lipi*.

The most important passages of the Epics, concerning writing, have been collected in the St. Petersburg Dictionary under the words mentioned, and by J. Dahlmann, Das Mahābhārata, 185 ff. Regarding the passages on writing in Manu, see the Index in Sacred Books of the East, Vol. XXV, under "Documents," and for the legal documents, described in the later Smṛtis, see Vol. II. of this Encyclopedia, Part 8, Recht und Sitte, § 35. An interesting collection of statements regarding MSS. in the Purāṇas is found in Hemādri's Dānakhaṇḍa, Adhy. 7, p. 544 ff. (Bibl. Ind.). The Kāmasūtra I, 3 (p. 33, Durgāprasād) enumerates *pustakavācana*, "the reading of MSS.," among the 64 Kalās.

B.—*Buddhistic literature.*[34]

[5] More important than the testimony of the Brahmans is that of the Ceylonese Tripiṭaka, where numerous passages bear witness not only to an acquaintance with writing, but also to its extensive use at the time when the Buddhist canon was composed. *Lekhā*, "writing", and *Lekhaka*, "a writer," are mentioned in the Bhikkhu-Pācittya 2, 2, and in the Bhikkhuni-Pācittiya 49, 2 ; and the former work praises writing as a branch of knowledge that is honoured in all countries. The Jātakas repeatedly speak of private[35] and official[36] letters. They also know of royal proclamations[37], of which Mahāvagga 1,43 likewise mentions an instance ; and they narrate that important family affairs or moral and political maxims were engraved on gold plates.[38] Twice we hear of debtor's bonds (*iṇapaṇṇa*[39]), and twice even of MSS. (*potthaka*[40]). A game called *akkharikā* is mentioned repeatedly in the Vinayapiṭaka and the Nikāyas[41] ; according to Buddhaghoṣa, its main feature was that letters were read in the sky. The Pārājika section of the Vinayapiṭaka (3,4,4) declares that Buddhist monks shall not "incise" (*chind*) the rules which show how men may gain heaven, or riches and fame in the next life, through particular modes of suicide. From this passage it follows (1) that the ascetics of pre-Buddhistic times used to give their lay-disciples rules, incised on bamboo or wooden tablets, concering religious suicide, which ancient Brahmans and the Jainas strongly recommended, and (2) that the knowledge of the alphabet was widely spread among the people.

Finally, Jātaka No. 125, and Mahāvagga 1, 49,[42] bear witness to the existence of elementary schools, in which the method of teaching and the matter taught were about the same as in the indigenous schools of modern India. The Jātaka mentions the wooden writing-board (*phalaka*), known (as well as the *varṇaka* or wooden pen) also to the Lalitavistara[43] and to Berūnī,[44] and still used in Indian elementary schools. The passage of the Mahāvagga gives the curriculum of the schools, *lekhā*, *gaṇanā* and *rūpa* which three subjects, according to the Hāthigumphā inscription of the year 165 of the Maurya era[45], king Khāravela of Kaliṅga learnt in his childhood. *Lekhā*, of course, means "writing," and *gaṇanā*, "arithmetic", i. e., addition, subtraction and the multiplication-table formerly called *aṅka* and now *āṁk*, while *rupa*, literally "forms," corresponds to applied arithmetic, the calculations with coins, of interest and wages, and to elementary mensuration. These three subjects are still "the three R's" taught in the indigenous schools called *gāmṭī nīśāḷ*, *pāṭhśāla*, *lehśaḍ* or *toll*.

These very plain statements of the Ceylonese canon refer certainly to the actualities of the period between B C. 500-400, possibly even of the sixth century.[46] Their antiquity is proved also by the fact that all the terms for writing, letters, writers,—*chindati*, *likhati*, *lekha*, *lekhaka*, *akkhara*,—as well as nearly all the writing materials, wood or bamboo, *paṇṇa* or leaves, and *suvaṇṇapaṭṭa* or gold plates, point to the oldest method of writing, the incision of the signs in hard materials. All traces of the use of ink are wanting, though the statements of Nearchos and Q. Curtius regarding the writing materials used at the time of Alexander's invasion (see below under C) make it very probable that ink was known in the fourth century B.C, and though an ink-inscription of the third or second century B. C. is found on the inner side of the lid of the relic vessel from Stūpa No. III. at Andher[47]. Moreover, the Ceylonese books are not acquainted with the words *lipi*, *libi*, *dipi*, *dipati*, *dipapati*, *lipikara* and *libikara* for "writing," "to write," and "writer," of which the first six are found in the [6] Aśoka edicts and the last two, as stated above, in Pāṇini's grammar. *Dipi*, and *lipi* are probably derived from the Old Persian *dipi*, which cannot have reached India before the conquest of the Pañjāb by Darius about B.C. 500, and which later became *lipi*[48].

C.—*Foreign Works.*

To the last quarter of the fourth century B. C. refer the statement of Nearchos,[49] according to which the Hindus wrote letters on well beaten cotton cloth, and the note of Q. Curtius,[50] which mentions the tender inner bark of trees as serving the same purpose, and clearly points to the early utilisation of the well known birch-bark. The fact that, according to these two writers, two different *indigenous* Indian materials were used in B. C. 327-325, shows that the art of writing was then generally known and was nothing new. To a slightly later time belongs the fragment No. 36 *a* of Megasthenes,[51] which speaks of mile-stones indicating the distances and the halting places on the high roads. In another often-discussed passage,[52] Megasthenes says that the Indians decided judicial cases according to unwritten laws, and adds in explanation that they knew no *γράμματα* and settled everything *ἀπὸ μνήμης*. According to the now usual interpretation, this statement has been caused by a misunderstanding. Megasthenes took the term *smṛti*, used by his informants, in the sense of *μνήμη*, "memory," while they meant it in the sense of "the sacred tradition concerning law," or "the lawbooks," which, according to Indian principles, can only be explained orally by one who knows the Dharma.

§ 3.—*Paleographic Evidence.*[53]

The results of a paleographic examination of the most ancient Indian inscriptions fully agree with the literary evidence, which bears witness to the widely spread use of writing during the fifty century B.C. and perhaps even during the sixth. The characters of the Aśoka edicts, which have to be considered first, prove very clearly that writing was no recent invention in the third century B. C. The alphabet of the edicts is not homogeneous. All the letters, with the exception of *U*, *jha*, *ṅa*, *ña*, *ṭha*, *ṇa*, *tha* and *na*, have several often very dissimilar forms, which are partly local and partly cursive varieties. The number of the variants of one letter sometimes amounts to nine or ten. Thus plate II, 1, 2, cols. II-XII, shows for *A*, *Ā*, no less than ten forms, among which the eight most important ones may be placed here side by side :—

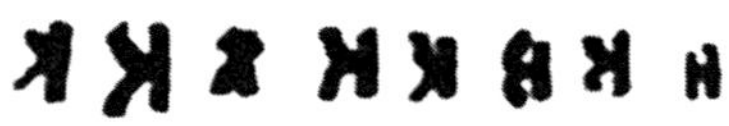

The first sign has hardly any resemblance to the last. But the sequence in the row shows their connection and their development. The first seven owe their existence to a predilection partly [7] for angles and partly for curves,—two mutually contradictory tendencies, which find their expression also in the forms of other letters of pl. II, such as *gha*, *ḍa*, *da*, *la*, &c. The signs Nos. 1,2,3 of the series given above, are due to the first tendency, and Nos. 6,7 to the second. Nos. 4,5 show the transition from the angle to the curve, and No. 8 is a cursive simplification of No. 6. These eight signs are not found in all the versions of the Aśoka edicts, but are divided locally as follows. The angular forms Nos. 1, 2, 3 appear only in the South, in Girnār, Śiddāpura, Dhauli, and Jaugada, side by side with Nos. 4 to 7. And it must be noted that the latter are rare in Girnār and Śiddāpura, but in the majority in Dhauli and Jaugada. In the versions discovered north of the Narmadā or the Vindhya, we find mostly only Nos. 4 to 7, but in Kālsī No. 8 also is common, and it occurs a few times in Rāmpūrva. Hence the angular forms of *A*, *Ā*, appear to be specially southern ones, and they are no doubt also the most ancient. The first inference is confirmed by a comparison of the most nearly allied inscriptions. The relic vessels from Kolhāpur[54] and Bhaṭṭiprolu (pl. II, cols. XIII-V), and the oldest Andhra inscription from the Nānāghāṭ (pl. II, cols. XXIII-XXIV) again show the angular *A*, *Ā*, either exclusively or together with the mixed forms Nos. 4,5, while the numerous inscriptions found further north on the Stūpas of Sāñci and Bharahut, in Pabhosa and Mathurā (pl. II, cols. XVIII-XX) on the coins of Agathocles, and in the Nāgārjunī cave (pl. II, col. XVII), offer either pure curved letters or mixed ones. An exception in Mahābodhi-Gayā[55] is probably explained by the fact that pilgrims from the south incised records of their donations at the famous sanctuary. Similar differences between northern and southern forms may be observed in the case of *kha*, *ja*, *ma*, *ra* and *sa*[56], and they are all the more important as the circumstances under which the Aśoka edicts were incised did not favour the free use of local forms[57]. But the existence of local forms always points to a long continued use of the alphabet in which it is observable.

Equally important is the occurrence of apparently or really advanced and cursive types which for the greater part reappear or become constant in the later inscriptions.

The subjoined table shows in line A the most important modern looking signs from the Aśoka edicts, and in line B the corresponding ones from later inscriptions.

Four among these signs, Nos. 2, 7, 10, 21, are, as will appear further on,[58] really archaic, but the remainder are partly secondary, partly tertiary cursive forms. To the last-mentioned belong in particular Nos. 4, 8, 11, 15 and 19. [8] Among the letters form the later inscriptions in line B, Nos. 9, 11, 12 and 19 appear in the Nāgārjunī cave inscriptions of Aśoka's grandson Daśaratha; Nos. 2, 6-8, 10, 13-16 and 21 in Khāravela's Hāthigumphā inscription and in the oldest Andhra inscriptions, inscriptions, Nāsik No. 1 and Nānāghāṭ, as well as in the archaic Mathurā inscriptions, all of which documents belong to the period between about B. C. 170 and 150. Nos. 1, 3 and 22 are still later, and occur first in the inscriptions of the Kuṣānas from Mathurā and in the Andhra and Ābhīra inscriptions from Nāsik of the first and second centuries A.D. Occasionally the Aśoka edicts show also the short top-stroke, the so-called *Serif*, which is so characteristic for the later alphabets and causes numerous modifications.[59] Very commonly, too, appear the upward strokes for medial *ā* and *e*, the cursive rounded *i* (in Girnār sometimes not distinguishable from *ā*), more rarely the later straight *o*-stroke, and once a looped *o*.[60] Finally, the Anusvāra sometimes stands, as is generally the case in later times, above the letter after which it is pronounced.[61]

The existence of so many local varieties, and of so very numerous cursive forms, proves in any case that writing had had a long history in Aśoka's time, and that the alphabet was then in a state of transition. The use of the cursive forms together with archaic ones may possibly be explained by the assumption that several, partly more archaic and partly more advanced, alphabets were simultaneously used during the third century B. C., and that the writers, intending or ordered to use lapidary forms, through negligence mixed them with the more familiar cursive letters, as has also happened not rarely in later inscriptions. It is possible to adduce in favour of this view the above-mentioned tradition of the Dṛṣṭivāda, according to which a larger number of alphabets was in use about B. C. 300. The conjecture would become a certainty, if it could be shown that the word *seto*, "the white (elephant)," which has been added to Dhauli edict VI. in order to explain the sculpture above the middle column, was incised at the same time as the preceding edicts. The two characters of *seto* show the types of the Kuṣāna and Gupta inscriptions.[62] Though it is difficult to understand that, in later times, anybody should have cared to add the explanation of the relief, keeping exactly the line of the edict, the possibility of the assumption that this was actually done, is not altogether excluded.

The Eraṇ coin with the legend running from the right to the left,[63] offers a contribution to the earlier history of the Brāhmī. It shows the ancient *sa* with the straight side-stroke, but the later *ma* with the semicircular top, and the *dha* turned to the left. The coin probably dates from the time when the Brāhmī was written both from the right to the left and from the left to the right. Even if one makes due allowance for the fact that coins often reproduce archaic forms long gone out of fashion, one can only agree with Cunningham (CAI. 101), who thinks that the coin is older than the Maurya period ; and one must allot it, if not to B. C. 400, at least to the middle of the fourth century. The time when the Brāhmi was written *βουστροφηδόν* probably lies somewhat before the Maurya period, since the Aśoka edicts show only few traces of the writing from right to left, in the *O* of Jaugada and Dhauli and in the rare *dha* of Jaugada and Delhi-Sivālik (plate II, 8, VI, and 26, V, VI).[64] In connection with this coin it is also necessary to mention the Patnā seals (C. ASR. 15, pl. 3. 1. 2), which very likely are older than the time of the Mauryas. The first with the legend *Nadaya* (*Naṃdāya*), "(the seal) of Nandā," shows a *da* open to the right, [9] and the second with the inscription *Agapalaśa* (*Aṃgapālaśśa*) shows an *A* in its original position (pl. II. 1. I). More important results for the history of the Brāhmi may be obtained from the Drāviḍī of the relic caskets of Bhaṭṭiprolu,[65] already referred to above. This alphabet contains, besides various characters agreeing with the southern variety of the Aśoka edicts, (1) three signs, *dh*, *d* and *bh*, in the position of the writing running from right to left ; (2) three signs, *c*, *j* and *ṣ*, which are more archaic than those of the Aśoka edicts and of the Eraṇ coin ; (3) two signs, *l* and *ḷ*, derived independently from the old Semitic originals ; (4) one new sign, *gh*, derived from *g*, the *mātṛkā gha* of the Brāhmī being at the same time discarded. The reasons for the assertions under 2 and 3 will be adduced in the next paragraph. But if the assertions themselves are true, it certainly follows that, whatever the age of the inscriptions may be, the Drāviḍa alphabet separated from the main stock of the Brāhmī long before the Eraṇ coin was struck, at the latest in the fifth century B. C.

This estimate carries us back to the period for which the Ceylonese canon proves the general use of writing in India, without however giving the name of the current alphabet. It seems therefore natural to conjecture that the alphabet known to the earliest Buddhist authors was a form of the Brāhmī ; and there are some further facts which favour this view. Firstly, recent discoveries have made it evident that the Brāhmī has been commonly used since the earliest times even in North-Western India, and that it was indeed the real national script of all Hindus.[66] In the ruins of Taxila, the modern Shāh-Derī in the Pañjāb, coins have been found which are struck according to the old Indian standard, and some of which bear inscriptions in Kharoṣṭhī, while the majority show legends in the oldest type of the Brāhmi, sometimes together with transcripts in Kharoṣṭhi.[67] These coins are certainly not later than the third century B. C. Perhaps they even date, as Cunningham thinks, from a much earlier time about B. C. 400. Some of them have been struck by *negamā* or guilds, those of the *Dojaka* or *Dujaka*, of the *Tālimata* and of the *Atakatakā* (?), and one with the inscription *Vaṭasvaka* probably was issued by a section of the tribe of the *Aśvakas* (*Assakenoi*), named after the *vaṭa*-tree, the Ficus religiosa. These finds decidedly establish the popular use of the Brāhmi in the Pañjāb, side by side with the Kharoṣṭhi, at least for the third century B. C. Mr. Rapson's discovery of Persian *sigloi* with letters in Kharoṣṭhī and in Brāhmī proves that both alphabets were used together much earlier.[68] For, in all probability these *sigloi* were current during the rule of the Akhaemenians over North-Western India, or before B. C. 331.

Secondly, Dr. Taylor's view regarding the origin of the Kharoṣṭhī has become more and more probable, and it must now be admitted that this alphabet was developed out of the later Aramaic characters after the conquest of the Pañjāb by Darius, which happened about B.C. 500[69]. And it becomes more and more difficult to refuse credence to the conjecture of A. Weber, E. Thomas and A. Cunningham, according to which the principles ruling the already developed Brāhmī have been utilised in the formation of the Kharoṣṭhi[70]. According to our present information, the Kharoṣṭhi is the only alphabet, besides the Brāhmī, to which the Buddhists possibly could refer. But as it was only a secondary script even in Gandhāra, as it was developed only in the fifth century, the possibility suggested becomes improbable, and the Brāhmi alone has a claim to be considered as the alphabet known to the authors of the Ceylonese canon.

§ 4.—*The origin of the Brāhma alphabet*[71]

[10] Among the numerous greatly differing proposals to explain the origin of the Brāhmī[72], there are five for which complete demonstrations have been attempted :—(1) A. Cunningham's derivation from indigenous Indian hieroglyphics[73] ; (2) A. Weber's derivation from the most ancient Phoenician characters[74] ; (3) W. Deecke's derivation from the Assyrian cuneiform characters, through an ancient South-Semitic alphabet which is also the parent of the Sabaean or Himyaritic script[75] ; (4) I. Taylor's derivation from a lost South-Arabian alphabet, the predecessor of the Sabaean[76] ; (5) J. Halévy's derivation from a mixture of Aramaic, Kharoṣṭhi and Greek letters of the last quarter of the fourth century B. C.[77]

Cunningham's opinion, which was formerly shared by some eminent scholars, presupposes the use of Indian hieroglyphic pictures, of which hitherto no trace has been found. On the other hand, the legend of the Eraṇ coin, which runs from the right to the left, and the letters seemingly turned round in the opposite direction which appear rarely in the Aśoka edicts and more frequently in the Bhaṭṭiprolu inscriptions, point to the correctness of the view taken as granted in all the other attempts at explanation, viz., that Semitic signs are the prototypes of the Brāhma letters.

Among the remaining four proposals, J. Halévy's *a priori* improbable theory may be at once eliminated, as it does not agree with the literary and paleographic evidence just discussed, which makes it more than probable that the Brāhmī was used several centuries before the beginning of the Maurya period, and had had a long history at the time to which the earliest Indian inscriptions belong. It is more difficult to make a choice between A. Weber's derivation from the oldest North-Semitic alphabet, and the view of W. Deecke and I. Taylor, who derive the Brāhmī from an ancient South-Semitic script. Neither the one nor the other derivation can be declared to be *a priori* impossible; for, the results of modern researches make a high antiquity probable for also the Sabaean script, and point to the conclusion that this alphabet not only is older than the oldest Indian inscriptions, but that it existed at a period for which no evidence for the use of writing in India is available.[78] But according to these results, the question has to be put in a manner somewhat differing from that in which Deecke and Taylor have put it. The point to be ascertained is no longer, whether the Brāhmī can be derived from an unknown predecessor of the Sabaean alphabet, but whether it can be derived directly from the actually known Sabaean characters.

In all attempts at the derivation of alphabets, it is necessary to keep in mind three fundamental maxims, without which no satisfactory results can be obtained :—

(1) For the comparison of the characters to be derived, the oldest and fullest forms must be used, and the originals from which they are derived must belong to the types of one and the same period.

(2) The comparison may include only such irregular equations as can be supported by analogies from other cases where nations have borrowed foreign alphabets.

(3) [11] In cases where the derivatives show considerable differences from the supposed prototypes, it is necessary to show that there are fixed principles, according to which the changes have been made.

If one wishes to keep to these principles in deriving the Brāhmī from Semitic signs, neither the Sabaean alphabet, nor its perhaps a little more archaic variety, the Lihyanian or Thammudaean[79], will serve the purpose, in spite of a general resemblance in the *ductus* and of a special resemblance in two or three letters. The derivations proposed by Deecke and Taylor do not fulfil the absolutely necessary conditions, and it will probably not be possible to obtain satisfactory results, even if all the impossible equations are given up, and the oldest Indian signs in every case are chosen for comparison. It would be necessary to assume that several Sabaean letters, such as *Aleph*, *Gimel*, *Zain*, *Teth*, *Phe*, *Qoph*, *Resh*, which show strong modifications of the North-Semitic forms, had been again made similar to their prototypes on being converted by the Hindus into *A*, *ga*, *ja*, *tha*, *pa*, *kha* and *ra*. In other cases, it would be impossible to show any connection between the Sabaean and the Indian signs. These difficulties disappear with the direct derivation of the Brāhmī from the oldest North-Semitic alphabet, which shows the same type from Phoenicia to Mesopotamia. The few inadmissible equations which Weber's earlier attempt contains, may be easily removed with the help of recently discovered forms, and it is not difficult to recognise the principles, according to which the Semitic signs have been converted into Indian ones.

An examination of the old Indian alphabet in plate II. reveals the following peculiarities :—

(1) The letters are set up as straight as possible, and with occassional exceptions in the case of *ṭa*, *ṭha* and *ba*, they are made equal in height.

(2) The majority consist of vertical lines with appendages attached mostly at the foot, occasionally at the foot and at the top, or rarely in the middle; but there is no case in which an appendage has been added to the top alone.

(3) At the top of the letters appear mostly the ends of verticals, less frequently short horizontal strokes, still more rarely curves on the tops of angles opening downwards, and,

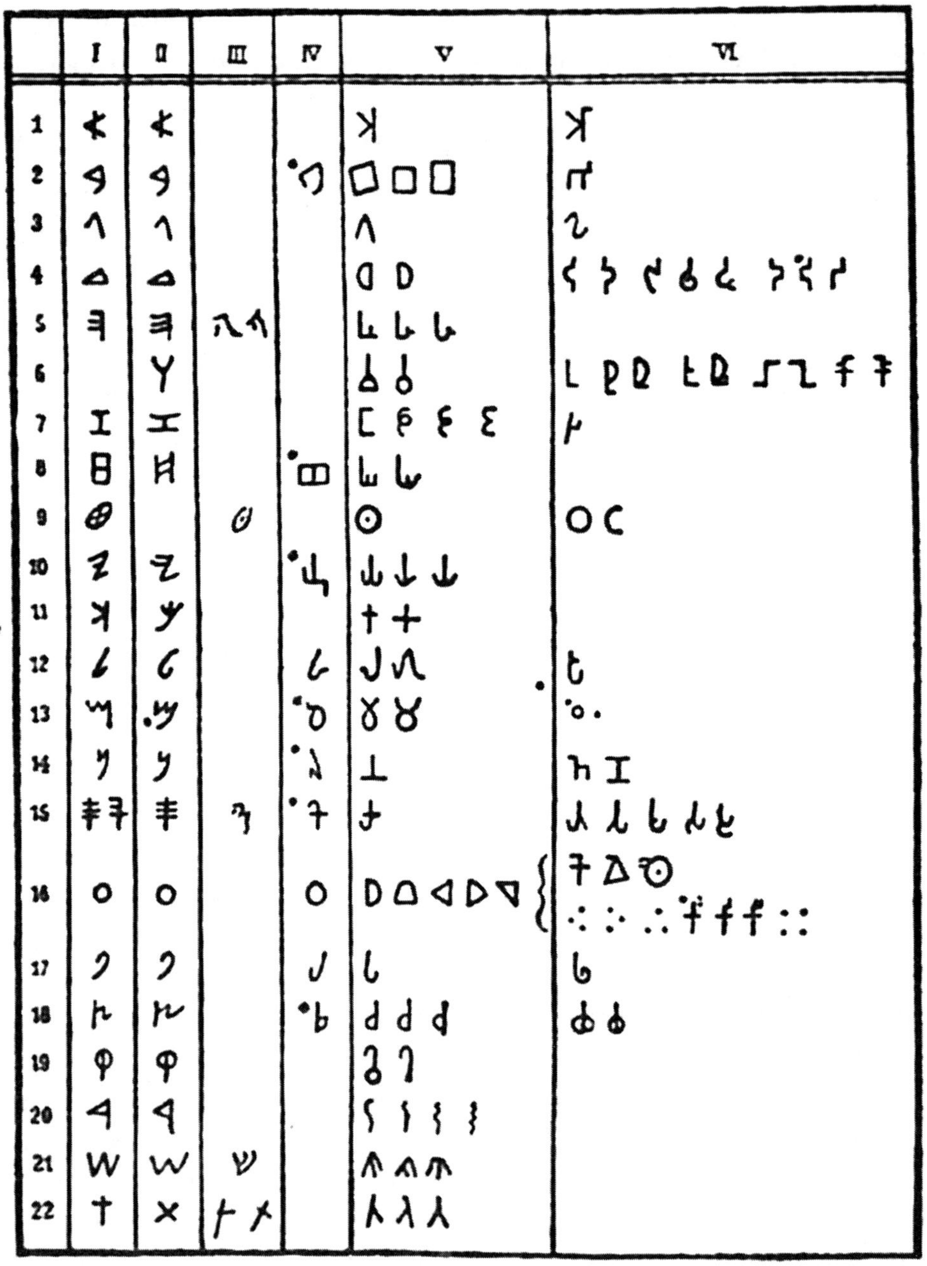

quite exceptionally, in *ma* and in one form of *jha*, two lines rising upwards. In no case does the top show several angles, placed side by side, with a vertical or slanting line hanging down, or a triangle or a circle with a pendant-line.

The causes of these characteristics of the Brāhmī are a certain pedantic formalism, found also in other Indian creations, a desire to frame signs suited for the formation of regular lines, and an aversion to top-heavy characters. The last peculiarity is probably due in part to the circumstances that since early times the Indians made their letters hang down from an imaginary or really drawn upper line[80], and in part to the introduction of vowel-signs, most of which are attached horizontally to the tops of the consonants. Signs with the ends of verticals at the top were, of course, best suited for such a script. Owing to these inclinations and aversions of the Hindus, the heavy tops of many Semitic letters had to be got rid of, by turning the signs topsy-turvy or laying them on their sides, by opening the angles, and so forth. Finally, the change in the direction of the writing necessitated a further change, inasmuch as the signs had to be turned from the right to the left, as in Greek.

[12] The details of the derivation, for which, with the exception of the evidently identical Nos. 1, 3-7, 9, 12, 16, 17, 19-22, only a greater or smaller degree of probability can be claimed, are shown in the subjoined comparative table, which has been drawn by Mr. S. Pepper of Vienna. Cols. I, II, showing the oldest Phoenician characters and those from Mesa's stone, have been taken from Ph. Berger's Histoire de l' E'criture dans l' Antiquité, pp. 185, 202. Col. III. comes from Euting's Tabula Scripturae Aramaicae of 1892. And cols. IV-VI, with the exception of the signs marked by asterisks as hypothetical, are taken from plate II. of this work. With respect to the single letters, I add the following explanatory remarks, brief abstracts of those in my Indian Studies, III. 2, p. 58 ff.

A.—*Borrowed Signs.*

No. 1, A, col. V, = *Aleph*, cols. I, II (Weber doubtfully), [13] turned from right to left except on the Patnā seal (above, § 3, and pl. II, 1, I), with transposition of the vertical line to the end of the angle.—No. 2, *ba*, col. V, *a*, *b*. *c*, = *Beth*, cols. I, II (Weber); the opening of the triangular top produced first a sign like that in col. IV, next the rhombus, col. V, *a*, and finally the square and the oblong, col. V, *b*, *c*.—No. 3, *ga*, col. V, = *Gimel*, cols. I, II.—No. 4, *dha*, col. V, *a*, *b*, = *Daleth*, cols I, II (Weber), set up straight with rounded back (compare the half-angular forms, pl. II, 26, IX, XIX, XXIII, and the triangular, pl. III, 24, VII-XIII), with or without the turn from right to left.—No. 5, *ha*, col. V, = *He* (Weber doubtfully), the Śiddāpura form, col. V, *a*, being probably derived from the *He* of col. III, *a* (Mina of Salmanassar, before B. C. 725), which was turned topsy-turvy and from right to left. The more similar *He* of the sixth century B. C. (col. III, *b*) cannot be the prototype, because it occurs in the period when the Brāhmi had been developed, and because then the Semitic *Aleph*, *Daleth*, *Cheth*, *Theth*, *Waw*, and *Qoph* had become cursive and had been changed so much that they could no longer have produced the Indian forms.—No. 6, *va*, col. V, *a*, *b*, = *Waw*, col. II (Weber doubtfully), turned topsy-turvy and with the lower end shut.—No. 7, *ja*, col. V, = *Zain*, cols. I, II (Weber); a displacement of the two bars produced the Drāviḍi letter, col. V, *a*; from this was derived, the letter being made with one stroke of the pen, the *ja* of the northern Brāhmi, col. V, *b*, with a loop, for which, owing to the use of ink, a dot was substituted in the *ja* of col. V, *c*. The usual Girnār form, col. V, *d*, was also derived from the Drāviḍa form, the letter being made with two strokes of the pen.

No. 8, *gha*, col. V, *a*, *b*, = *Cheth*, cols. I, II (Taylor), the Semitic sign being laid on its side, col. IV (on account of its often sloping position), and the upper horizontal bar being changed into a vertical.—No. 9, *tha*, col. V, = *Theth*, col. I (Weber), with the substitution of a dot for the cross in the centre, just as in the Assyrian letter, col. III.—No. 10, *ya*, col. V, = *Yod* (Weber), the *Yod* of cols. I, II, being laid on its side, col. IV, the central stroke being lengthened; and the pendant on the right being turned upwards, hence first the *ya* of col. V, *a*, and later the cursive forms in col. V, *b*, *c*. —No. 11, *ka*, col. V, *a*, *b*, = *Kaph*, the upper side-bar of a form like that in col. II. having been converted into the top of the vertical, and the sign being then set up straight.—No. 12, *la*, col. V, = *Lamed*, cols. I, II (Weber), preserved in its original position in the slightly differentiated *ḷ* of the Drāviḍī, col. VI (see below, B, 4, *c*), and in the Eraṇ from, col. IV, with the *Serif* on the top of the curve, turned from right to left in the usual form of the Aśoka edicts, cal V, *a*, and turned with a tail on the right, but without the *Serif*, in the Drāviḍī *l*, col. V, *b*.—No 13, *ma*, col. V, = *Mem* (Weber), derived from a form like that in col. II, with the change of the bent pendant into a loop, as in the hypothetical form in col. IV (analogous development in Euting, TSA. col. 58, *a*), and with superposition of the angle on the loop, col. V, *a* (analogous development in Euting, TSA. col. 59, *c*), whence the cursive form with semicircle at the top in col. V, *b*.—No 14, *na*, col. V, = *Nun* (Taylor), the *Nun* in cols. I, II, being turned topsy-turvy as in col. IV, and the hook at the foot being converted into a straight stroke, for which development the *n̄a*, col. VI, *a*, formed out of the hypothetical sign by a regularisation of the hook and the addition of a differentiating bar at the top (see below B, 4, *d*), appears to be a witness.

No. 15, *sa*, *ṣa*, cols. V, IV, = *Samekh* (Weber doubtfully); a *Samekh* like that of col. I, *b*, being made cursive by the Hindus, as shown in col. IV, and turned topsy-turvy, [14] whereby the Drāviḍa *ṣ*, col. V, was obtained, which originally served both for *s* and *ṣ*. Later, this sign was divided into the signs for the etymologically connected *sa* and *ṣa*. By transferring the cross-bar to the outside of the curve, arose the *sa* of the southern Brāhmi in col. VI, *a*, and (turned round) that in col. VI, *b*, while the removal of the bar to the inside of the curve produced the *ṣa* of the same script, col. VI, *c*. The Drāviḍī adopted the new *sa* for its *s*, and retained the old sign for *ṣ*. The northern Brāhmi developed out of the southern *sa* that with the curve, col. VI, *d*, and out of this a new *ṣa*, col. VI, *e*. An immediate derivation of the Drāviḍa *ṣ* from the *Samekh* of the sixth century B.C. in col. III. is not possible, for the reasons stated under No. 5, and because the characteristic ancient cross-bar is wanting in it.—No. 16, *E*, col. V, = *Ain*, cols. I, II (Weber), the Indian sign being changed slightly or not at all in the ancient forms of Kālsī, col. IV and col. V, *b*, as well as in that of Sāñci and Hāthigumphā, col V, *a*, but later made triangular, col. V, *c*, *d*, *e*, in order to avoid a confusion with *ṭha* and *dha*.—No. 17, *pa*, col. V, = *Phe*, cols. I, II (Weber), turned topsy-turvy; in its original position in the Eraṇ form, col. IV; turned sideways in col. V.

No. 18, *ca*, col. V, = *Tsade*, cols. I, II, turned topsy-turvy, the second hook on the right being bent at the same time towards the vertical as in the hypothetical form of col. IV, whence arose, with the turn sideways, the angular or round *ca* of the Brāhmī in col. V, *a*, *b*, and the tailed one of the Drāviḍī, col. V, *c*.—No. 19, *kha*, col. V, = *Qoph*, cols. I, II, turned topsy-turvy with the addition of a curve at the top, col. V, *a*, in order to distinguish the letter from *va*. Owing to the use of ink, the circle at the foot was converted into a dot, col. V, *b*.—No. 20, *ra*, col. V, = *Resh*, cols. I, II (Weber), the triangular head of the letter being opened and the vertical attached to the base of the former triangle, whence arose the forms in col. V, *a*, *b*, and later the ornamental ones, col. V, *c*, *d*, in which the angles were repeated.—No. 21, *śa*, col. V, = *Shin*, cols. I, II (Weber), the two angles, standing side by side, being placed the one inside the other, and the sign being then turned topsy-turvy, col. V, *a*, *b*, *c*. The more closely resembling Aramaic *Shin* of the Sixth century B.C., col. III, cannot be the prototype of *śa*, for the same reasons as those stated above under No. 5, and is merely an analogous transformation, which the Arameans, Phoenicians and Ethiopians have made independently at various periods. The older form with two angles has been preserved in the western sign for 100 = *śu* (see my Indian Studies, III.2 71, 117).—No. 22, *ta*, col. V, = *Taw*, cols. I, II (Weber); from a form like that of Sinjirli, col. III, *b*, or the Assyrian of the time of Salmanassar, col. III, *a*, was derived the *ta* of col. V, *a*, *b*, and hence the regularised from of col. V, *c*.

B.—*Derivative consonants and initial vowels.*

The derivative signs, invented by the Hindus themselves, have been formed by means of the following contrivances :—

(1) One of the elements of a phonetically cognate letter is transposed: (*a*) in *sa* and *ṣa*, where the cross-bar of the oldest sign has been displaced (see above, A, No. 15); (*b*) in *da*, which has been derived from *dha* (Weber) by dividing the vertical stroke, and by attaching the two pieces to the upper and lower ends of the curve, whence first the *da* of the Drāviḍī and of the Patna seal. No. 4, col. VI, *a* was derived, and, with the turn to the left, the ordinary form of the Brāhmī, No. 4, col. VI, *b*, and further the angular *da*, No. 4, col. VI, *f*.

(2) A borrowed or derivative letter is mutilated in order to obtain one with a similar phonetic value: (*a*) from *da*, No. 4, col. VI, *a*, comes [15] by the removal of the lower end the half round *ḍa* of Kālsī and the later southern inscriptions, col. VI, *c*; similarly, from the angular *da*, col. VI, *g*, the ordinary angular *ḍa*, col. VI, *h* of the Aśoka edicts (Weber); (*b*) from *tha*, No. 9, col. V, comes *ṭha*, col VI, *a*, by the removal of the central dot; and from the latter again *ṭa*, col. VI, *b*, is derived by bisection, the round *ṭha* being considered as the product of an unaspirated letter and a curve of aspiration, which appears (see below, 5) in various other letters (Weber); (*c*) from the triangular *E*, No. 16, col. V, *c*, *d*, *e*, comes the *I* with three dots, col. VI, B, *a*, *b*, *c*, which just indicate the outlines of the older sign (Prinsep), the derivation being suggested by the fact that gramatically *e* is the guṇa-vowel of *i*, for which therefore a lighter form of *e* appeared suitable; (*d*) through a bisection of the lower portion of *va*, No. 6, col. V, *b*, and a straightening of the remaining pendant, is derived *U*, col. VI, *a* (see my Indian Studies, III 2. 74), the derivation being suggested by the fact that *u* commonly

represents *va* in weak grammatical forms (*samprasāraṇa*); (*e*) if the later small circle (pl. IV, 38, VI) is the original form of the Anusvāra, No. 13. col. VI, *a*, *b*, and the dot a cursive substitute, the sign may be explained as a mutilated small *ma*, which has lost the angle at the top, and has been thus treated like the small vowelless consonants appearing in the inscriptions of the first centuries A. D. (see. e. g., pl. III, 41, VIII); compare also the derivation of the Kharoṣṭhi Anusvāra from *ma* (see below, §9, B, 4).

(3) Short horizontal strokes, which originally, before the change in the direction of the writing, stood on the left, are used to derive the long vowels $\bar{A}$, No. 1, col. VI, and $\bar{U}$, No. 6, col. VI, *d*, from short *A* and *U*. On account of the peculiar shape of *I*, a dot is used instead for the formation of $\bar{I}$, No. 16, col. VI, B, *g*.

(4) Short horizontal strokes, originally added on the right, denote a change in the quality of the sounds: (*a*) in *O*, No. 6, col. VI, *f*, *g*, derived from *U*, col. VI, *a* (with the bar in the original and the later position), because grammatically *o* is the guṇa-vowel of *u*; (*b*) in *AI*, No. 16, col. VI, A, *b*, derived from *E*, because grammatically *ai* is the vṛddhi-vowel of *e*; (*c*) in the *ḷ* of the Drāviḍi, No. 12, col. VI, from the original form of *la* (*Lamed*), cols. I, II, in which case the bar still stands on the right, because the letter has not been turned; (*d*) in *ña*, No. 14, col. VI, *a*, from the original inverted *Nun*, col. IV; compare above under A, No. 14; (*e*) in *ṅa* (see my Indian Studies, III. 2, pp. 31, 76; also page 35, below, §16, C, 12) from *na*, No. 14, col. V, with a displacement of the lower horizontal stroke towards the right, the letter being kept in its original position; (*f*) in *ṇa*, No. 14, col. VI, *b*, from *na*, the bar protruding at both sides of the vertical in order to avoid the identity with *nā*, *ne* and *O*.

(5) The aspiration is expressed by a curve in the *gh* of the Drāviḍī, No. 3, col. VI, formed out of *g*, and in the ordinary Brāhmī *ḍha*, No. 4, col. VI, *d*, from *ḍa*, col. VI, *c*, in *pha*, No. 17, col. VI, from *pa*, col. V, and in *cha*, No. 18, col. VI, *a*; in the last sign the curve has been attached to both ends of the vertical, and this proceeding led to the development of the cursive *cha* of col. VI, *b*. More rarely a hook is substituted for the curve, and then the original sign is mutilated; thus *bha*, No. 2, col. VI, is derived from *ba* by omitting the base stroke, and *jha*, No. 7, col. VI, from the Drāviḍa *j*, col, V, *a*, by dropping both bars at the ends of the vertical. Both the hook and the curve are cursive substitutes for *ha*, which in the Tibetan alphabet[81] is used again in order to form *gha*, *bha*, &c.

(6) [16] The *ḷa* of the Brāhmi, No. 4, col. VI, *e*, has been derived, by the addition of a small semicircle, for which we have an open angle in Sāñci (pl. II, 41, XVIII), from the half round *ḍa* of col. VI, *c*, the derivation being very probably suggested by the phonetic affinity of *ḍa* to *ḷa*, which two letters are frequently exchanged in Vedic and classical Sanskrit and in the Prākṛt dialects.

C.—*Medial vowels and absence of vowel in ligatures.*

(1).—The system of the Brāhmi.

In accordance with the expressions of the Sanskrit phonologists and grammarians, who take into account the spoken language alone[82] and who call the *k*-sound *ka-kāra*, the *g*-sound *ga-kāra*, &c., the medial *a* is inherent in all consonants, and consequently medial *ā* is expressed by the stroke which distinguishes *A* from *Ā*.

The other medial vowels are either the full initial vowel-signs or cursive derivatives from them, which are placed mostly at the top or rarely at the foot of the consonants. The identity of the medial *o* with the initial *O* is distinctly recognisable in all letters with verticals at the top, as in *ko*, No. 6, col. VI, *h*, *i*, where, on the removal of the dagger-shaped *k* below the second cross-bar, the signs in col. VI, *f*, *g*, reappear ; compare also *go* in *mago*, Girnār edict I, line 11, where an initial *O* has been placed above *g*. In the Jaugada edicts, where only the *O* of col. VI, *f*, occurs, the medial *o* has invariably the same form. But in Girnār we have both forms of *o*, though there is only the *O* of col. VI, *g*. Similarly, the full initial *U* is recognisable in the combinations with consonants ending in verticals, as in *ku*, pl. II, 9, V ; *ḍu*, 20, VII ; *du*, 25, V ; *bhu*, 31, III, V (compare § 16, D, 4) ; and in the *dhu* of Kālsī, No. 6, col. VI, *b* : more usually *u* is represented cursively, either by the horizontal stroke of *U*, as in *dhu*, No. 6, col. VI, *c*, or by its vertical as in *cu*, pl. II, 13, III, and *dhu*, 26, II, &c. Medial *ū* is identical with *Ū*, if combined with consonants ending in verticals ; elsewhere it is cursively expressed by two lines, commonly placed horizontally, as in *dhū*, No. 6, col. VI, *e* : but in the later inscriptions we occasionally find the *Ū* of the period used for the medial vowel.[83] Medial *i* was probably at first expressed by the three dots of the initial *I* (*ki*, No. 16, col. VI, B, *d*), which afterwards were joined cursively by lines and converted into the angle used in most of the Aśoka edicts (*ki*, col. VI, B, *e*). The medial *ī* has been developed out of the latter form by the addition of a stroke, indicating that the vowel is long (*kī*, col. VI, B, *f* ; see above, under B, 3). In order to express medial *e*, the triangle of the initial *E* has been reduced cursively first to an angle, open on the left, as in *ge*, pl. II, 11, III, and more commonly to a straight line (*ke*, No. 16, col. VI, A, *a*). In accordance with the form of the initial *AI*, which consists of *E* and a horizontal bar, medial *ai* is expressed by two parallel horizontal strokes (*thai*, No. 16, col. VI, A, *c*).

The absence of a vowel is indicated by interlacing the sign for the consonants immediately following each other, and in such ligatures the second sign is often mutilated ; see below, § 16, E, 2. This proceeding appears to be a practical illustration of the term *saṃyuktākṣara*, "a joined or ligature syllable," by which the phonologists and grammarians denote a syllable beginning with more consonants than one.

2.—The system of the Drāviḍī.

The notation of the medial vowels in the inscriptions of Bhaṭṭiprolu differs from the usual one in so far as medial *a* is marked by the Brāhmī sign for *ā*, and medial *ā* by a horizontol stroke from the end of which a vertical one hangs down ; see *ka*, pl. II, 9, XIII ; *kā*, 9, XIV. Hence the consonats have no inherent *a*. The device is no doubt of later origin, and has been invented in order to avoid the necessity for ligatures.

§ 5 —*The time and the manner of the borrowing of the Semitic Alphabet.*[84]

[17] According to the preceding discussion, the great majority of the Brāhma letters agree with the oldest types of the North-Semitic signs, which are found in

the archaic Phoenician inscriptions and on the stone of Mesa, incised about B.C. 890. But two characters, *ha* and *ta*, are derived from Mesopotamian forms of *He* and *Taw*, which belong to the middle of the eighth century B.C., and two, *sa*-*ṣa* and *śa*, resemble Aramaic signs of the sixth century B. C. As the literary and epigraphic evidence leaves no doubt that the Hindus were not unlettered during the period B.C. 600-500, and as the other signs of the Aramaic alphabet of this period, such as *Beth*, *Daleth*, *Waw*, &c, are too far advanced to be considered as the prototypes of the corresponding Brāhma letters, it becomes necessary to regard the seemingly modern forms of *sa*, *ṣa* and *śa* as the results of an Indian development, analogous to that of the corresponding Aramaic characters. This assumption, of course, remains tenable only as long as the two Aramaic letters are not shown to be more ancient by new epigraphic discoveries, which event, to judge from the results of the Sinjirli finds, does not seem to be impossible. But, for the present, they must be left out of consideration in fixing the *terminus a quo* for the importation of the Semitic alphabet into India ; and this *terminus* falls between the time of the incision of Mesa's inscription and of those on the Assyrian weights, from about B.C. 890 to about B.C. 750, probably a little more towards the lower than towards the upper limit, or, roughly reckoning, about B.C. 800. And various circumstances make it probable that this was actually the time when the Semitic letters became known to the Hindus.

As the *ha* and the *ta* of the Brāhmī are derived from forms of *He* and *Taw* not found in the Phoenician inscriptions but only in Mesopotamia, it appears probable that this is the Semitic country from which the letters were brought over.[85] It agrees with this inference, that the most ancient Indian works speak of sea-voyages in the Indian Ocean at a very early period, and sea-borne trade, carried on by Hindu Vāṇias in the same waters, is mentioned in later, but still ancient, times. The well-known Bāveru Jātaka[86] bears witness to an early export trade of the Vāṇias to Babylon ; and the form of the word, in which the second part *ilu* is represented by *eru*, points to its having arisen in Western India, where *ra* is occasionally substituted for *la*, as in the Girnār and Shāhbāzgarhī form *Turamaya* for *Ptolemaios*. Several other Jātakas, e.g., No. 463, which describe sea-voyages, name the ancient ports of Western India, Bharukaccha (the modern Broach) and Śūrpāraka (now Supārā), which were centres of the trade with the Persian Gulf in the first centuries A.D. and much later. As according to the Jātakas the Vāṇias started from these towns, it is probably that these trade-routes were used much earlier. Two of the most ancient Dharmasūtras likewise bear witness to the earlier existence of trade by sea in India and particularly on the western coast. Baudhāyana, II, 2, 2, forbids Brahmans to undertake voyages by sea, and prescribes a severe penance for a breach of the rule. But he admits, I, 2, 4, that the "Northerners," were not strict in this respect. As the other offences of the "Northerners," mentioned in the same passage, such as dealing in wool, selling animals with two rows of teeth, i.e. horses and mules, show, the term applies to the inhabitants of western and north-western India. It naturally follows that the sea-voyages referred to were made to western Asia. The same author, I,18,14, and the still older Gautama Dharmasūtra, 10,33, mention the duties payable to the king on merchandise imported by sea.[87] In accordance with my estimate of the age of the Dharmasūtras and of the materials out of which the Jātakas have been made up, I look upon these statements as referring to the 8th-6th centuries B.C.[88] From still earlier times dates the well-known Vedic myth of the shipwreck of Bhujyu "in the ocean where there is no support, no rest for the foot or the hand," and of his being saved on the "hundred-oared galley" of the Aśvins.[89] The scene of action must of course lie in the Indian Ocean, and the story points to the inference [18] that the Hindus navigated these waters during the earliest Vedic period. As, in addition, Semitic legends such as that of the Flood and of Manu's preservation by a miraculous fish occur in the Brāhmaṇas,[90] we have a sufficient number of facts to furnish some support for the conjecture that Hindu traders, who probably learnt the language of the country, just as their modern descendants learn Arabic and Suahili and other African languages, may have imported from Mesopotamia not only the alphabet, but perhaps also other technical contrivances, such as brick-making which was so important for the construction of the ancient Brahmanical altars. With this assumption, which under the circumstances stated appears at least not quite unfounded, the Indian Vāṇias are credited with having rendered the same service to their countrymen which Sambhota or Thonmi did to the Tibetans, when he fetched the elements of their alphabet from Magadha, between A.D. 630 and 660.[91]

In any case, it is *a priori* probable that the Vāṇias were the first to adopt the Semitic alphabet[92]; for they, of course, came most into contact with foreigners, and they must have felt most strongly the want of some means for recording their business transactions. The Brahmans wanted the art of writing less urgently, since they possessed, as passages of the Ṛgveda show,[93] from very early times a system of oral tradition for the preservation of their literary treasures.

Nevertheless, the oldest known form of the Brāhmi is, without a doubt, a script framed by learned Brahmans for writing Sanskrit. This assertion is borne out not only by the remnants of the Gayā alphabet of Aśoka's stone-masons, which must have contained signs for the Sanskrit vowels *AI* and *AU*, and which is arranged according to phonetic principles, but also by the influence of phonetic and grammatical principles which is clearly discernible in the formation of the derivative signs. The hand of the phonologist and grammarian is recognisable in the following points: (1) the development of five nasal letters and of a sign for nasalisation in general from two Semitic signs, as well as of a complete set of signs for the long vowels,[94] which latter are very necessary for the phonologist and grammarian, but not for men of business, and are therefore unknown in other ancient alphabets; (2) the derivation of the signs for the phonetically very different, but grammatically cognate, *śa* and *ṣa* from one Semitic sign (*Samekh*); (3) the notation of *U* by the half of *va*, from which the vowel is frequently derived by saṃprasāraṇa; (4) the derivation of *O* from *U* (*o* being the guṇa-vowel of *u*) by the addition of a stroke; of *I* by a simplification of the sign for its guṇa-vowel *E*; of *AI*, the vṛddhi-vowel, from *E* the guṇa-vowel of *I*; and of *ḷa* from *ḍa*, the former consonant being frequently a substitute for the latter, as in *īḷe* for *īḍe*; (5) the non-expression of medial *a*, in accordance with the teaching of the grammarians who consider it to inhere in every consonant; the expression of medial *ā* by the difference between *A* and *Ā*, and of the remaining medial vowels by combinations of the initial ones, or of cursive simplifications of the same, with the consonants, as well as of the absence of vowels by ligatures of the consonants, which apparently illustrate the grammatical term *saṃyuktākṣara*. All this has so learned an appearance and is so artificial that it can only have been invented by Pandits, not by traders or clerks. The fact that the Vāṇias and the accountants until recent times used to omit all medial vowels in their correspondence and account books, permits even the inference that an Indian alphabet, elaborated by such men, would not possess any such vowel-signs. And it is immaterial for the correctness of this inference, whether the modern defective writing is a survival from the most ancient period or is due to the introduction of the Arabic alphabet in the middle ages.

A prolonged period must, of course, have elapsed between the first introduction of the Semitic alphabet by the merchants, its adoption by the Brahmans which probably did not take place at once, and the elaboration of the 46 radical signs of the Brāhmī together with its system of medial vowels and ligatures.

As, according to the results of the preceding enquiry, the elaboration of the Brāhmi was completed about B. C. 500, or perhaps even earlier, the *terminus a quo*, about B. C. 800, may be considered as the actual date of the introduction of the Semitic alphabet into India. This estimate is, however, [19] merely a provisional one, which may be modified by the discovery of new epigraphic documents in India or in the Semitic countries. If such a modification should become necessary, the results of the recent finds induce me to believe that the date of the introduction will prove to fall earlier, and that it will have to be fixed perhaps in the tenth century B.C., or even before that.

II.—THE KHAROṢṬHI SCRIPT.

§ 6.—*How it was deciphered.*

The Indian alphabet running from right to left, the *Kharoṣṭhī lipi*,[95] has been deciphered exclusively by European scholars among whom Masson, J. Prinsep, Ch. Lassen, E Norris, and A. Cunningham must be particularly mentioned.[96] The coins of the Indo-Grecian and Indo-Scythian kings with Greek and Prākṛt inscriptions furnished the first clue to the value of the letters. The results, which the identifications of the royel names and titles seemed to furnish, were partly confirmed, partly rectified and enlarged, by the discovery of the Shāhbāzgarhi version of the Aśoka edicts and E. C. Bayley's Kāngrā inscription in Brāhmī and Kharoṣṭhī. The characters of the Aśoka edicts are readable with full certainty, with the exception of a few ligatures (see below, § 11, C, 3, 4). Similarly, the inscriptions of the Śakas offer no difficulties, and the new MS. of the Dhammapada from Khotan[97] is in general not difficult to read. But considerable portions of the inscriptions of the Parthian Guduphara and of the Kuṣāna kings Kaniṣka and Huviṣka, still resist the attempts of decipherers and interpreters.

§ 7.—*Use and characteristics.*

In its form, known to us at present, the Kharoṣṭhī is an ephemeral, chiefly epigraphic, alphabet of North-Western India. The majority of the inscriptions written in Kharoṣṭhī have been found between 69°—73°30′E. Long. and 33°—35° N. Lat., in the ancient province of Gandhāra, the modern eastern Afghanistan and the Northern Pañjāb; and the oldest documents are confined to the districts the capitals of which were Taxila (Shāh-Derī) to the east of the Indus, and Puskalāvatī or Carsādā (Hashtnagar) to the west of the river. Single inscriptions have turned up further south-west in Bhāwalpur near Multān, south in Mathurā, and south-east in Kāngrā, and single words or letters in Bharahut, Ujjain and Maisūr (Śiddāpura Aśoka edicts[98]). Coins, cameos and MSS. with Kharoṣṭhī characters have been carried much further north and north-east. The period during which, according to the documentary evidence at present available, the Kharoṣṭhi seems to have been used in India, extends from the fourth century B. C. to about the third century A.D., the earliest letters occuring on the Persian *sigoli* (§ 8) and the latest perhaps on the Gandhāra sculptures and the Kuṣāna inscriptions.[99] As the note in the Fawanshulin of A.D. 668 (see above, § 1) shows, the Buddhists preserved a knowledge of the existence of the alphabet much longer.

Hitherto, the Kharoṣṭhi has been found (1) in stone-inscriptions, (2) on metal plates and vases, (3) on coins, (4) on cameos, and (5) on a longer known small piece of birch bark from a Stūpa in Afghanistan[100] and on the Bhūrja MS. of the Dhammapada from Khotan. The latter MS. has probably been written in Gandhāra during the Kuṣāna period. The dialect of its text shows characteristic affinities to that of the Shāhbāzgarhī version of the Aśoka edicts, and its characters agree very closely with those of the Wardak vase.[101] On the metal plates and vases, [20] the letters frequently consist of rows of dots, or have been first punched in this manner and afterwards scratched in with a stilus[102]. On stone vases they are sometimes written with ink.[103]

In spite of its frequent utilisation for epigraphic documents, the Kharoṣṭhī is a popular script, destined for clerks and men of business. This is proved by the throughout highly cursive character of the letters, by the absence of long vowels, which are useless for the purposes of common daily life, by the expression of groups of unaspirated double consonants by single ones (*ka* for *kka*) and of unaspirated and aspirated ones by the latter alone (*kha* for *kkha*), and by the invariable use of the Anusvāra for all vowelless medial nasals.[104] The discovery of the Khotan MS. makes it very improbable that there existed another form of the script which, being more similar to the Brāhmi in completeness, would have been more suitable for the Brahmanical Śāstras.

§ 8.—*Origin*[105]

The direction of the Kharoṣṭhī from right to left made it *a priori* highly probable that its elements had been borrowed from the Semites; and the almost exact agreement of the forms for *na*, *ba*, *ra* and *va* with Aramaic signs of the transitional type induced E. Thomas to assume a closer connection of the Kharoṣṭhī with this alphabet[106]. His view has never been disputed; but of late it has been given a more precise form by I. Taylor and A. Cunningham, who assign the introduction of the Aramaic letters into India to the first Akhaemenians[107]. The reasons which may be adduced for this opinion are as follows:—
(1) The Aśoka edicts from the western Pañjāb use for "writing, edict," the word *dipi*, which evidently has been borrowed from the Old Persian, and they derive from it the verbs *dipati*,

'he writes' and *dipapati*, "he causes to write;" see above, § 2, B. (2) The districts where Kharoṣṭhī inscriptions occur, especially in earlier times, are just those parts of India which probably were subject to the Persians, be it with or without interruptions, from about B. C. 500 to 331. (3) Among the Persian *sigloi*, there are some marked with single syllables in Kharoṣṭhī and Brāhmī[108], whence it may be inferred that they were struck in India during the Persian period, and that the Kharoṣṭhī was current during a great part of the fourth century B.C., certainly before the fall of the Persian empire in B.C. 331. Some considerable variations in the Kharoṣṭhī letters of the Aśoka edicts, as well as the strongly cursive forms of several ligatures, such as *sta*, *spa* &c. (see below, § 11, C, 2, 3), likewise point to the conclusion that the alphabet had had a long history before the middle of the third century B.C. (4) Recent discoveries in Semitic epigraphy make it extremely probable that the Aramaic, which was used already in Assyria and Babylon for official and business purposes side by side with the cuneiform writing, was very widely spread during the rule of the Akhaemenians. Numerous Aramaic inscriptions of this period have been found in Egypt, Arabia, and Asia Minor, and one even in Persia. Besides, Egypt has furnishnd a number of official Aramaic papyri, and Asia Minor many coins with Aramaic legends, struck by Persian satraps[109]. In addition, there is the curious statement in the Book of Ezra, IV, 7, according to which the Samaritans sent to Artaxerxes a letter written in the *Ārāmī* script and language. Taking all these points together, there are sufficient reasons to warrant the assertion that Aramaic was commonly employed not only in the offices of the satraps, but also in the royal secretariate at Susa. The ultimate cause for the official use of the Aramaic script and language during the Akhaemenian period was, no doubt, that numerous Aramaeans held appointments as clerks, accountants, mint-masters and so forth in the Persian Civil Service. [21] When the Persian empire was rapidly built up on the ruins of more ancient monarchies, its rulers must have found the employment of the trained subalterns of the former governments, among whom the Aramaeans were foremost, not only convenient, but absolutely unavoidable. In these circumstances, it is but natural to assume that, after the full organisation of the administration by Darius, the Persian satraps introduced Aramaean subordinates into the Indian provinces, and thereby forced their Indian subjects, especially the clerks of the native princes and of the heads of towns and villages, to learn Aramaic. At first, the intercourse between the Persian and the Indian offices probably led to the use of the Aramaic letters for the north-western Prākṛt, and later to modifications of this alphabet, which were made according to the principles of the older Indian Brāhmī[110], and through which the Kharoṣṭhī finally arose. The adoption of the Arabic alphabet, during the middle ages and in modern times, for writing a number of Indian dialects, is somewhat analogous, as it likewise happened under foreign pressure, and as its characters were and are used either without or with modifications. (5) With these last conjectures agrees the general character of the Kharoṣṭhī, which is clearly intended for clerks and men of business; see above, § 7. (6) Finally, they are confirmed by the circumstance that the majority of the Kharoṣṭhī signs can be most easily derived from the Aramaic types of the fifth century B.C. which appear in the Saqqārah and Teima inscriptions of B. C. 482 and of about B. C. 500, while a few letters agree with somewhat earlier forms on the later Assyrian weights and the Babylonian seals and gems, and two or three are more closely allied to the later signs of the Lesser Teima inscription, the Stele Vaticana, and the Libation-table from the Serapeum. The whole *ductus* of the Kharoṣṭhi, with its long-drawn and long-tailed letters, is that of the characters on the Mesopotamian weights, seals and cameos, which re-occurs in the inscriptions of Saqqārah, Teima and the Serapeum. Others[111] have compared the writing of the Aramaic papyri from Egypt, which partly at least, like the Taurinensis, belong to the Akhaemenian period. But it does not suit so well. Many of its signs are so very cursive that they cannot be considered as the prototypes of the Kharoṣṭhi letters, and its *ductus* is that of a minute current handwriting. Some special resemblances appear to be, on a closer investigation, the results of analogous developments. Taking all these points together, the Kharoṣṭhi appears to have been elaborated in the fifth century B.C.

§ 9.—*Details of the derivation.*

The subjoined comparative table illustrates the details of the derivation. The signs in col. I. have been taken (with the exception of No. 10, col. I, *a*) from Euting's Tabula Scripturae Aramaicae, 1892, cols. 6, 8, 9, 11 and 12; those in col. II, from the same work, cols. 13, 14, 15, 17, 19 and those in cols. III, IV from plate 1 of this manual; and all have been reproduced by photolithography.

A.—*Borrowed signs.*[112].

Preliminary remarks.—The changes of the Aramaic signs have been caused chiefly by the following principles: (1) by a decided predilection for long-tailed signs with appendages at the upper end, the foot being left free for the addition of *u*, *ra* and the Anusvāra, and by an aversion to appendages at the foot alone; (2) by an aversion to signs with heads containing more than two lines rising upwards, [22] or with transverse strokes through the top-line, or with pendants hanging down from it,—all of which peculiarities would have been awkward for the insertion of the vowels *i*, *e* and *o*; (3) by a desire to differentiate the signs which, altered according to these principles, would have become identical.

No. 1, *A*, col. III, = *Aleph*, col. I, *a* (Saqqārah), with a cursive change of the head to a curve; the position and the size of the letter make a connection with the forms in col. I, *b*, or col. II, improbable.—No. 2, *ba*, col. III, = *Beth*, col. I, *a*, *b* (Teima, Saqqārah), with a cursive curve for the angle at the right; the cursive forms of the *Beth* of the papyri, [23] col. II, *b*, *c*, are further developed than the Kharoṣṭhi signs.—No. 3, *ga*, col. III, = *Gimel*, derived from col. I. or a similar form (compare col. II, and Euting, TSA. 1, *a*), with a cursive loop on the right and a curve on the left; similar loops are common in later ligatures, see pl. I, 33, 35, 36, XII; 34, XIII; and they occur even in *ja*, pl. I, 12, XII.—No. 4, *da*, col. III, = *Daleth*, derived from a form like that in col. II, *b*, which, according to col. I, *a*, occurs already about B. C. 600 on Assyrian weights.—No. 5, *ha*, col. III, = *He*, derived from a form like that in col I, *a* (Teima), with the transposition of the pendant in the middle of the curve to the right end of the foot in order to facilitate the insertion of *i*, *e* and *o* (see preliminary remarks, 2, page 20f., above, and below under No. 17).—No. 6, *va*, col. III, = *Waw*, col. I (Teima, Saqqārah); the papyri in col. II. show more advanced forms.

No. 7, *ja*, col. III, *a*, = *Zain*, derived from a form like those in col. I, *a*, *b* (Teima), the left corner being turned upwards still further, whence the usual Kharoṣṭhī letter in col. III. is derived by omitting the stroke at the foot; the papyri, col. II, show more

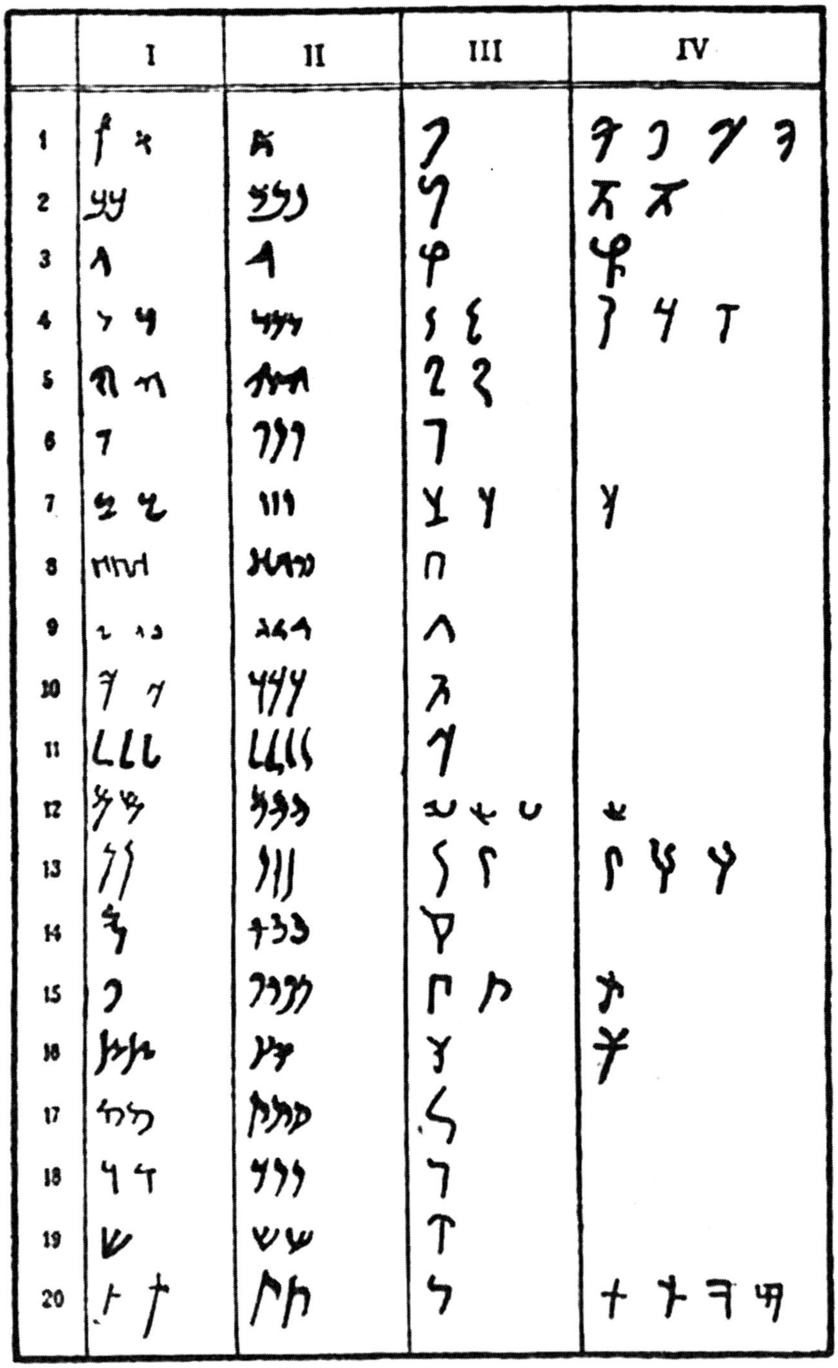

advanced forms unsuitable for comparison.—No. 8, *śa*, col. III, = *Cheth*, col. I (Teima), the sound of the Indian *śa* being very similar to a palatal χa, as in German *ich*.—No. 9, *ya*, col. III, = *Yod*, derived either from a form like col. I, *b*, or directly from one like col. I, *a* (Assyrian weights), with the omission of the bar on the right (see preliminary remarks, 1);

analogous forms occurring in later Palmyranian and Pahlavi (E.TSA. cols. 21-25, 30-32, 35-39, 58).—No. 10, *ka*, col. III, = *Kaph*, derived by a turn from right to left from col. I, *b* (Assyrian weights, Babylonian seals, &c.), and with the addition of a top-stroke, in order to distinguish the new sign from *la* (No. 11, col. III) and from *pa* (No. 15, col. III); the signs of the papyri, col. II, differ entirely.—No. 11, *la*, col. III, = *Lamed*, a form like those in col. I, *a*, *c* (Teima) being turned topsy-turvy owing to the aversion to signs with appendages at the foot alone (preliminary remarks, 1), and the curved line being broken and attached lower in order to distinguish the new letter from *A*.

No. 12, *ma*, col. III, *a*, *b*, = *Mem*, derived from a form like that in col. I, *a*, *b* (Saqqārah) with a curved head, by the omission of the transverse line and a rudimentary indication of the vertical standing originally on the right, whence comes the semicircular ordinary *ma* of the Aśoka edicts, col. III, *c*, still more mutilated on account of the vowel-signs ; the forms of the *Mem* of the Papyri, col. II, are unsuited to be considered the prototypes of the Kharoṣṭhī *ma*.—No. 13, *na*, col. III, *a* = *Nun*, col. I, *a*, *b* (Saqqārah), a later derivative being the *na* of col. III, *b* ; the *Nun* of the papyri, col. II, is again unsuited for comparison.—No. 14, *sa*, col. III, = *Samekh*, col. I (Teima), with transposition of the slanting bar to the left end of the top-stroke from which it hangs down, and with connection of its lower end with the tail of the sign, which has been pushed forward towards the left (see the figures in B.IS. III. 2 ; 105) ; analogous developments appear in Nabataean (E. TSA. cols. 46, 47) and in Hebrew.—No. 15, *pa*, col. III, *a*, = *Phe*, col. I (Teima), turned from right to left to distinguish it from *A* ; in the more usual *pa* of col. III, *b*, the curve has been pushed lower down.—No. 16, *ca*, col. III, = *Tsade*, derived from an acute-angled from like col. I, *a*, *b* (Teima), with the omission of the second hook on the right (see preliminary remarks, 2) and with the development of a hook below the head, because the vertical was made separately ; the analogous *Tsade* of col. II, *b*, has been developed, because the right stroke of the head was made separately and drawn to the vertical.

No. 17, *kha*, col. III, = *Qoph*, derived from a form like col. I, *a*, *b* (Serapeum) with the conversion of the central pendant into an elongation of the top-stroke on the left ; similarly, the pendant has been transferred to the right end of the letter in the Teima form (E TSA. col. 10).—No. 18, *ra*, col. III, = *Resh*, col. I, *a*, *b* (Saqqārah), with complete removal of the angular protuberance on the right.—No. 19, *śa*, col. III, = *Shin*, col. I (Teima), turned topsy-turvy owing to the aversion to tops with more than two strokes rising upwards (preliminary remarks, 2), and with a lengthening of the central stroke owing to the predilection for long-tailed signs.—No. 20, *ta*, col. III, = *Taw*, derived from a form like that in col. I, *a* (Assyrian weights) or in col. I, *b* (Saqqārah), with the transposition of the bar to the top of the [24] vertical, as in col. II, *a*, the new sign at the same time being turned from right to left in order to avoid the resemblance to *pa* (No. 15), and being broadened in order to distinguish it from *va* and *ra* (Nos. 6, 18) ; the older form and the intermediate steps appear in *tha* (No. 20, col. IV, *a*) and *ṭa* (No. 20, col. IV, *b*) where the original *Taw* has been preserved, and in *ṭa* (No. 20, col. IV, *c*) where the bar stands at the top ; compare below, B, 1, *c*, and B, 2.

B.—*Derivative Signs.*

(1) Aspiration.—The aspiration is expressed by the addition of a curve or a hook, which probably represent a cursive *ha* (Taylor), and for which cursively a simple stroke appears; at the same time, the original *mātṛkā* is sometimes simplified.—(*a*) A curve or a hook is added to the right of the vertical of *ga* in *gha*, No. 3, col. IV, to the top of *da* in *dha*, No. 4. col. IV, *a*, and to the end of the second bar of *ṭa*, No. 20, col. IV, *c*, from which it rises upwards, in *ṭha*, No. 20, col. IV, *d* (properly *ṭho*).—(*b*) A hook, a curve, or cursively a a slanting stroke, appears to the right of *ba* in *bha*, No. 2, col. IV, *a*, *b*, the head of *ba* being converted at the same time into a straight line and pushed somewhat more to the left, in order to avoid the identity with *ka*, No. 10, col. III.—(*c*) In the following aspirates appear only cursive straight strokes, added on the left in *jha*, No. 7, col. IV, and *pha*, No. 15, col. IV, and on the right in *cha*, No. 16, col. IV, *ḍha*, No. 4, col. IV, *c*, and *tha*, No. 20, col. IV, *a*, all of which letters show, however, additional peculiarities. In *cha*, the little pendant on the left of *ca* has beeen made horizontal and combined with the stroke of aspiration to a cross bar. In *ḍha*, the head of *ḍa* has been flattened into a straight line. *Tha* has been formed out of the ancient Aramaic *Taw*, No. 20, col. I, *a*, turned from right to left, and the stroke of aspiration continues the bar of *Taw* towards the right.

(2) Linguals.—*ṭa* has been formed out of the older *Taw*, turned from the right to the left, by the addition of a short bar, which in the Aśoka edicts usually stands on the right and lower than that on the left, as in No. 20, col. IV, *b*. In col. IV, *c*, the sign of lingualisation stands on the left, below the *ṭa* with the bar at the top. This form of *ṭa*, which appears rarely in the Aśoka edicts, must formerly have been common, as the *ṭha* has been derived from it (see above, B, 1, *a*). The *ḍa* of No. 4, col. IV, *b*, exactly resembles the common Aramaic *Daleth* in col. I, *b* (Teima) and may be identical with it. If the alphabet imported into India contained two forms for *ḍa* (col. I, *a*, *b*), both may have been borrowed, and the more cumbrous one may have been used for the expression of the fuller sound. It is, however, also possible that the *ḍa* has been formed out of the *da* of No. 4, col. III, *a*, by the addition of the bar of lingualisation, placed vertically on the right. The *ṇa*, No, 13, col. IV, *a*, is likewise derived from *na*, col. III, *a b*, by the addition of a straight stroke going downwards; compare what has been said above, §4, B, 4, regarding the use of a short stroke for denoting the change of the quality of a borrowed or derivative sign in forming the *AI*, *O*, *ṅa*, *ña* and *ṇa* of the Brāhmi.

(3) The palatal *ña*, No. 13, col. IV, *b*, *c*, consists of two *na* (col. III, *a*) joined together (E. Thomas), and illustrates the modern Indian name for *ña* and *ṇa*, which the Pandits often call the big *nakāras*. The sign, which is really not necessary for a clerk's alphabet, has perhaps been framed only because it existed in the Brāhmi, the Pandit's alphabet.

(4) Medial vowels, absence of vowel in ligatures, and Anusvāra.—Long vowels are not marked, and *a* inheres, just as in the Brāhmi, in every consonant. Other vowels are marked by straight strokes. In the case of *i*, the stroke passes through the left side of the top-line or top-lines of the consonant; in *u*, it stands to the left of the foot; in *e*, it descends on the left side of the top-line; in *o*, it hangs down from this line, see *ṭho*, No. 20, col. IV, *d*; for further details see below, §11, B. Joined to *A*, the same strokes form *I*, *U*, *E* and *O*

(No. 1, col. IV, *a-d*). The absence of a vowel between two dissimilar consonants, except nasals, is expressed, as in the Brāhmī, by the combination of the two signs into a ligature, in which the second letter is usually connected with the lower end of the first. But *ra* stands invariably at the foot of the other consonant, whether it may have to be pronounced before or after it. Double [25] consonants, except nasals, are expressed by single ones, and non-aspirates and aspirates by the aspirates alone. Nasals immediately preceding other consonants, are always expressed by the Anusvāra, which, in the Aśoka edicts, is attached to the preceding *mātṛkā*.

The non-expression of *a*, and the rules regarding the formation of the ligatures, no doubt, have been taken over from the Brāhmī, only minor modifications being introduced. And it seems probable that the use of straight strokes for *i*, *u*, *e* and *o* comes from the same source. For, already in the Brāhmī of all the Aśoka edicts, *u*, *e* and *o* are either regularly or occasionally expressed by simple strokes, and in Girnār *i* is represented by a shallow curve, often hardly distinguishable from a straight stroke; moreover, *i*, *e* and *o* stand in Brāhmī, just as in the Kharoṣṭhī, at the top of the consonants, and *u* at the foot. A connection of the two system of medial vowel-signs is therefore undeniable, and that of the Brāhmī must be regarded as the original one, since its signs, as has been shown above, §1, C. 1, evidently have been derived from the initial vowels.

The notation of *I*, *U*, *E* and *O* by combinations of *A* with the medial vowel-signs is peculiar to the Kharoṣṭhī, and is attributable to a desire to simplify the alphabet. Among the later Indian alphabets, the modern Devanāgarī offers an analogy with its ओ and औ, and the Gujarātī with its એ *E*, ઐ *AI*, ઓ *O*, and ઔ *AU*. Several among the foreign alphabets derived from the Brāhmī, as e.g. the Tibetan, show the principle of the Kharoṣṭhī fully developed.

The Anusvāra, which is used, as in the Brāhmī, for all vowelless nasals, is derived from *ma* (E. Thomas). In *maṃ*. No. 12, col. IV, it still has the full form of *ma*, but usually it undergoes cursive alteration; see below, §11, B, 5.

§ 10.—*The varieties of the Kharoṣṭhī of Plate I*[113].

According to Plate I, the Kharoṣṭhī shows four chief varieties, viz. :—(1) the archaic one of the fourth and third centuries B.C., found in the Aśoka edicts of Shāhbāzgarhī (photolithograph of edict VII. in ZDMG. 43, 151, and of edict XII. in EI. 1,16) and of Mansehra (photolithograph of edicts I-VIII. in JA. 1888, II, 230, = Senart, Notes d'E'pigraphie Indienne, 1), with which the signature in the Aśoka edicts of Śiddāpura (photolithographs in EI. 3,138-140), the legends on the oldest coins (autotypes in C. CAI. pl.3, Nos. 9, 12, 13) and the syllables on the Persian *sigloi* (autotypes in J. RAS. 1895, 865) fully agree.

(2) The variety of the second and first centuries B.C. on the coins of the Indo-Grecian kings, which is imitated by some later foreign kings (autotypes in P. Gardner's Catalogue of Indian Coins in the British Museum, pl. 4-21).

(3) The variety of the Śaka period, first century B. C. to first century A D. (?), on the Taxila copper-plate of Patika (lithograph in J. RAS 1863, 222, pl. 3, and collotype in EI. 4, 56), and on the lion-capital of the satrap Śoḍāsa or Śuḍasa from Mathurā, which

occurs also on some sculptures from Gandhāra (autotype in J. ASB. 58, 144, pl. 10; Anzeig phil. hist. Cl. WA. 1896), on the Kaldawa stone (WZKM. 10, 55, 327) and on the coins of several Śaka and Kuṣāna kings (autotypes, P. Gardner, op. cit., pl. 22-25).

(4) The strongly cursive script of the first and second centuries A.D. (?), which begins with the Takht-i-Bahi inscription of Gondopherres (autotype in JA. 1890, I, = S.NI. 3, pl. 1, No. 1) and is fully developed in the inscriptions of the later Kuṣāna kings Kaniṣka and Huviṣka (autotype of the Zeda inscriptions in JA. 1890, I, = S.NEI. 3, pl. 1, No. 3, of the Manikyāla stone, JA. 1896, I, = S.NEI. 6, pl. 1, 2, of the Sü Bihār inscription, IA. 10, 324, lithograph of the Wardak vase, J.RAS. 1863, 256, pl. 10)[114], and occurs also in the MS. of the Dhammapada from Khotan; see above, §7.

§ 11.—THE ARCHAIC VARIETY.[115]

A.—*The radical signs.*

(1) [26] A small stroke, rising upwards at an acute angle, may be added at the foot of every letter ending with a straight or slanting line, in order to mark its end (plate I, 1, II; 6, II, V; 7, II; 8, II; &c). If a letter ends with two slanting lines, like *ya* and *śa* (34, II), the upstroke may be added to the left. In the Aśoka edicts of Mansehra, *ḍha* receives instead occasionally a straight base-stroke (18, V).

(2) *Ca* has three varieties, (*a*) head with obtuse angle (10, I. II, IV); (*b*) head with curve (10, V); (*c*) head with curve connected by a vertical with the lower part (10, III). —(3) The head of *cha* is likewise sometimes anglar (11, I, IV) and sometimes round (11, II), and loses occasionally the cross-bar below the head, as in the later types.—(4) The full form of *ja* occurs at least once in Shāhbāzgarhī (12, I, V) and oftener in Mansehra, where once (edict V, l. 24) the bar stands to the left of the foot. The left side stroke of *ja* is often curved (12, III)—(5) In *ña*, the second shortened *na* (see above, §9, B, 3) is sometimes added on the right (14, I, V) and sometimes on the left (14, III, IV). Occasionally, the right side of the letter is converted cursively into a vertical, as in the later inscriptions (14. IX).

(6) The normal form of *ṭa* is that of 15, I, II; but the bar on the left stands occasionally lower than that on the right (15, V; 38, II), or both bars stand on the left (38, VI), or the bar on the right is omitted (commonly in Mansehra) (15, III).

(7) *Ta* (20) is mostly shorter and broader than *ra* (31), and either its two lines are of equal length, or the vertical one is shorter. Forms like 20, V, are rare.—(8) *Di* (22, II) shows twice, in Shāhbāzgarhī edict IV, l. 8, and Mansehra edict VII, l. 33 (where the transcript in ZDMG. has erroneously *dri*), a curve to the right of the foot, which is probably nothing but an attempt to clearly distinguish *da* from *na*.—(9) *Dha* with the left end turned upwards (23, V) is rare and a secondary development (see above, §9, B, 1). In the abnormal *dha* of 38, VIII (*dhra*), from Mansehra, the second bar is a substitute for a very sharp bend to the left (23, V).—(10) The *na* with the bent head (24, III) occurs not rarely in the syllable *ne*.

(11) The greatly mutilated *ma* (29, I) is more common than the forms with remnants of the old pendant (compare above, §9, A, No. 12). It appears invariably in connection with vowel signs and owes its existence to such combinations.

(12) *La* with a curve on the left, as in the later inscriptions (32, VIII), is rare in the Aśoka edicts, but occurs in Mansehra edict VI, l. 29.

(13) The cursively rounded *śa* of 34, III, is rare; but once, in Shāhbāzgarhī edict XIII, l. 1, appears a *śa* hardly distinguishable from *ya*.—(14) The *sa* with a triangular head (36, II), and that with a rounded head (36, I, III, IV), are cursive developments from the old polygonal from (36, V). The vertical stroke of *sa* is occasionally omitted, as in Mansehra [27] edict VI, l. 27.

(15) The common forms of *ha* with a curve (37, I, IV) or a short hook (37, III, V) at the foot, are cursive developments of the *ha* of 37, II; see above, §9, A, No. 5.

B.—*Medial vowels and Anusvāra*

(1) The *i*-stroke goes regularly across the left side of the horizontal strokes of the consonants (6, III; 7, III; 15, II, III; &c.); in letters with two horizontal or slanting top-strokes, it passes through both (14, III; 16, III; 38, III, VI; &c.), likewise through both the top-strokes of *ṇa* (19, X). In *I* (2, I), *di* (22, II), and *ni*, it stands just below the head, and in *yi* (30, II) it hangs in the left side.

(2) The *e*-stroke corresponds in form and position to the upper half of the *i*-stroke (4, I; 6, IV; 12, II; 19, III; &c.); in *E* (4, II) it may also stand straight above the head of *A*.

(3) The *o*-stroke mostly corresponds in its position to the lower half of the *i*-stroke (5, I; 12, IV; 14, IV; &c.), but it stands further to the right in the angle, formed by the upper part of the letters, in *go*, *gho* (9, II) and *so* (36, IV).

(4) The *u*-stroke stands regularly at the left lower end of the consonant (3, I; 8, III; 10, IV; 12, III; &c.), but a little higher up if the foot of the consonant is curved to the left (*U*, 3, II), or to the right (*du*, 22, IV), or has a hook on the right (*pru*, 25, V; *hu*, 37, IV). In *mu* it stands to the left of the top of *ma* (see *mru*, 29, V).

(5) The Anusvāra has the full form of *ma* (see above, §9, B, 4) only occasionally in *maṃ* (29, IV). More commonly it is represented cursively by a straight stroke as in *maṃ* (38, XI), or by two hooks at the sides of *ma* as in *maṃ* (38, X). In combination with other consonants ending in a single slanting or vertical line, the Anusvāra is marked by an angle, opening upwards, which the foot of the consonant bisects (8, IV; 11, IV; 17, V; 19, V; &c.). or, rarely in Shāhbāzgarhī, oftener in Mansehra, by a straight line, a substitute for the curve of *ma*, as in *thaṃ* (21, V). If the foot of the consonant has some other appendage, the Anusvāra is attached higher upto the vertical, as in *ñaṃ* (14, V); *ḍaṃ* (18, V); *vraṃ* (33, V); *haṃ* (37, V). The angular Anusvāra is always divided in *yaṃ* (30, V) and in *śaṃ*, and the one half is added to the right end of the *mātṛkā*, and the other to the left. This may also be done in *kaṃ* and in *bhaṃ* (28, IV).

C.—*Ligatures.*

(1) *Bhye* (38, IX), *mma* (38, XII) and *mya* (38, XII, *b*) show no changes or only very slight ones in the combined letters. In other cases, one or the other is usually mutilated.

(2) For *ra*, which must be pronounced sometimes before and sometimes after its Mātṛkā (exception in *rṭa* in Mansehra edict V, 1. 24), appears, besides slightly mutilated forms (in *rṭi*, 38, IV, and *rva*, 39, I), (*a*) a slanting line, with or without a bend, which goes through the middle of the vertical of the combined consonant (as in *gra*, 38, I; *rṭa*, 38, II; *rṭi*, 38, III); (*b*) also a curved or straight stroke at the foot of the combined sign (*rṭi*, 38, V; *kra*, 6, V; *gra*, 8, V; *tra*, 20, V; *dhra*, 23, V; 38, VIII; *pru*, 25, V; *bra*, 27, V; *vraṃ*, 33, V; *śru*, 34, V; *stri*, 39, VIII, IX). In combination with *ma*, the *ra*-stroke stands invariably at the right top, as in *kru* (29, V), and in *kra* and *bhra* (28, V), occasionally at the right end of the hooks of those letters. Sometimes, especially in Mansehra, a curve open above, as in *thra* (21, IV), is substituted for the straight stroke. The stroke and the curves, of course, are cursive substitutes for a full *ra*, attached to the foot of the combined consonants.

(3) In *vru* (39, II) the two consonants have been pushed the one into the other, so that the vertical does duty both for the *va* and the *ra*. The same principle is followed in the formation of the ligature *sta* (which consists only in Shāhbāzgarhī edict I, 1. 2, *srestamati*, of *sa* with a *ta* hooked into the vertical, 39, IV). At the same time *sa* is mutilated, the middle of its top remaining open and the hook on the left being omitted. This is clearly visible in *sti* (39, V) and *stri* (39, IX), while *sta* (39, III), *sti* (39, VI), *stu* (39, VII) and *stri* (39, VIII) are made more negligently. The ligature of *sa* and *pa* is formed according to [28] the same principles, but the *sa* is mutilated still more and merely indicated by a little hook at the top of the vertical of *pa* in *spa* (39, X) and *spi* (39, XII).[116] In *spa* (39, XI) the hook stands on the side-limb of *pa*.

(4) The ligature in 38, VII seems to have two different meanings. In Shāhbāzgarhī edict X, 1. 21, the sign appears in the representative of the Sanskrit *tadātvāya*, which in the dialect of the Aśoka edicts might be either *tadatvaye* or *tadattaye*, and in Mansehra it occurs frequently in the representative of the Sanskrit *ātman*. As the Kuṣāna inscriptions offer a similar sign (31, XIII) in the representative of the Sanskrit *satvānām*, we have probably to read *tva* in Shāhbāzgarhī edict X, 1. 21, and to assume that the curve at the foot of *ta* represents a *va*, just as it stands in *thra* (21, IV) for the similar *ra*. This explanation is confirmed by the ligatures 30, XIII, and 37, XIII, which most probably are equivalent to *śva* (*īśvara*) and *sva* (*visharasvamini*). In Mansehra (especially edict XII) the sign 38, VII, has to be read *tma*.[117].

§ 12.—CHANGES IN THE LATER VARIETIES[118].

A.—*The radical signs.*

(1) The meaningless upward stroke connected with the foot of the verticals occurs only occasionally on the Indo-Grecian coins (7, VI; 20, VI; 36, VI). More frequently it appears detached to the left of the signs, as in *A* (1, VI), and even with *ha* (37, VI). A cursive substitute is the very common dot, as in *ha* (37, VII); compare also *ma* (29, VII). Finally, various letters, like *ta* (20, VII) and *na* (24, VII), receive on the Indo-Grecian coins a horizontal base-line (see above, §11, A, 1). In the variety of the Śaka period, the ends of the verticals show sometimes a meaningless hook, as in *ca* (10, VIII) and in *sa* (36, IX), or a straight stroke on the right, as in *ṣi* (35, VIII). The same hook appears also in the cursive script of the Kuṣāna

period (*ṣa*, 35, X), or a horizontal stroke to the left, as in *A* (1, XI), *ka* (6, X), *dha* (23, XI), *na* (24, XII), *bi* (27, XI), *ya* (30, X), as well as curves both to the right and left, as in *kha* (7, X), *ca* (10, XII), *dhi* (16, XI), *ghi* (9, X), *ba* (27, X), *mi* (29, XI), where the curve has been added to the vowel-stroke.

(2) In the Śaka and Kuṣāna varieties, the head of *ka* is commonly converted into a curve (6, VIII), and in the Kuṣāna variety this curve is connected with the side-limb of *ka* (see 6, X).—(3) In all the later varieties, the top of *kha* is made longer and curved to the right (7, VI-XI ; 39, XIV).

(4) In the Śaka type, we have a cursive form of *ca*, derived from 10, III, in which the left end of the lower portion of the sign is attached to the short vertical below the top. Similar, still more cursive, forms are common in the Kuṣāna variety ; see 10, X, and XII. —(5) All the later varieties show the *cha* without the cross-bar, and the vertical is occasionally made to slant so that the sign looks like *mo*.—(6) In the later varieties, the left side-limb of *ja* is nearly always rounded, and in the Kuṣāna variety the head of the sign often consists of a shallow curve, from the left end of which the vertical hangs down (12, XI). Hence is developed the looped *ja* (12, XII) of the Bimāran vase. The full *ja* with the bar across or to the left of the foot occurs on the Indo-Grecian coins (12, VII).—(7) In all the later varieties, one side of *ña* invariably shows a vertical (14, VIII, IX).

(8) The only known *ṭa* of the Śaka period in the ligature *ṣṭe* (22, XIII) shows the archaic form with one bar on the left ; compare 15, III. In the Kuṣāna variety, the two bars to the right and left (15, I) are converted into a straight line, whereby *ṭa* becomes *ṭha* (15, X-XII). The small strokes at the top of *ṭu* (15, XI) are, as FLEET's impression of the *Sū* Bihār inscription shows, due to rents in the copper. The correct reading of the word, in which it occurs, is *kuṭubini* instead of *kichubini* (Hoernle).—(9) In all [29] the later varieties, *ṭha* (16, VIII, X, XI) loses the hook at the end of the second bar.

(10) On the Indo-Grecian coins, *ta* (20) is very similar to *ra* ; in the Śaka inscriptions, it is only one-third of the size of *ra*, and in the Kuṣāna variety the two letters are again very similar.

(11) The Śaka *da* of *do* (22, IX) is derived from the form 22, II, while the signs 22, VIII and X, come from the ordinary *da* of the Aśoka edicts. The Kuṣāna form (22, XI) shows an inverted curve at the head.

(12) The inscription of Gondopherres and some coins of that king and of Azilises (P. Gardner, Cat. Ind. C. Br. Mus. p. 94, No. 22), show—the first in the king's name—a peculiar sign (26, X) usually read *pha*, but possibly meant for *fa*, as O. Franke proposes, ZDMG. 50, 603.—(13) In the Kuṣāna variety, the right end of the horizontal top of *bha* is occasionally connected with the vertical (28, X), and sometimes the top-stroke is connected with the side-limb, just as in *ku* (6, XI). —(14) The fuller *ma* (29, VI) is common on the Indo-Grecian coins, and for its slanting stroke the later coins often show a dot (29, VII). In the *mu* of the Śaka and Kuṣāna varieties (29, IX, XII) *ma* is laid on its side, the right part of the semicircle rises high up, and the left is bent downwards ; compare the late *muṃ* (33, XIII).

(15) In the Kuṣāṇa inscriptions, *ya* often becomes a curve or rhombus-like figure, open below (30, XI, XII).—(16) In the later varieties, the left limb of *la* (32, VIII, X) is invariably round, and in the Kuṣāṇa type it is often attached to the top of the vertical (32, XI, XII).—(17) In later times, the head of *va* (33, VIII, X) is invariably rounded.

(18) Equally, *śa* (34, VIII, X) is often made round and similar to *ya*.—(19) In later times, *sa* (36, VII-XI) invariably loses the line connecting the left side of the head with the tail, and the new form becomes in the Kuṣāṇa inscriptions often highly cursive ; see 36, XII.

B.—*Medial vowels and Anusvāra.*

(1) Medial *i* often crosses the vertical low down ; see *I* (2, VII, VIII, X), *di* (22, XI), *ni* (24, XI), &c. ; and in the Kuṣāṇa variety it gets a hook in *mi* (29, XI). Medial *o* like-wise is occasionally attached low down to the vertical, see *ro* (31, XI) ; *ho* (37, XII).

(2) The *e*-stroke stands in *E* invariably on the right of the *A* (4, VI-VIII), and it may sink down as low as the foot. The short stroke is then converted into a long bent line (4, X, XII) or receives a hook at the end (4, XI). Occasionally *e* stands also at the foot of other letters, as in *śe* (34, IX, Mathurā lion-capital).

(3) On the Indo-Grecian coins, medial *u* keeps its old form ; but in *ju* (12, VII) the stroke rises upwards on account of the base-line of *ja*, likewise in *pu* (25, VII) on account of the bend in the *pa*. In later times, *u* is represented by a curve or a loop, as in *U* (3, VIII), *ku* (6, XI), *khu* (7, XI), &c. ; in *mu* (29, IX, XII), the curve opens to the right.

(4) The Anusvāra is marked by a *ma*, laid on its side, which either is connected with its *mātṛkā*, as in *Aṃ* (1, VII), *Iṃ* (2, VII), *ṭhiṃ* (16, XI), or stands separate to the left, as in *yaṃ* (30, VII), or may be placed below (see *mahaṃtasa* in the Taxila copper-plate, line 1).

C.—*Ligatures.*

(1) The ligatures of the Indo-Grecian coins, such as *kra* (6, VII), *khre* (39, XIV), *stra* (38, XIV), and those of the Śaka inscriptions, *ṣṭe* (22, XIII), *khsa* (25, XIII), *sta* (23, XIII), show only small changes. The same remark applies to the ligatures on the coins of the Śakas and the older Kuṣāṇas, where, however, some new groups appear, such as *psa* (26, XIII), *rma* (28, XIII ; compare the shape of *ma* in P. Gardner, op. cit., pl. 25, 1, 2), *śpa* (29, XIII), which has been mostly misread *spa* on account of the Greek Spalyrises, *śva* (30, XIII) with the *va* turned into a curve (see above, § 11, C, 4), and the doubtful representative of *dphi* (27, XIII) in *Kadphises*, the upper part of which is plainly *pi*, while the lower one does not correspond to any known letter.

(2) Among the ligatures of the cursive Kuṣāṇa inscriptions, some, like *gra* (8, XI), *bhra* (28, XII), exactly agree with the archaic forms, and [30] during this period we still find even the old *vra* (*rva*) (39, I) in the word *sarva*. The ligatures *tva* (31, XIII),

ṭsa (32, XIII), often misread as *tsa*, *ṣka* (35, XIII), and *ṣṭu* (36, XIII) show the new Kuṣāna forms of the component parts. But the *sa* of *sva* (37, XIII) is badly mutilated, and the loops of *rya* (34, XIII), *rva* (33, XII), *ṣya* (35, XII), and *sya* (36, XII)[119] are new cursive formations. In all words where one would expect *sta*, the Kuṣāna inscriptions show *ṭha* (16, X, XI). Probably the omission of the bar on the right (compare 23, XIII) is merely cursive, and the sign has to be read both *ṭha* and *sta*, as the case may require. The MS. of the Dhammapada has both signs.

III. THE ANCIENT BRĀHMĪ AND DRĀVIDĪ FROM ABOUT B. C. 350 TO ABOUT A. D. 350.

§ 13.—*How it was deciphered.*

The first scholar who read, in 1836, an inscription in the oldest Brāhma characters, the legend on the coins of the Indo-Grecian king Agathocles, was Ch. Lassen[120]. But the whole alphabet was deciphered by J. Prinsep in 1837-38[121]. His table[122] is, with the exception of the signs for *U* and *O*, quite correct, as far as it goes. Since his time, six missing signs have been found, among which *I*, *Ū*, *śa*, *ṣa* and *ḷa* have been given in Plate II of this manual, while *ṅa*, discovered by Grierson in Gayā, is figured in my Indian Studies, III. 2, pp. 31, 76, and on §16, C below. The existence of *AU* in the third century B. C. is assured by the Gayā alphabet of Aśoka's masons[123]. *Ū* and *śa* have been first recognised by Cunnigham[124]. One form of *ṣa* has been first pointed out by Senart[125] and another by Hoernle[126]. I have found *ḷa* in the Sāñci votive inscriptions[127]. Regarding *I*, compare below, §16, C, 4.

§ 14.—*Common characteristics of the ancient inscriptions.*

The forms of the Brāhmī and Drāviḍī, used during the first 600 years, are known at present only from inscriptions on stones, copper-plates, coins, seals and rings[128], and there is only one instance of the use of ink from the third or second century B C.[129]. The view of the development of the characters during this period is, therefore, not complete. For, in accordance with the results of all paleographic research, the epigraphic alphabets are mostly more archaic than those used in daily life, as the very natural desire to employ monumental forms prevents the adoption of modern letters, and as, in the case of coins, the imitation of older specimens not rarely makes the alphabet retrograde. The occurence of numerous cursive forms together with very archaic ones, both in the Aśoka edicts (see above, § 3) and also in later inscriptions, clearly proves[130] that Indian writing makes no exception to the general rule. And it will be possible to use the numerous cursive letters for the reconstruction of the more advanced alphabets, which were employed for manuscripts and for business purposes.

The full recognition of the actual condition of the Indian writing is obscured also by the fact that the inscriptions of the earliest period, with two exceptions, are either in Prākṛt or in a mixed language (Gāthā dialect), and that the originals, from which they were transferred to stone or copper, were drafted by clerks and monks who possessed little or no education. In [31] writing Prākṛt these persons adopted nearly throughout —(in writing the mixed dialect less constantly)—the practically convenient popular orthography, in which the notation of long vowels, especially of ī and ū and of the Anusvāra, is occasionally neglected as a matter of small importance, and in which double consonants are mostly represented by single ones, non-aspirates are omitted before aspirates, and the Anusvāra is put for all vowelless medial nasals[131]. This mode of spelling continues in the Prākṛt inscriptions with great constancy until the second century A. D. The constant doubling of the consonants appears first in a Pāli inscription of *Hāritīputta Sātakaṇṇi*, king of Banavāsī, which has been recently found by L. Rice[132]. The longer known inscription of the same prince (IA. 14, 331) does not show it. Besides, we find in some other, partly much older, Prākṛt documents, faint traces of the phonetical and grammatical spelling of the Pandits. Thus, the Aśoka edicts of Shāhbāzgarhī offer some instances of *mma* (see above, § 9, B, 4), the Nāsik inscriptions Nos. 14, 15, and Kuḍā No. 5, have the word *siddha*, and Kaṇheri No. 14 *āyyakena*[133]. Such deviations from the rule indicate that the writers had learned a little Sanskrit, which fact is proved also for the writer who drafted the Kālsī edicts by the, for the Pali absurd, form *baṃhmane*, for *baṃbhane* (Kālsī edict XIII, 1. 39).

With the exception of the Ghasundī (Nāgarī) inscription, which contains no word with a double consonant, all the documents in the mixed dialect offer instances of double consonants which sometimes even are not absolutely necessary. Pabhosa No. 1 has *Bahasatimittrasa* and *Kaśśapīyānaṃ*, No. 2 has *Tevaṇīputtrasya*, Nāsik No. 5 has *siddham*, and Kārle No. 21 has *Setapharaṇaputtasya*[134]. And the Jaina inscriptions from Mathurā furnish numerous analogous cases[135]. The only known Sanskrit inscriptions of this period, the Girnār Praśasti from the reign of Rudradāman and Kaṇheri No. 11[136], in general show the orthography approved by the phonologists and grammarians, with a few irregularities in the use of the Anusvāra, e.g., *pratānaṃ ā* (Girnār Praśasti, 1. 2), *saṃbaṃdhā* (1, 12), which have been caused by the influence of the popular orthography, but are found in the best MSS. written by Pandits. The orthographic peculiarities, just discussed, have therefore nothing to do with the development of the alphabet, but merely show that in ancient, as in modern, India the spelling of the clerks differed from that of the learned Brahmans, and that both methods, then as now, mutually influenced each other and caused irregularities.

A second peculiarity[137], found in many inscriptions in Prākṛt and in the mixed dialect, is the frequent erroneous employment of the signs for the sibilants. In the Aśoka edicts of Kālsī, of Śiddāpura, and of Bairāt No. II[138], on the Bhaṭṭiprolu vases, in the cave inscriptions of Nāgārjunī and of Rāmnāth[139], and in the Mathurā inscriptions of the Kuṣāna period, nay even in the two oldest Ceylonese inscriptions, *ṣa* or *śa* are used often for *sa*, and *śa* for *ṣa*, and *sa* for *śa* and *ṣa*. The reasons for this promiscuous use of the sibilants are, first, the circumstance that the school alphabet, which the clerks learned, was originally intended for Sanskrit and contained more sibilants than the ancient vernaculars possessed, and secondly, the negligent pronunciation of the classes destitute of grammatical training.

The western and southern Prākṛts very probably possessed, then as now, both the palatal and the dental sibilants, and it was probably the custom, as is done also in our days, to exchange the two sounds in the same words. The natural consequence was that the feeling for the real value of the signs for *śa* and *sa* disappeared among the Prākṛt-speaking classes, while the *ṣa* of their school-alphabet, for which there was no corresponding sound in their vernaculars, must have appealed to them as a sign suitable to express sibilance. The Sanskrit inscriptions of all centuries, especially the land-grants which were drafted by common clerks, the MSS. of works written in the modern Prākṛts, and the documents from [32] the offices of modern India, with their countless mistakes in the use of the sibilants, offer abundant proof for the correctness of this explanation of the errors in the old inscriptions. The explanation is also confirmed by the occasional occurence of *ṇa*[140] for *na*,—once in the separate edicts of Dhauli and once of Jaugada,—though *na* alone is permissible for their dialect. In these cases, too, the error seems to have been caused by the fact that the school alphabet contained both *ṇa* and *na*. The clerks, who had learned it, each made once a slip, and put in the, for them, redundant sign. The different opinion[141], according to which the exchange of the sibilants in the Aśoka edicts indicates that the values of the Brāhma signs were not completely settled in the third century B. C., rests on the, now untenable, assumption that the Brāhmī was elaborated, not for writing Sanskrit, but for the Prākṛt dialects.

§ 15.—*The varieties of the Brāhmī and Drāviḍī in Plates II and III.*[142].

Plates II. and III. show the following fifteen scripts of the first period :—

(1) The variety of the Eraṇ coin, running from the right to the left (pl. II. col. I), which probably dates from the 4th century B. C.

(2) The older Maurya alphabet of the Aśoka edicts[143] (pl. II, cols. II-XII), which occurs also with local variations on the Persian *sigloi*[144] and the old coins from Taxila, &c[145], in the majority of the inscriptions on the Bharahut Stūpa (pl. II, 6, XVIII ; 45, XI), in Gayā[146], Sāñci[147], and Parkham[148], on the Patnā seals, on the Sohgaura copper-plate[149], and on the stone of Ghasundī or Nagarī (pl. II, col. XVI), and probably prevailed at least in the latter half of the 4th and in the 3rd century B. C.

(3) The Drāviḍī of Bhaṭṭiprolu (pl. II, cols. XIII-XV), which is connected with the southern variety of the Maurya type, but includes many very archaic signs ; about B.C. 200.

(4) The later Maurya alphabet of Daśaratha's inscription (pl. II, col. XVII), closely related to the characters on the coins of the Indo-Grecian kings Agathocles and Pantaleon[150] ; about B. C. 200 to 180.

(5) The Suṅga alphabet of the Toraṇa of Bharahut (pl. II, col. XVIII), which agrees with that of the Pabhosa inscriptions (pl. II, col. XIX), of the later votive inscriptions on the rails of the Bharahut and Sāñci Stūpas[151], of the oldest Mathurā inscriptions[152] (pl. II, col. XX), of the Riwā inscription[153], and so forth[154] ; 2nd to 1st centuries B.C.

(6) The older Kaliṅga alphabet of the Kaṭak (Hāthigumphā) caves (pl. II, cols. XXI, XXII) ; about B. C. 150.

(7) The archaic alphabet of the western Dekhaṇ in the Nānāghāṭ inscription (pl. II, cols. XXIII, XXIV), which is found also in Nāsik No. 1, in Pitalkhorā, and in Ajaṇṭā Nos. 1, 2[155]; from about B.C. 150 to the 1st century A.D.

(8, 9) The precursors of the later northern alphabets, the alphabet of the inscriptions of the Northern Kṣatrapa Śoḍāsa and of the archaic votive inscriptions from Mathurā (pl. III, cols. I, II), 1st century B.C. to 1st century A.D. (?), and the Kuṣāna alphabet of the reigns of Kaniṣka, Huviṣka and Vāsudeva (pl. III, cols. III-V), 1st and 2nd (?) centuries A.D.

(10-15) The precursors of the later southern alphabets, the alphabet of Kāṭhiāvāḍ from the time of the Western Kṣatrapa Rudradāman (pl. III, col. VI), about A.D. 150; the archaistic type of the western Dekhaṇ from the time of the Kṣatrapa Nahapāna (pl. III, col. VII), beginning of the 2nd century A.D. (?); the more modern-looking alphabet of the same district (occasionally with only faint traces of southern peculiarities) from the time of Nahapāna (pl. III, cols. VIII, IX), of the Andhra king Gotamīputa Sātakaṇi (col. X), of the Andhra king Puḷumāyi (col. XI), of the Andhra king Gotamīputa Siriyaña Sātakaṇi (col. XII), of Nāsik No. 20 (col. XIII), and of the Ābhīra king Īśvarasena (col. XIV), 2nd century A.D.; the ornamental variety of the same district with more fully developed southern peculiarities, from the Kuḍā and [33] Junnar inscriptions (cols. XV, XVI), 2nd century A.D.; the highly ornamental variety of the eastern Dekhaṇ from Jaggayyapeṭa (cols. XVII, XVIII), 3rd century A.D. (?); and the ancient cursive alphabet of the Prākṛt grant of the Pallava king Śivaskandavarman (cols. XIX, XX), 4th century A.D. (?).

§16.—THE OLDER MAURYA ALPHABET: PLATE II.

A.—*Geographical extension and duration of use*[156].

The older Maurya alphabet was used over the whole of India, and it seems to have found its way into Ceylon at the latest about B.C. 250. For, the two oldest Ceylonese inscriptions[157], from the time of the king Abaya Gāmini, which probably belong to the end of the 2nd or the beginning of the 1st century B.C., show characters which appear to have been developed from those of the Aśoka edicts. And the close relations between Aśoka and Tissa of Ceylon, reported by the Southern Buddhists, make an importation of the Brāhmī from Magadha into Ceylon not improbable. It is, however, possible that the Brāhmī alphabet was introduced even earlier into Ceylon by Indian colonists[158].

The upper limit of the use of the older Maurya alphabet cannot be fixed with any certainty. But the shape of some of the characters on the Persian *sigloi* (above § 15, 1) makes it probable that even its more advanced forms existed before the end of the Akhaemenian rule in India (B.C. 331). Its oldest primary forms, no doubt, go back to much earlier times, as also the statements of the tradition, discussed above, tend to show. [34] The lower limit of the use of this type cannot be very distant from the end of Aśoka's reign (about B.C. 221), and must fall about B.C. 200. This estimate is supported by the character of the writing in the inscriptions of Aśoka's grandson Daśaratha[159], which were incised "immediately after his coronation" (*ānaṃtaliyaṃ abhiṣitena*), i.e., probably just about the end of the 3rd century B.C., and of the legends on the coins of the Indo-Grecian kings Pantaleon and Agathocles, who ruled in the beginning of the 2nd century B.C.[160]. The letters of the Nāgārjunī cave inscriptions (pl. II, col. XVII) are sharply distinguished from those of the Aśoka edicts, partly by the far advanced forms of *ja, ta, da, la* and partly by the invariable and considerable reduction of the vertical strokes. The second peculiarity re-occurs on the coins of the two Indo-Grecian kings, which show also a further development of the northern *ja* of pl. II, 15, III. Though the shortened letters were by no means unknown to the writers of the Aśoka edicts (see table on p. 7), their constant use for epigraphic documents is, to judge from the available materials, a characteristic of the types of the second and subsequent centuries. And I believe that all inscriptions showing long verticals must be assigned to the 3rd century B.C., and those with short ones to later times.

B.—*Local varieties.*

The peculiar circumstances, under which the Aśoka edicts were incised, were most unfavourable to a full expression of the existing local varieties. First, the fact that all of them were first drawn up in the imperial secretariate at Pāṭaliputra and then forwarded to the Governors of the provinces, must have proved a serious obstacle. As the differences in the grammatical forms and small alterations in the text indicate, the edicts were copied by the provincial clerks before they came into the hands of the stone-masons. It is a matter of course that the scribes of the Rājukas, in copying them, were influenced by the forms of the letters in the originals, and that they imitated them, be it involuntarily or out of respect for the head office. Further, it is probable that the provincial clerks were not always natives of those districts in which they served; and this circumstance must have contributed to efface or to modify the use of the local varieties. Most of Aśoka's governors will, no doubt, have been sent from Magadha, the home of the Maurya race, and many will have been transferred in the course of their service from one province to another. Those acquainted with the conditions of the Civil Service in the Native States of India, which still preserve the ancient forms common to the whole of Asia, will regard it as probable that the governors, on taking charge of their posts, imported their subordinates, or at least some of them, be it from their native country or from the districts which they formerly governed. The case of Paḍa, the writer of the Śiddāpura edicts, confirms this inference. As he knew the Kharoṣṭhī, he probably had immigrated, or been transferred, to Maisūr from the north of India.

In spite of these unfavourable conditions it is possible to distinguish in the writing of the Aśoka edicts at least two, perhaps three, local varieties. First, there is a northern and a southern one, for which, as in the case of the later alphabets, the Vindhya or, as the Hindus say, the Narmadā, forms the dividing line. The southern variety is most strongly expressed in the Girnār and Śiddāpura edicts, less clearly in the Dhauli and Jaugada edicts, by differences in the signs for *A, Ā, kha, ja, ma, ra, sa*, the medial *i*, and the ligatures with *ra* (see below, under C, D). A comparison of the characters of the most closely allied northern and southern inscriptions confirms the assumption that the differences are not accidental. If the characters of the Śiddāpura edicts do not always agree with those of Girnār, [35] the discrepancies will have to be ascribed to the northern descent of the writer Paḍa or to his service in a northern office.

Even the writing in the northern versions is not quite homogeneous. The pillar edicts of Allahabad, Mathia, Niglīva, Paḍeria, Radhia, and Rāmpūrvā, form one very closely connected set, in which only occasionally minute differences can be traced, and the edicts of Bairāt No. I, Sahsarām, Barābar, and Sāñci, do not much differ. A little further off stand the Dhauli separate edicts (where edict VII. has been written by a different hand from the rest), the Delhi-Mirat edicts, and the Allahabad Queen's edict, as these show the angular *da*. Very peculiar and altogether different is the writing of the rock edicts of Kālsī, with which some letters on the coins of Agathocles and Pantaleon (but also some in the Jaugada separate edicts) agree. Perhaps it is possible to speak also of a north-western variety of the older Maurya alphabet.[161]

C.—*The radical signs or Mātṛkās.*

Signs beginning with verticals show already in the Aśoka edicts occasionally a thickening or a very short stroke (*Serif*) at the upper end, as in *cha* (pl. II, 14, II), *pa* (28, VII); compare the cases noted EI. 2, 448, and B. ASRSI, 1, 115.

(1, 2)[162] In addition to the eight forms of *A*, *Ā*, given on page 21 above, the plate shows a ninth in col. XI. with an open square at the top (compare *ma*, 32, XI, XII); a tenth, with the angle separated from the vertical, occurs in No. 1 of the Śiddāpura inscriptions, edict I, line 2, 3. The forms with the bent vertical (cols. VII, XI) have been caused by writing the upper and lower halves of the letter separately. The addition of the stroke, marking the length of the vowel, to the right top of the vertical (cols. VIII, IX), is a peculiarity of Girnār.

(3) The forms of *I* in cols. III, IV, are the common ones; that in col. X, which agrees with the *I* of the Gupta period and later types, is rare. (4) The rare *Ī*, which, as may be inferred from the Gayā alphabet of the masons, existed already in the 3rd century B.C., occurs also in the Mahābodhi-Gayā inscriptions, pl. 10, Nos. 9, 10, where Cunningham reads *Iṃ*, because it appears in the representative of the Sanskrit *Indra*. Though this reading is possible, I consider it improbable, as it would be necessary to assume for *I* a not traceable form, consisting of two dots side by side with a third dot above on the left, thus, ∴. In later times (see pl. VI, 4, V, VII) the angles of the square are turned towards the top and the bottom lines.

(5, 6) Hultzsch (ZDMG. 40, 71) admits that the sign 6, XVIII, looks like *Ū*, but prefers to read *O* for linguistic reasons, which seems to be unnecessary according to E. Müller, *Simplified Pāli Grammar*, 12 f. The existence of *Ū* in the 3rd century may be inferred from the Gayā alphabet of the masons.

(7) Add the horseshoe-form of *E* (Kālsī edict V, 16, &c.) from the comparative table on page 26 above, No. 16, col. V, *b*. The half-round *E* of col. XXII occurs also in Sāñci Stūpa I, No. 173. The *AI*, which has been placed in this row (col. XXI), existed in the 3rd

century, as may be inferred from the Gayā alphabet of the masons.—(8) Regarding the *O* of Dhauli and Jaugada in col. VI, see above, § 4, B, 4, *a*.

(9) The dagger-shaped *ka* occurs occasionally in all versions of the Aśoka edicts, most rarely in Girnār.—(10) The oldest among the seven forms of *kha* is that in col. II (Kālsī) and col. VI (Jaugada separate edicts and Bharahut Stūpa inscription). Hence come first the northern *kha*, with the loop on the right, col. III (Kālsī and Bharahut), and a form, nearly identical with that of col. XVIII, in Jaugada separate edict I, 1. 4. The next derivative from this is the *kha* with a bent vertical and a dot at the foot, in cols. IV, V. Likewise of northern origin is the *kha* with the triangle at the foot, in *khya*, 43, V; compare Mahābodhi-Gayā, pl. 10, No. 3, and Bharahut. Another derivative from the primary form in col. III, is the *kha* of cols. VII, IX-XII, with a point at the foot of the perfectly straight vertical, and it occurs both in the south in Girnār, Śiddāpura, Dhauli, and Jaugada, and in the north in Allahabad, Delhi-Mirat, Mathia, Radhia, Rāmpūrvā, and Bairāt No. I. The *kha*, consisting of a simple hook with the omission of the dot, in col. VIII, is confined to the southern versions and is particularly common in Girnār.—(11) The *ga*, which is originally pointed at the top, is sometimes slightly rounded, in cols. IV, VI, X-XII.—(12) The primary angular *gha* appears occasionally in Kālsī (col. III) and in the Jaugada separate edicts.—I add here the figure of *ṅa* from the Gayā alphabet of the masons, which has been discovered after the preparation of the plates; compare my Indian Studies,  III. 2, pp. 31, 76.

(13) The primary *ca* with tail (see above, § 4, A, 18) occurs also in Sāñci Stūpa I, Nos. 269 and 284 (EI. 2, 368).—(14) The primary *cha* with unequal [36] halves in cols. VI, VII, becomes first a circle, bisected by the vertical, cols. III, IV, and hence is derived the later usual form with two loops in col. II, and in the Gayā alphabet.—(15) The forms of *ja*, all of which have been derived from the *j* of the Drāviḍī (cols. XIII-XVI) may be divided (*a*) into essentially northern forms with a loop in col. III (Kālsī and Mathia), or with a dot in cols. IV, V (Allahabad, Delhi-Sivālik, Delhi-Mirat, Bairāt No. I, Niglīva, Paḍeria, Dhauli, Jaugada, and Śiddāpura), or with a short central stroke in col. II (Kālsī, Jaugada separate edicts, Sahsarām and Rūpnāth), and (*b*) into southern forms, those in cols. VIII, X, XI, XVI (Girnār, Dhauli, Jaugada, and Ghasundi) and that in col. IX (Girnār).

(18) In addition to the semicircular *ṭa*, we often find secondary forms, flattened above or below or at both ends, as in cols. II, XI, XVI.—(20) With the round-backed *ḍa* of Kālsī in col. III, compare also the similar *ḍi* in the Allahabad Queen's edict, line 3.

(23) From the primary *ta* in col. III, and 43, III (*tu*), which is often turned sideways (see comparative table at page 26 above No. 22, V, *b*), comes (*a*) the form with the round side-limb in cols. IV, V, XVI, as well as that in col. VI, and 43, col. II (*ti*), and (*b*) the very common *ta* with the angle just below the vertical in col. XI, from which finally the tertiary form with the semicircle for the angle in col. XII (common in later times) appears to be derived.—(25) From the primary rounded *da* in cols. II, III, comes (*a*) the angular form in cols. IV, V (Delhi-Mirat, Delhi-Sivālik, Allahabad Kosambī edict, and Allahabad Queen's edict), and (*b*) the cursive *da* in cols. VII, IX (Girnār, Jaugada, &c., rarely).—(26) The original *dha* of

cols. V-VII appears only in Delhi-Sivālik (rarely) and in the Jaugada separate edicts (constantly).

(28, 29) The angular *pa* and *pha* of col. XII. and col. VI, occurs here and there in various versions.—(30) Add the *ba* of the comparative table, page 26 above No. 2, V, *a*, which is not rare in Kālsī and other versions.—(31) The secondary *bha* with the straight stroke on the right, col. XVI, and that with the rounded back, col. VI (Jaugada separate edicts), appear also in Bharahut (constantly), Sāñci (often), Barābar and Kālsī.—(32) The secondary *ma* with the semicircle at the top occurs throughout in the northern inscriptions, except in the Sohgaura copper-plate, which offers a *ma* with an open square, similar to that of Śiddāpura, cols. XI, XII. The older *ma* with the angle above the circle, cols. VIII-X, is a southern form, and is confined to Girnār (exclusively) and Dhauli and Jaugada (rarely).

(33) The notched *ya* in cols. IV, V, VII, XI, is used either constantly or chiefly in Delhi-Sivālik, Delhi-Mirat, Mathia, Radhia, Rāmpūrvā, Niglīva, Paḍeria, and Kālsī. It is also very common in Dhauli, Jaugada, and Śiddāpura. But in Girnār the *ya* with the curve below is the usual one, cols VIII, X, XII, besides which that with the angle, col. IX, is found occasionally. In writing the notched *ya*, the left half of the sign has been made first, and the right half has been added afterwards. In the *ya* with the curve below, the vertical and the curve have been drawn separately, as may be seen from *iyaṃ* in No. 1 of the Śiddāpura inscriptions edict I, line 4.—(34) Add the forms of *ra* from Girnār given in the comparative table on page 26 above, No. 20, V, *a* and *c*. The corkscrew-like *ra* of Ghasundī, col. XVI, and the tertiary, almost straight-lined form, of Rūpnāth (between cols. VII, VIII), seem to be northern cursive forms of the letter.—(35) The angular *la* of cols. III, V, appears occasionally in most versions, whereas the highly cursive form in col. VII is confined to the Jaugada separate edicts.—(36) Add the modern-looking *va* of the comparative table on page 22 above, No. 19 (Kālsī). The *va* of Śiddāpura in col. XII, flattened below, and the triangular one of Ghasundī in col. XVI, appear occasionally in other versions. The *va* of col. IX, which resembles a *ca* turned round from right to left, is found also in *Vesagame*, Sohgaura, line 2.

(37) Add the broad-backed *śa* of the comparative table on page 26, No. 21, VI *c*; and compare the *śa* in Kālsī edict XIII, 1, lines 35, 37, 38; 2, lines 17, 19.—(38) The conjectural reading of the signs of Kālsī in cols. II, III, is based on Senart's *Inscriptions de Piyadasi*, 1, 33 f. The *ṣa* from which the later forms have been derived is that of col. XVI.—(39) The primary *sa* with the straight side-limb has been preserved only in the south (Girnār and Śiddāpura). The cursive form in col. VII occurs also in Kālsī.

(40) Add the probably primary *ha* of Śiddāpura in the comparative table on page 26 above, No. 5, V, *a*, which [37] is found also in Kālsī. The cursive *ha* of col. VII is confined to the Jaugada separate edicts; a somewhat different cursive occurs in *mahamāta*, Allahabad Kosambī edict, line 1.

(41) A certain *ḷa* is not found in the known inscriptions of the 3rd century, as the *ḷī* of Sāñci, in col. XVIII, belongs without doubt to the 2nd century B. C. But it is possible that the *ḍa* with the dot, 20, col. VI (Radhia), has to be read *ḷa*. The sign

appears in Delhi-Sivālik, Mathia, and Radhia (edict V) in the representative of the Sanskrit *duḍī* or *dulī*, and in Mathia and Radhia in the representative of *dvādaśa*, which in Pāli usually becomes *duvāḍasa*. The dot may be, as in *kha* and *ja*, a substitute for a circle. If such a modification of *ḍa* was really used for *ḷa*, the sign must have been derived from the angular *ḍa* nearly in the same manner as the later *ḷa* was framed out of the round-backed *ḍa* (see above, § 4, B, 6).

D.—*Medial vowels and Anusvāra.*

(1) The originally straight stroke for *ā* is often turned upwards in Kālsī (see, for instance, *śā*, 37, III) and occasionally in other versions, after the manner prevalent in later times. In *khā* (10, V, VI), *jā* (15, VI, &c.), *ṭā* (18, II), *ṭha* (19, II), *thā* (24, II), the *ā*-stroke is added to the middle of the letter. Bharahut offers also a *jā* like that of 15, XXI.

(2) The angular *i* (see, for instance, *khi*, 10, II) becomes, regularly in Girnār (see *ḍhi*, 21, IX) and rarely in the Jaugada separate edicts (see *khi*, 10, VII), a shallow curve, which in *khi* (10, VIII), in *ni* (27, IX), and other letters ending in verticals, may be attached to the middle of the consonant, and which frequently is very much like *ā*. In Kālsī edict XIII, 2, 10, the medial *i* of *ti* (43, II) stands twice to the left of its consonant, likewise in *ti* in Allahabad edict I (end), and in *hi* in the Sohgaura copper-plate, line 4.—(3) The medial *ī* of Girnār usually consists of a shallow curve bisected by a vertical (*dī*, 25, IX); but in *ṭī* (18, IX) it is marked by two vertical strokes, and in *thī* (24, IX) by two slanting ones.

(4) The full *u* which is identical with *U* occurs in the *dhu* (26, III) of Kālsī several times. It is also recongnisable in *ku* (9, V), *gu* (11, IX), *ḍu* (20, VII), and other letters ending in verticals, which latter have to do double duty as parts of the consonants and of the vowel; see below, the remarks on some ligatures under E, 1. Elsewhere we have secondary forms; (*a*) such as omit the horizontal, in *dhu* (26, II), *pu* (28, III), &c; (*b*) such as omit the vertical, in *tu* (23, V), &c. In *tu* the *u*-stroke is occasionally turned upwards, as in 23, VIII, and 43, III; compare the later *tū* of pl. III, 21, XIX.—(5) The identity of medial *ū* with *U* is still recognisable in letters ending in verticals, as in *bhū* (31, X), &c., where the vertical again does double duty. But mostly the vowel is expressed by two strokes, either parallel as in *dhū* (26, X) and in *yū* (33, VII) or placed otherwise as in *pū* (28, VIII, XVI).

(6) Signs like *ge* (11, IV) perhaps offer still remnants of the hook-form of medial *e*, into which the originally super-imposed triangle no doubt was reduced at first (see above, § 4, C, 1); and the *e*-strokes of *khe* (10, III), *ge* (11, III), and *gye* (42, VII), which slant downwards from the left to the right, may have to be interpreted in the same way. In *je* (15, VII), *ṭe* (18, V), *ṭhe* (19, XII), and *the* (24, XII), the vowel stands opposite to the middle of the consonant; in *khe* it is often attached to the left end of the hook.—(7) Medial *ai* occurs only in *trai* (23, IX) and *thai* (24, X), both in Girnār, and in *mai* (32, XII; Śiddāpura).

(8) Medial *o* preserves mostly the original shape of *O* very faithfully (see above, § 4, C, 1). The later cursive *o* with the two bars at the same height appears however in

go (11, V; Delhi-Sivālik) and *ho* (40, V; Delhi-Sivālik), as well as in the *yo* of the Persian *sigloi*. In *mo* (32, VII, X; Jaugada separate edicts, Mathia, Radhia, and Girnār), the *o* has been formed in a similar manner. In the second form, the bars stand opposite the middle, and indicate that analogous *mā* and *me* existed already in the 3rd century B. C., just as later; see pl. III, 30, X, XVII. In the *no* of Kālsī edict V, line 14 we have a looped *o*, similar to that in *lo* of pl. III, 33, XX, and in later signs.

(9) The Anusvāra mostly stands opposite the middle of the preceding Mātṛkā, as in *maṃ* (32, VIII). But in connection with *i* it is placed regularly in [38] Delhi-Sivālik, Delhi-Mirat, Mathia, Radhia, Jaugada, and Dhauli, inside the angle of the vowel, as in *ṭiṃ* (18, VI). There are also other cases in which it occasionally appears, as in the later scripts, above its Mātṛkā, and sometimes, as in *mam* (32, II), it sinks to the foot of the latter; see above, § 4, B, 2 *c*.

E.—*Ligatures*.

(1) In the ordinary ligatures of the Aśoka edicts (42, II-VII, X-XII; 43, V-VIII, XI, XII; 44, III-VII, XI, XII; 45, IV, V, X), in those of Bharahut (45, XI) and of Ghasundi (42, 43, XVI), the consonants are placed below each other in their natural order and suffer no material changes. Occasionally, however, as in *kyā* (42, II, IV), *kye* (42, III), *gyā* (42, VI), and *gye* (42, VII), a single vertical stroke does duty both for the upper and the lower consonant, just as in the modern ligatures क्त, क्क, and so forth; compare also the Kharoṣṭhī ligatures, § 11 above, C, 3.

(2) But there are cases of greater irregularities, especially in Girnār, where (*a*) the second sign is sometimes greatly mutilated or made cursive, as in *vya* (44, II), *mya* (44, VIII), *sṭi* and *stu* (45, VIII, IX); (*b*) the sign for the second consonant is sometimes placed first (Girnār and Śiddāpura) for convenience sake[163], as in *stā*, *sṭi* (42, VIII, IX), *tpa*, *tpā* (43, IX, X), *vyā* (44, X, ?); and (*c*) in ligatures with *ra*, this sign is either (both in Girnār and Śiddāpura) inserted in the vertical lines of the other consonant (*kra*, 9, X; *tram*, 23, X; *dra*, 25, XII; *brā*, 30, X; *vra*, 36, X; *sru*, 39, X), or (in Girnār alone) is indicated by a small hook at the top of the combined sign (*trai*, 23, IX; *pra*, *prā*, 28, IX, X; &c.). The position of *ra* always remains the same, whether it is to be pronounced before or after the combined consonant, and thus 36, X, has the value both of *rva* and of *vra*. The insertion of *ra* in the left vertical of *ba* in *brā* (30, X) probably goes back to the period when the writing went from the right to the left. Otherwise it ought to stand in the right vertical.

§ 17.—The Drāviḍī of Bhaṭṭiprolu: Plate II.

To the remarks on the value of the Drāviḍī of Bhaṭṭiprolu for the history of writing in India (above, page 23), and to the explanations of its peculiar signs (above, § 6, A, 3, 7, 12, 15, 18; B, 4 c, 5; and C, 2), I have now to add the reasons for the assumed reading of the sign in pl. II, 38, XIII-XV. It seems to me certain that originally it had the value of *ṣ*. For there can be no doubt that it expresses a sibilant, and that the Drāviḍī is, like the Brāhmī, an alphabet invented in order to write Sanskrit (see above, § 6, C, 2). As signs for two of the three Sanskrit sibilants are easily recognisable,—the palatal in 37, XIII, XIV, and the dental in 39, XIII, XIV, XV,—the third sign can only have been intended to express the lingual sibilant. But it is a different question, whether in the words of the Prākṛt Bhaṭṭiprolu inscriptions, in which the sign occurs, the lingual sibilant was actually pronounced, or whether, owing to the negligent orthography of the clerks, the sign has been put where the pronunciation was *ś* or *s*. A certain answer to this question is for the present impossible. It could be given only if we knew more about the ancient Prākṛt of the Kistna districts [39] than is actually the case. But the correct use of *śa* in *śamaṇudeśānaṃ* (Bhaṭṭiprolu, No. X) indicates that the dialect possessed two sibilants; and it can only be doubted, whether *ṣ* has been put erroneously for *ś*, as often happens in the Jaina inscriptions from Mathurā (compare EI. 1, 376), or whether it was still the lingual sibilant. Another point in the character of the Drāviḍī, which requires special mention, is, that its signs, which agree with those of the Brāhmī, in several cases present characteristic peculiarities of the southern variety. This may be seen (1) in the angular *A*, *Ā*; (2) in the *kh* (10, XIII, XV) consisting, like that of Girnār, merely of a vertical, with a hook at the top; (3) in the *dh*, which has the same position as that of the Jaugada separate edicts and the Nānāghāṭ inscriptions; (4) in *m*, which, though turned topsy-turvy, retains the angle of the *ma* of Girnār; and (5) in *s*, which mostly has the straight side-limb, as in Girnār and Śiddāpura.

As the inscription on the crystal prism (No. X), found with the stone vessels, shows the ordinary Brāhmī except in the *da* opening to the right, it follows that the Drāviḍi was not used exclusively even in the Kistna districts, but together with the common old Indian alphabet. The small number of the inscriptions hitherto found, makes it impossible to say anything definite regarding the spread of this alphabet. And it is equally difficult to fix with certainty the time and the duration of its use. As king Kubiraka or Khubiraka (Kubera) is not known from other sources, we can only fall back on the never absolutely certain paleographic indications. The signs, which agree with the Brāhmī, point to the time immediately after Aśoka, or about B.C. 200. In favour of this estimate is particularly the occurrence of the long verticals, the invariably round *g*, and the *r*, which is always represented by a straight line.

§18.—*The last four alphabets of Plate II.*

In addition to the inscriptions of Daśaratha (col. XVII), which very probably belong just to the end of the 3rd century B.C. (see above, § 16, A), only those of the Ceta king Khāravela of Kaliṅga (cols. XXI, XXII) and those of the Andhra queen Nāyanikā in the Nānāghāṭ cave (cols. XXIII, XXIV) can be dated approximately. Khāravela's inscription must have been incised between B.C. 157 and 147, as the king's thirteenth year is said to correspond to the year 165 of "the time of the Muriya (Mauriya) kings[164]," and it fixes also the time of the Nānāghāṭ inscription. For, according to line 4, Khāravela assisted in the second year of his reign a western king called Sātakaṇi This Sātakaṇi probably is identical with the first Andhra prince of that name mentioned in the Purāṇas, whose inscribed image is found in the Nānāghāṭ cave. Hence the date of the large inscription, which was incised during the regency of Sātakaṇi's widow Nāyanikā, cannot be much later than B.C. 150[165].

Paleographic evidence is almost the only help for fixing the time of Dhanabhūti's inscription on the *toraṇa* of the Bharahut Stūpa (col. XVIII), which was incised "during the rule of the Suṅgas," as well as that of the Pabhosa cave inscriptions (col. XIX) and of the oldest votive documents from Mathurā (col. XX), all of which offer (see above, § 15, 5) the Suṅga type of the ancient Brāhmi. To judge from the evidently close connection of their characters, partly with the younger Maurya alphabet and partly with the Kaliṅga script, the signs of cols. XVIII, XIX, probably belong to the second century B.C. Those of col. XX may date from the first century B.C., as the elongation of the lower parts of the verticals of *A*, *Ā* (1, 2), the broad back of *śa* (37), the cursive *ḷa* (41) and the subscribed *ra* in *dra* (42), which is twisted to the left, point to a later time.

The tendency to shorten the upper vertical lines, mentioned already above (§ 16, A), is, though here and there not fully carried through, common to all the four scripts. The broadening of the letter or of the lower parts of *ga*, *ta*, *pa*, *bha*, *ya*, *la*, *sa* and *ha*, is found only in the last [40] three alphabets; and the thickening of the tops of the upper verticals, and the use of the so-called *Serif*, are particularly remarkable only in the Suṅga and Kaliṅga alphabets. Tendencies in the direction of later developments are found, not only in the letters of col. XX, already mentioned, but also in the round *ḍa* (20, XXII, XXIII), so characteristic for the latter southern alphabets, in *ṇa* with the curved upper horizontal line (22, XVIII, XIX) in the partly or entirely angular *ma* (32, XIX, XXII), in the semicircular medial *ī* of *kī* (9, XXII), *bī* (30, XXII), and *vī* (36, XXIV), as well as in the detached *o* of *go* (11, XXII), *ṭho* (19, XXIV) and *tho* (24, XXIV). The single medial *au* of the plate, in *pau* (28, XVIII), deserves to be noted.

As regards the geographical distribution of these types, the younger Maurya alphabet belongs not only to the north-east (Bihār), but also to the north-west, where its *ja* and *ṣa* are found on the coins of the two Indo-Grecian kings, mentioned above (§ 15, 4). The Kaliṅga alphabet is of course that of the south-eastern coast, and the type of the Nānāghāṭ inscriptions that of the western Dekhaṇ. Finally, the Suṅga type probably represents the script of the centre of India. It, however, extends also to the west, as the same or very similar characters are found in the caves of the Marāṭhā country; compare § 15 above, 5, note 153.

Very little can be said regarding the duration of the use of these scripts. The Indo-Grecian coins show that the younger Maurya characters were used in the first half of the 2nd century B.C.[166] The Kaliṅga script is visible also in the inscriptions of Khāravela's next descendants.[167] If Burgess has correctly fixed the time of the Pitalkhorā caves,[168] it would follow that the script of the Nānāghāṭ inscriptions continued to be used in the first century A. D.

§ 19.—THE PRECURSORS OF THE NORTHERN ALPHABETS.

A.—The Alphabet of the Northern Kṣatrapas : Plate III.

Immediately connected with the latest forms of the Suṅga type in the oldest Jaina inscriptions from Mathurā (pl. II, col. XX) is the alphabet of the Northern

Kṣatrapas on the coins and in the inscriptions of the Mahākṣatrapa Rājuvula or Ramjubula and of his son Śoḍāsa or Suḍasa, who ruled in the first century B. C. or A. D. (?) over the same town[169]. And some "archaic" votive inscriptions from Mathurā, as well as legends on certain Indian coins, exhibit the early letters of the same type[170].

The characteristics of this type (pl. III, cols. I, II) are the equalisation of all the upper verticals, except in *la* (33, I); the constant use of the *Serif*, occasionally replaced, as in *bha* (29, I), by a nail-head or wedge; and the constant use of angular forms for *gha* (10, I), *ja* (13, I, II), *pa* (26, I, II), *pha* (27, I), *ma* (30, I, II), *la* (33, I), *ṣa* (36, I), and *ha* (38, I, II). Other, mostly cursive, innovations are found in the peculiar *ca* (11, I); in the slanting angular *ḍa* (18, I); in *da* (23, I); in the broadened *bha* (29, I, II); in *ra* with the curve at the end (32, I, II), which occasionally reappears also later (see pl. IV, 33, IV) in northern inscriptions; in the medial vowels *ā* (which in *hā*, 33, II, rises upwards, but in *rā*, 32, I, keeps its ancient form), *i* (in *di*, 23, 1), *o* (in *gho*, 10. I, and *śo*, 35, II); and in the position of the Anusvāra above the line (in *ṇāṃ*, 20, I). The *ka* shows, besides the old form in 7, I, II, the later one with the bent bars in *kṣa* (40, I). The upper part of the abnormal *va* (34, II) with two triangles, which sometimes is found also in the Kuṣāna inscriptions[171] and elsewhere, [41] probably represents a hollow wedge. The inscriptions of this class for the first time show[172] the medial *ṛ* which consists, exactly like that of the Kuṣāna inscriptions in *vṛ* (34, III), of a straight line slanting towards the left.

B.—The alphabet of the Kuṣāna inscriptions: Plate III.

The next step in the development of the Brāhmī of Northern India is illustrated by the inscriptions from the time of the Kuṣāna kings Kaniṣka, Huviṣka and Vāsuṣka or Vāsudeva (plate III, cols. III-V), the first among whom made an end of the rule of the older Śakas in the eastern and southern Pañjāb. The inscriptions with the names of these kings, which run from the year 4 to the year 98 (according to the usually accepted opinions. of the Śaka era of A. D. 77-78, or of the 4th century of the Seleucid era)[173], are very numerous in Mathurā and its neighbourhood, and are found also in eastern Rājputāna and in the Central Indian Agency (Sāñci)[174]. In spite of great variations in the single letters, which occasionally exhibit the more modern forms in the older inscriptions and the earlier forms of the Northern Kṣatrapa type in the later documents, the alphabet possesses a very characteristic appearance, and nobody who once has seen the squat and broad letters of the Kuṣāna period will ever make a mistake by assigning them to other times.

As regards the details, the following innovations deserve special mention[175]:— (1) Side by side with more ancient signs, the *A* of col. IV shows a form leading up to the modern *A* of the Nāgarī of Western India; compare also pl. IV. 1, IX, XI ff. (2) The bar denoting the length of *Ā* is attached low down (2, III, IV); compare pl. IV, 2, VII ff. (3) Three strokes, one of which is set up vertically, take the place of the three dots of *I* (3, III). (4) The horizontal stroke of *U* occasionally shows a curve at the left end (4, IV). (5) The base of the triangular *E* (5, IV, V) is mostly at the top; compare pl.

IV, 5, X ff. (6) The *kha* (8, III-V) is mostly triangular below, and its hook is often small. (7) One of the two originally horizontal strokes of *ṇa* is always turned into a curve notched in the middle, and sometimes both are changed in this manner, as in 20, III, IV; occasionally the vertical is split up into two lines, which are attached to the ends of the left horizontal line, each bearing a portion of the curved top-bar (20, V). (8) The *ta* shows sometimes, but rarely, a loop, as in *sti* (43, IV). (9) The lower end of *da* (23, III-V) is drawn further to the right, and the bulge on the right becomes larger. (10) The *dha* (24, III, IV) becomes narrower and pointed at the ends. (11) The horizontal stroke of *na* is curved (25, III) or looped (25, IV), whereby the still more modern looking form in 25, V, is developed. (12) The *ya* (31, III-V) mostly has a hook or circle on the left limb, and in ligatures is either looped as in *ryya* (42, III), or bipartite as in *ryya* (41, V). (13) The *va* is occasionally rounded on the left (34, V), or becomes similar to *ca*, as in *rvva* (42, IV). (14) The *śa* (35, III-V) becomes narrower, and its middle stroke lies horizontally across the interior; sometimes the left down-stroke bears a *Serif* at the end, or the right one is made longer, just as in *ga* (9, V); compare pl. IV, 36, I ff. (15) The central bar of *ṣa* (36, III-V) goes straight across the interior of the letter. (16) The left limb of *sa* is occasionally, but rarely, turned into a loop (37, IV); compare plate IV, 38, I ff.

All these peculiarities, as well as the advanced forms of the medial vowels, of *ā* in *rā* (32, IV), of *u* in *ku* (7, IV, V) and in *stu* (43, V)[176], and of *o* in *to* (21, IV), reappear constantly in the northern alphabets of the next period, those of the Gupta inscriptions (pl. IV, cols. I-VII) and of the Bower MS. (pl. VI, cols. I-III), or are precursors of the forms of those documents. The literary alphabets used in Mathurā during the first two centuries A.D., very likely were identical with or closely similar to the later ones, and the admixture of older forms, observable in the inscriptions of the Kuṣāṇa period, may be due purely to an imitation of older votive inscriptions.

Attention must be called to the medial *ṛ* in *tṛ* (21, IV) and [42] in *vṛ* (34, III), for which we have also once[177] the form of pl. IV, 3, III; likewise to the rather common final *m*, which resembles that in *ddham* (41, VIII), and to the Visarga, which looks exactly like the modern one (compare 40, 41 IX) and first appears in hese inscriptions[178]. The broad strokes of the letters and their thick tops indicate that they imitate an alphabet written with ink.

§20 —THE PRECURSORS OF THE SOUTHERN ALPHABETS

A.—The alphabet of the Kṣatrapas of Mālva and Gujarāt: Plate III.

While the inscriptions of Northern India thus show in the first and second centuries A.D. the beginning of the development of a new local variety of the Brāhmī, we find in the documents from Western and Central India, as well as from the Dekhaṇ, the first steps leading up to the later southern alphabets. The inscriptions and coins of the Kṣatrapa dynasty of Mālva and Gujarāt, descended from Caṣṭana or Tiastanes, illustrate the western writing, and col. VI, taken from the Girnār Praśasti of the reign of Rudradāman (about A. D. 160)[179] gives a specimen of it. This script agrees with the later southern alphabets

(§ 27, below) in the following characteristic points :—(1) in the curves at the ends of *A* and *Ā* (1, 2), *ka* (7), *ṅa* (15), *ra* (32), and of medial *u* and *ū* (not in the plate) ; (2) in the round-backed *ḍa* (18) ; (3) in the *ba* (28), notched on the left ; (4) in the *la* (33) with the vertical bent to the left ; and (5) in the medial *ṛ* (see *sṛ*, 37), which is difficult to distinguish from *ra*. Its other letters, for instance, *śa* (35) and the tripartite subscribed *ya* of *lya* (42), partly agree with those of the inscriptions of Śoḍāsa, and partly,—for instance, *kha* (8), *na* (25) with the bent base-line, *pa* (26) with the notch in the left vertical, *ya* (31) with the curve on the left, and the frequently rounded *va* (34),—with the types of the Kuṣāna period. Peculiar is its *ṭa* (16). Its cursive medial *ū*, which is used only in *nū* (25) and in *rū* (compare pl. VII, 33, III), and the *au* in *yau* (31), besides which the older form of pl. II, 28, XVIII, is used, appear here for the first time.

The letters on the somewhat older coins[180] of Rudradāman's grandfather Caṣṭana and of his father Jayadāman, which probably were struck in Ujjain, exhibit no material differences. Among the later Kṣatrapa inscriptions[181], that from Junāgaḍh, incised during the reign of Rudradāman's son Rudrasiṃha, fully agrees with the Girnār Praśasti. The Gunda inscription of the same prince from the year 103 (or, according to the usual assumption, from A. D. 180), and the Jasdan inscription of Rudrasiṃha's son Rudrasena from the year 127 (?) or A. D. 204-205, show a few more advanced characters. Both these documents offer the bipartite subscribed *ya* ; and the second has several times the northern *ma* of the Gupta period (pl. IV, 31, I ff.), as well as the *e* standing above the line (compare, for instance, *ne*, pl. VII, 27, V). The same *ma*, or a similar sign with a straight base-stroke, appears also frequently on the coins of the later Kṣatrapas[182]. Its occurrence probably indicates a northern influence, perhaps that a northern alphabet was used at the same time ; compare § 28 below, A.

B.—*The alphabets of the cave-inscriptions of the western Dekhaṇ and the Koṅkaṇ : Plate III.*

[43] The writing of the western Dekhaṇ and the Koṅkaṇ in the caves of Nāsik, Junnar, Kārle, Kaṇheri, Kuḍā, &c., shows three varieties, an "archaistic" or retrograde type, a more advanced one with mostly faint traces of southern peculiarities, and an ornamental one. The first two appear in the oldest dated inscriptions of the Śaka Uṣavadāta or Usabhadāta (Ṛṣabhadatta)[183], the son-in-law of the Kṣaharāta king and Kṣatrapa Nahapāna from the years 41 to 45 of, according to the usual assumption, the Śaka era[184], or from A. D. 118 to 122 The Kārle inscription No. 19 (col. VII) offers the "archaistic" or retrograde type, among the letters of which *gha* (10), *ja* (13), *da* (23), *bha* (29), *ya* (31), *la* (33), *sa* (37) and *ha* (38) come close to the forms in the older alphabets of pl. II, especially to those of the oldest Andhra inscriptions in cols. XXIII, XXIV. The same variety is found in some other, partly older, inscriptions of the same caves[185], and must be regarded as a direct development from the ancient Andhra type. It shows only very faint traces of the southern peculiarities enumerated above. The curves at the ends of the verticals are only rudimentary. The vertical of *la* is curved, but to the right. The triangular *dha* (24), which appears here for the first time, is found also in other alphabets of this plate (see col. XI ff.) ; the abnormal *kha* (8) is confined to Kārle No. 19.

Against this rather clumsy alphabet, we find in Uṣavadāta's inscriptions from Nāsik (cols. VIII, IX) very neatly made letters, the *ductus* of which resembles that of Śoḍāsa's inscriptions (col. I) and of the Girnār Praśasti (col. VI). They show no trace of archaic forms, and the traces of the southern peculiarities are faint or entirely wanting. Only the southern *ḍa* (18) is distinct and constant. Noteworthy are *śa* (35, 42, VIII), which agrees with that of col. VI, the final *m* in *ddham* (41, VIII), and the tripartite subscribed *ya* in *bhyoḥ* (41, IX).

Very similar to this script is that of the Nāsik inscriptions (No. 11, *a*, *b*, =col. X) of the Andhra king Gotamiputa Sātakaṇi, who destroyed the Kṣaharāta dynasty,—possibly just Nahapāna and Uṣavadāta,—and of his son Siri-Puḷumāyi, Puḷumāi or Pulimāvi (Nāsik No. 14=col. XI), who is mentioned by Ptolemy as Siri-Polemaios or Polemios[186]. The only material difference occurs in the triangular *dha* (24, XI ; compare col. VII), which however is by no means constant. Nearly of the same type are the alphabets shewn in col. XII, from the Nāsik inscription of the somewhat later Andhra king Gotamiputa Siriyaña Sātakaṇi, in col. XIII from the undated inscription Nāsik No. 20, and in col. XIII from Nāsik No. 12, incised during the reign of the Ābhīra king Īśvarasena[187]. In col. XIV, however, we have a peculiar form of *ta* (21) developed from a looped form, a looped *na* (25) somewhat differing from the northern form in col. IV, a *ra* (32) with a stronger curve, and a *la* (33) with the vertical bent towards the left ; further, in col. XIII a looped *ta* (21) and in col. XIV, a *ta* (21) and a *na* (25) derived from looped forms, a *ya* (31) with a curve on the left, a *la* (33) bent towards the left, a cursive subscribed *ña* in *jñaḥ* (40), and apeculiar, *r*-like, medial *u* in *du* (23), which reappears in later southern inscriptions ; compare, for instance, *bhu*, pl. VII, 30, XII, and the *ū* in *tū*, pl. III, 21, XVII, XIX.

Cols. XV, XVI, give two somewhat differing specimens of the ornamental variety of this period according to the undated inscriptions of Kuḍā (Nos. 1—6, 11, 20) and of Junnar (No. 3). Both agree in the ornamental treatment of medial *i* and *ī*. But the Kuḍā inscriptions extend it to the curves at the ends of all verticals, and show notches in the left [44] strokes of *pa* (26) and *ba* (28 ; compare col. VI). In col. XVI, there are two other noteworthy signs, the bipartite subscript *ya* in *yya* (40), and the *śi* with the horizontal bar in *śri* (41 ; compare 35, III-V). Ornamental forms, resembling those of cols. XV, XVI, are found also in the approximately datable inscriptions of Puḷumāyi in Kārle Nos. 20, 22, and of the minister of the queen of his successor Vāsiṭhīputa Sātakaṇi in Kaṇheri No. 11. The first two of these documents show a looped *ta* and a *ṇa* like that of col. XVII ; the third exhibits the neat characters of Western Kṣatrapa inscriptions. It is, therefore, certain that during the 2nd century A. D. all these three varieties were used promiscuously in the western Dekhaṇ and the Koṅkaṇ[188] and the inscriptions from the Amarāvatī Stūpa[189] prove that they occurred also on the eastern coast of India. The contemporaneous employment of more advanced types and of more archaic ones with an admixture of more modern signs will have to be explained in this, as in other cases, by a desire to select archaic and monumental forms for epigraphic purposes and a failure to completely carry out this intention.

C.—*The alphabet of the Jaggayyapeṭa inscriptions* : *Plate III.*

In the Kistna districts of the eastern coast, a still more ornamental alphabet, found in the Jaggayyapeṭa inscriptions from the time of the Ikṣvāku king Sirivīra Purisadatta (cols. XVII, XVIII), as well as in some Amarāvati inscriptions[190], was developed out of the ornamental variety just discussed, probably somewhat later, in the 3rd century A.D. One of its most prominent characteristics is the very considerable elongation of the verticals of *A*, *Ā*, *ka*, *ña*, *ra* and *la*, as well as of the medial *i*, *ī* and *u*. To a later time point the cursive forms of *tha* and *ha*, which latter agrees with the northern Gupta form (pl. IV, 39, I, VI), and the medial *e* of *me* (30), which, with its downward curve, agrees with the *e* of the later southern inscriptions (compare 30, XIX, XX, and pl. VII, 35, XII), and the medial *ū* in *tu* (21 ; compare col. XIX, and pl. VII, 30, XX). The medial *ū* of *t*‾ (40), in which the stroke expressing the length of the vowel has been attached to the head of the consonant, is entirely abnormal.

D.—*The alphabet of the Pallava Prākṛt land-grants* : *Plate III.*

The highly cursive writing of the Prākṛt land-grants of the Pallava kings Vijayabuddhavarman and Śivaskandavarman from Kāñci (Conjeveram) in the Tamil districts[191], shows in its *ductus* a certain relationship to the Jaggayyapeṭa inscriptions. But it is not doubtful that these documents are much later, though it is for the present impossible to fix their dates exactly. The use of Prākṛt for official purposes perhaps indicates that they are not later than the first half of the 4th century A.D. The broad *E* (5, XX) with the rudimentary vertical to the right (compare pl. VII, 6, XI ff.), the *ḍa* with a tail in *ṇḍam* (40, XX ; compare pl. VII, 19, IV f.), the subscribed *tha* open on the right in *ttha* (41, XIX ; compare pl. VII, 45, XX), and the constantly looped *o* in *lo* (33, XX ; compare pl. VII, 34, III f., XIII, XVII) point to the later period.

IV. THE NORTHERN ALPHABETS FROM ABOUT A.D. 350[192].

§ 21.—*Definition and varieties.*

[45] By the term "northern alphabets" I understand with Burgess, Fleet[193], and others, that large group of epigraphic and literary scripts, which from about A.D. 350 conquers the whole wide territory north of the Narmadā, with the exception of Kāṭhiāvāḍ and northern Gujarāt, and which, spreading in the course of time more and more, finally is used in a number of varieties for nearly all the Aryan languages of India. Their origin is to be found in the cursive forms, which first appear in the addition to the Aśoka edict VI of Dhauli, and in a number of signs of the Kālsī version (see above, page 21 f.) and later are found, occasionally or constantly, in some of the Jaina votive inscriptions of the Kuṣāṇa period (see above, § 19, A). Their general type is that of a cursive alphabet with signs reduced at the top to the same height, and made throughout, as much as possible, equal in breadth. As the occurrence of ancient MSS. and various peculiarities of the letters, such as the formation of wedges out of the *Serifs* at the ends of the verticals, clearly prove, they were always written with a pen or a brush and ink. Their most important common characteristics are :—(1) The absence of curves at the lower

ends of the verticals of *A*, *Ā*, *ka*, *ña*, &c. (with occasional exceptions for *ra*); (2) the use of the *Serif* at the left down-strokes of *kha*, *ga*, and *śa*; (3) the division of the original vertical of *ṇa* and of its upper bar; (4) the use of a looped *na* and of a *ta* without a loop; (5) the transformation of the lower portion of *ma* into a small knob or loop attached to the left of the letter; (6) the shortening of the vertical of *la*; (7) the turn of the medial *i* to the left, which is soon followed by the twist of medial *ī* to the right; (8) the development of curves, open to the left, at the end of the originally horizontal medial *u*; and (9) the use of a curve, open to the right, for medial *ṛ*.

While all the alphabets represented in plates IV, V, VI show these common characteristics or further developments from them, they may be divided, according to other peculiarities, into seven larger groups, most of which again comprise several varieties :—

(1) The epigraphic North-Indian alphabet of the 4th and 5th centuries, commonly called the Gupta alphabet, which, according to Hoernle's researches[194] has an eastern and western variety, among which the second again has two branches, and with the the western variety of which the literary alphabet of the Bower MS. and of some other documents from Kashgar is closely connected.

(2) The acute-angled or Siddhamātṛkā (?) alphabet with wedges at the verticals of the letters, which is first found in the palm leaves of Horiuzi, and towards the end of the 6th century in the Mahānāman inscription from Gayā and in the Lakkhāmaṇḍal Praśasti.

(3) The Nāgarī with its long-drawn, tailed, letters, and long top-strokes, the first certain traces of which occur in the 7th century.

(4) The Śāradā alphabet, a northern variety of the Western Gupta type, first found about A. D. 800.

(5) The eastern Proto-Bengālī alphabet with much rounded, cursive letters, and with hooks or hollow triangles at the tops of the verticals, first traceable in the 11th century.

(6) The hooked alphabet of Nepāl, [46] which is closely connected with the Proto-Bengālī occurs in MSS. from the 11th century onwards.

During the 4th and 5th centuries, the rule of these alphabets to the north of the Narmadā is by no means undisputed. In the west we find, as far north as Bijayagaḍh (Bhartpur), inscriptions in southern characters, or with an admixture of southern letters (see below, § 27). In the 6th and 7th centuries this mixture no longer occurs. Only the so called "arrow-head" type (see below, § 26, C), the seventh variety on plates IV-VI, which appears in rather late times in Bengal and Nepāl, offers an instance of the importation of a southern script into Northern India.

On the other hand, we meet, from the 7th century, with inscriptions in northern characters first on the coast, in the west in Gujarāt,[195] and in the east even beyond Madras.[196] Documents of this kind appear from the middle of the 8th century also in the central Dekhaṇ, and during the 12th and 13th centuries they penetrate as far as Vijayanagara in the Kanarese country (see below, § 23). But they never come into sole use beyond the northern limit of the Dravidian districts.

The ancient MSS. hitherto found in Kashgar, Japan and Nepāl, the oldest of which probably were written in the 4th century,[197] show only northern letters. The palm-leaf MSS. of Western India, which begin in the 10th century, agree with the inscriptions of the period, and prove that the northern Nāgarī was generally used in Rājputāna, Gujarāt[198] and in the northern Dekhaṇ as far as Devagiri (Daulatābād).[199] The gradual advance of the northern characters towards the south probably is explained by the predilection of many southern kings for northern customs, and by the immigration of northern Brahmans, castes of scribes, and Buddhist and Jaina monks, to which facts the statements in various inscriptions and the historial tradition bear witness.[200]

§ 22.—THE SO-CALLED GUPTA ALPHABET OF THE 4TH AND 5TH CENTURIES A. D.: PLATE IV.

A.—*Varieties.*

The differences between the eastern and western varieties of the so called Gupta [47] alphabet appear in the signs for *la*, *ṣa* and *ha*.[201] In the eastern variety the left limb of *la* (plate IV, 34, I-III, V, VI) is turned sharply downwards; compare the *la* of the Jaugada separate edicts (see above, § 16, C, 35). Further, the base-stroke of *ṣa* (IV, 37, I-III, V, VI) is made round and attached as a loop to the slanting central bar. Finally, the base-stroke of *ha* (IV, 39, I-III, V, VI) is suppressed, and its hook, attached to the vertical, is turned sharply to the left, exactly as in the Jaggayyapeṭa inscriptions (see above, § 20, C). In the western variety these three letters have the older and fuller forms.

The specimens of the eastern variety in plate IV have been taken from the oldest Gupta inscription, Hariṣeṇa's Allahabad Praśasti (cols I-III), which certainly was incised during the reign of Samudragupta[202], probably between A. D. 370 and 390, and from the Kahāuṃ Praśasti of A. D. 460 (cols. V, VI) of the time of Skandagupta. It appears, besides, in Fleet's Gupta Inscriptions (CII. 3) Nos. 6-9, 15, 64, 65, 77; in Bhagvānlāl's inscripitions from Nepāl, Nos. 1-3 [203]; and in Cunningham's Gayā inscription of Saṃvat 64[204]. The fact that Fleet's No 6 is found far west, near Bhilsa in Mālva, may be explained by its having been incised, during an expedition of Candragupta II to Mālva, at the command of his minister, who calls himself an inhabitant of Pāṭaliputra. Nothing is known regarding the origin of Fleet's No. 77, which is incised on a seal, purchased in Lahore, but possibly manufactured in Eastern India.

The western variety of the Gupta alphabet again appears in two forms, a cursive round-hand and an angular, monumental, type. The second form, which shews very characteristic thick top-lines and a hooked *ra* (33), is represented in plate IV, col. IV, by the alphabet of the Bilsaḍ Praśasti of A. D. 415. Another fine example is found in Fleet's No. 32, from the Meharaulī iron pillar near Delhi. Specimens of the cursive form are given in col. VII from the Indor copper-plate of A. D. 465, in col. VIII from Toramāṇa's Kura inscription probably of the second half of the 5th century[205], and in col. IX from the Kārītalāī copper-plate of Jayanātha of Uccakalpa, dated the year 174 or probably A.D. 423[206].

The same type is found in Fleet's Nos. 4, 13, 16, 19, 22-31, 36, 61, 63, 66, 67, 69, 74, 76, and in the Jaina votive inscriptions fron Mathurā, New Series, Nos. 38, 39[207]. It deserves to be noted that Fleet's No. 13 from Bhitarī is found in a district where one would expect the eastern variety. Fleet's No. 61, the Jaina inscription from Udayagiri in Mālva, shows a mixture of the northern characters with southern ones, as it offers throughout *A*, *Ā*, with a curve, and once a southern *r*. Perhaps the same may be said of Fleet's No. 59, the Bijayagaḍh inscription from Bhartpur in Rājputāna, where *ra* shows a curve at the end and medial *i* and *ī* resemble those in plate III, col. XVI. The characters on the Gupta coins[208] are frequently retrograde, and offer, e. g., the angular *ma* of the Kuṣāna period.

B.—*Characteristics of the epigraphic Gupta alphabet.*

The following particularly important or characteristic peculiarities of the Gupta inscriptions deserve to be noticed in detail :—

(1) The lower parts of the right-hand vertical of *A*, *Ā*, *ga*, *ḍa*, *ta*, *bha*, and *śa* are so much elongated, and those of *ka* and *ra* remain so long, that these eight signs have about double the length of those without verticals. This is particularly visible in the older stone inscriptions ; on the copper-plates they are often shortened.

(2) The right-hand portion of *gha*, *pa*, *pha*, *ṣa* and *sa* shows an acute angle, whereby later the development of tails or verticals on the right of these signs has been caused.

(3) Since the middle of the 5th century, the lower portion of the left limb of *A* (1, IX, XI) shows the curve, open to the left, which appears in all the later forms of the letter ; the sign of the length of *Ā* (2, VII-IX) [48] is attached to the foot of the right vertical.

(4) In addition to the *I* of the Kuṣāna period (3, I, V), there occur, owing to the predilection for letters flattened at the top, the also later frequent *I* with two dots above (3, VII), and that consisting of a short horizontal line with two dots below (3, IX), which latter is the parent of the later southern *I* (plates VII, VIII, and § 28 below) and of that of the Nāgarī (below, § 24, A, 4).

(5) The rudimentary curves at the left end of *U*, *Ū* and *O* are more fully developed in the 5th century ; compare above, § 19, B, 4.

(6) The guttural *ṅa* begins to appear instead of the Anusvāra before *śa* and *ha* (11, VII), perhaps in consequence of the faulty pronunciation, blamed in the Śikṣās[209].

(7) The third horizontal line of *ja* (14, I-III, VII, VIII) begins to slant downwards, and occasionally shows a curve at the end, whereby later the new forms of cols. XXI-XXIII are caused.

(8) The palatal *ña* (16, I, II ; 42, I, VI, VII, XI) is frequently made cursive and round, and is occasionally laid on the side in order to save space ; compare also *jñaḥ*, plate III, 40, XIV. But older, angular, forms likewise occur (42, V).

(9) The *ṭa* (17, I-III, IX) is often flattened down at the top.

(10) The *ṇa* of 21, I, II, shows a little stroke at the right end, caused by an inexact formation of the hook on the right, and in the second sign a cursive loop on the left ; in 21, III, the letter has been laid on the side and somewhat resembles the Nāgarī *ṇa*.

(11) The *tha* (23, I, V-IX) is mostly elliptical or flattened on the right, and a cross-bar often replaces the dot in the centre; but the old form likewise survives (23, II, III.)[210].

(12) The *ya* (32, 1-IX) is mostly tripartite, but sometimes, particularly in *ye*, *yai* and *yo*, transitional forms with the loop, like the later ones in 32, XIII, XVI, appear, which lead up to the bipartite *ya*[211]. The old st instance of the independent looped *ya* is found in Fleet's No. 59 of A. D. 371, but the Kuṣāna inscriptions show the looped subscript *ya* even earlier (see above, §19, B, 12).

(13) The left limb of *sa* (38, I-III, V, VI, VIII) often becomes a loop, as happens already in some Kuṣāna inscriptions (§19, B, 16). A substitute for the loop is the triangle (probably giving the outlines of a wedge), which occurs in the three most ancient inscriptions from Nepāl; compare the later *sa* of 38, XII. But the older hook is equally common.

(14) The rare *ḷa* (40, I-III) is found also in Fleet's No. 67, line 1.

(15) The signs for the medial vowels agree in many particulars with those of the Kuṣāna period. But the open semicircle for *ā* in *ṭā* (17, II), which is found also in *ṇā*, is an innovation. Further, the medial *i*, for instance, of *khi* (8, III, VI, IX), is drawn further to the left than in the earlier inscriptions. In some inscriptions like Mathurā, New Series, Nos. 38, 39, the medial *ī* consists merely of a curve, going to the right, though the form with two horns (as in *dī*, 24, I), and a looped one (as in *bhī*, 30, IV), are more common. Medial *u* is mostly represented by the still used curve, which in *ru* (33, III, VI) appears abnormally at the end of *ra*; but in *gu* (8, II, VI), *tu*, *bhu* (30, I) and *śu* (36, III) the vowel rises upwards. For medial *ū* there are, besides an old form in *gū* (9 IV), other combinations in *bhū* (30, II, VI) and *ḷū* (42, II) and a later very common, cursive form in *dhū* (25, II, VI). One of the Mātrās of *ai* and *o* is often placed vertically, as in *gai*, 32, III; in *go*, 9, III; and in *ṇo*, 21, III.

(16) The desire to save space causes the cursive *ña*, *ṭa* (see *ṣṭa*, 45, IX) and *tha* (see *sthā*, 45, V; *stha*, 46, IX) to be laid on the side, in case they form the second elements of ligatures. From the 5th century, *rya* (45, VII) is expressed by a full *ra* with a subscript *ya*.

(17) The first certain Virāma (see *ddham*, 43, VII), consisting of a horizontal stroke above the small final, dates likewise from the 5th century; the nothern Jihvāmūlīya (*hka*, 46, II) and the Upadhmānīya (*hpā*, 46, III) occur already in the 4th century.

C.—The Gupta alphabet in manuscripts.

Among the types of the Bower MS., which belongs, according to Hoernle's and my own opinion[212], to the 5th century, I have given [49] in plate VI, cols. I-IV, only the alphabet of the portion which Hoernle marks *A*, since the published parts of his *B* and *C* are not sufficiently extensive for a paleographic enquiry. Its characters differ very little from those of the epigraphic documents of the Gupta period, especially from the copper-plates. The *Serifs* at the tops of the vertical strokes, however, are made more carefully and neatly throughout worked up with the latter into real wedges. If a letter like *gha* (plate VI, 18, I-IV) has several upstrokes, the *Serifs* are added regularly to all of them. Similarly, the lower ends of vertical strokes more regularly bear *Serifs* or are converted into wedges or little buttons. The greater regularity of the writing is what may be expected in a good MS., the material of which offers fewer difficulties than stone or copper. The invariable use of the *Serifs* has led to the formation of the *ka* (15, IV), with the loop on the left[213] (compare 15, I, III), which appears occasionally in the Bower MS., but is noticeable only later, since A.D. 588-89 (see plate IV, 7, XIII), in the inscriptions. Further, the Bower MS., offers in rare cases, e.g. in *prayojayet* (fol. 31*a*, 11), an archaic form of the bipartite *ya*. Finally, it makes us acquainted with some signs which, owing to the rarity of the sounds expressed by them, cannot occur frequently in the inscriptions and hitherto have not been traced in those of the 4th and 5th centuries. To these belong the long *I* (4, I), in which the upper and lower dots of the ancient sign (compare plate VI, 4, V, VII) have been converted into a straight stroke, and further the short *Ṛ*, which clearly consists of a *ra* and a medial *ṛ* (compare above, § 1; and below, § 24, A, 7), also the *AU* (14, I, II) which fully agrees with the epigraphic character of A.D. 532 (plate IV, 6, X), and the subscript *ṛ* of *nṛ* (34, III) which consists of two *ṛ*, placed horizontally side by side.

§ 23.—*The acute-angled and Nāgarī types : Plates IV, V, VI.*

About the beginning of the sixth century we find in the northern inscriptions, both of Eastern and Western India (plate IV, cols. X-XII)[214], distinct beginnings of a new development which first leads to the forms of the Gayā inscription of AD. 588-89 (plate IV, cols. XIII, XIV) and of the probably not much later Lakkhāmaṇḍal Praśasti (plate IV, cols. XV, XVI)[215]. Their chief characteristic is that the letters slope from the right to the left, and show acute angles at the lower or at the right ends, as well as that the tops of the vertical or slanting lines invariably bear small wedges, and their ends either show the same ornaments or protuberances on the right. These peculiarities are observable in a large number of inscriptions of the next four centuries, and it seems to me advisable to class the characters of the whole group as those of the "acute-angled alphabet". Formerly[216] the term "nail-headed" was frequently applied to them. Of late this has been given up and no new generic name has been proposed. Thus Fleet says, in his edition of the Gayā inscription[217], only that the letters belong to the nothern class of alphabets. Possibly the Indian name may have been Siddhamātṛkā (*lipi*). For Berūnī[218] states that an alphabet [50] of this name was used in his time (about A.D. 1030) in Kashmir and in Benares, while the Nāgarī was current in Mālva. If the usual writing of Benares resembled that of Kashmir, it cannot have had the long horizontal top-strokes which always characterise the Nāgarī. Berūnī's note is, however, too brief and vague for a definite settlement of the question.

The two inscriptions, mentioned above, which, like the other contemporaneous cognate documents, are connected with the western Gupta alphabet, mark the first step in the development of the acute-angled alphabet during the sixth century. And to the same subdivision belong, among the MSS., the Horiuzi palm-leaves, which according to the Japanese tradition certainly existed in the second half of the 6th century[219]. If fourteen years ago, when I wrote my paleographical essay on these leaves in the *Anecdota Oxoniensia* the facsimiles of the Gayā and Lakkhāmaṇḍal inscriptions had been accessible, it would have sufficed to compare their letters in order to prove the correctness of the statements of the Japanese.

The characters of Aṃśuvarman's inscription of A.D. 635 (plate IV, col. XVII) and of the nearly contemporaneous Aphsaḍ Praśasti of Ādityasena (plate IV, cols. XVIII, XIX) show the further progress of the acute-angled alphabet during the 7th century. It must, however, be noted that Aṃśuvarman's inscriptions and other Nepalese documents of the same time have the round *ṣa* and thus are allied with the eastern Gupta character, while the Aphsaḍ Praśasti and its allies from India proper are connected with the western variety of the old northern alphabet[220]. Fleet calls this second variety, on account of the more marked twist of the lower ends of the strokes, "the Kuṭila variety of the Magadha alphabet of the 7th century."[221] I feel disinclined to adopt the term "*Kuṭila*", which was first used by Prinsep[222], and since has been employed by many other writers, because it is based on an erroneous rendering of the expression *kuṭila akṣara* in the Deval Praśasti[223]. I would remove it from the paleographic terminology. Kielhorn likewise avoids it in his paleographic remarks on various inscriptions of this period[224].

During the 8th-10th centuries, the development of the acute-angled or Siddhamātṛkā alphabet progresses more and more in the direction of its successor, the Nāgarī alphabet, which latter in its old North-Indian form is distinguished merely by the substitution of straight top-strokes for the wedges on the verticals. Documents with a mixture of wedges and straight top-strokes are also found; and occasionally it becomes difficult to decide how a particular inscription is to be classed.

To this third and last variety[225] of the acute-angled alphabet belong the characters of the Multai copper plates (plate IV, col. XX) of A.D. 708-709[226], of the Dighvā-Dubaulī plate, probably of A.D. 761 (plate IV, col. XXI)[227], of the Gwalior inscription of A.D. 876 (plate V, col. II), and of the Ghosrāva inscription of the 9th or 10th century (plate V, col. VI)[228], as well as, among the MSS. those of the Cambridge MS. No. 1049 (plate VI, col. VII), dated in the year 252[229], probably of Aṃśuvarman's era of A.D. 594[230], or in A. D. 846. An intermediate position between the acute-angled and the Nāgarī alphabets, is occupied by the letters of the Pehoa Praśasti of about A.D 900 (plate V col. III) of the Deval Praśasti of A.D. 992 or 993 (plate V, col. VIII) and of the copper-plates of the Paramāra king Vākpati II of A.D. 974 (plate V, col. X)[231]. They, no doubt, show the wedges; but these are so broad that they produce the same effect as the long straight top-strokes, and that, e.g., the open tops of *A*, *Ā*, *gha*, *pa*, &c., are closed, just as in the Nāgari inscriptions. Specimens of the mixture of wedges and straight top-strokes, mentioned above, are found in the Rādhanpur and Vaṇi-Diṇḍorī copper-plates of the Rāṣṭrakūṭa king [51] Govinda III of A D. 807-808 (plate V, col. IV)[232], and the Harṣa inscription of the Cāhamāna Vigraha II of A.D. 973 (plate V, col. IX)[233].

The last-mentioned two inscriptions are, however, by no means the oldest documents, in which Nāgarī letters occur. The first undoubtedly genuine specimens[234] are found in the signatures of the Gurjara princes on the copper-plates of Kaira (of A.D. 628 and

633), of Dabhoi (A.D. 642), of Nausāri (A.D. 705), and of Kāvi (A.D. 736)[235], the texts of which are written in a southern alphabet. In the first-mentioned three signatures, the Nāgari letters are in the minority, as most of the signs show either more archaic northern or southern forms. Only in the fourth signature the Nāgarī is used throughout and is fully developed. But the most ancient document, written throughout in Nāgarī, is the Sāmāngaḍ grant of the Rāṣṭrakūṭa king Dantidurga of A.D. 754 (plate IV, col. XXII)[236]. Much of the same type are the characters of the Kaṇheri inscriptions Nos. 15 and 43 (plate V, col. V)[237], which were respectively incised in A.D. 851 and 877 during the reigns of the Śilāhāra princes Pullaśakti and Kapardin II.

The Sāmāngaḍ and Kaṇheri inscriptions, together with some others of the 9th century[238], show the archaic variety of the southern Nāgari, the fully developed form of which is exhibited in the copper-plates of Kauṭheṃ (plate V, col. XVII)[239], which were incised during the reign of the Cālukya king Vikramāditya V. in A.D. 1009-10. The southern Nāgarī, of the 8th-11th centuries, which differs from its northern sister of the same period chiefly by the want of the small tails slanting to the right from the ends of the verticals, and in general by stiffer forms, besides occurs in numerous inscriptions of the Śilāhāras and Yādavas from the Marāṭhā country and the Koṅkaṇ, as well as of a Raṭṭa prince from the Belgaum collectorate[240]. Its latest development during the 13th-16th centuries is found in the inscriptions of the kings of Vijayanagara or Vidyānagara in the Kanarese country[241]. It still survives in the Bālbodh or Devanāgarī of the Marāṭhā districts, and in Southern India it has produced the so-called Nandināgari which is still used for MSS[242].

In Northern and Central India, the Nāgarī appears first on the copper-plate of the Mahārāja Vināyakapāla of Mahodaya (plate IV, col. XXIII)[243], probably of A. D. 794, which however exhibits some archaisms and peculiarities in the signs for *kha*, *ga*, and *na*, found also in later inscriptions from Eastern India. The fact that an earlier inscription from the Kanarese country, the incision of which is due to a Brahman from Northern India (see EI. 3, 1 ff.), shows a mixture of Nāgarī and acute-angled letters, makes it probable that the northern Nāgarī was in use at least since the beginning of the 8th century. From the next century, we have only a few inscriptions in northern Nāgari[244]. But after A. D. 950 their number increases, and in the 11th century the script becomes paramount in nearly all the districts north of the Narmadā.

The characters of the Sīyaḍoṇī inscriptions from Central India (plate V, col. VII), the dates of which run from A. D. 968, and those of the copper-plate of the first Caulukya of Gujarāt, incised in A. D. 987 (plate V, col. XI)[245], show the forms of the northern Nāgari of the 10th century. The copper-plates of the Rāṣṭrakūṭa (Gāhaḍavāla) king Madanapāla of Kanauj in Northern India, dated A. D. 1097 (plate V, col. XII), the Udaypur Praśasti of the Paramāras of Mālva (probable date about A. D. 1060) in the west of Central India (plate V, col. XIII), the Nanyaurā plates of the Cāndella Devavarman of A. D. 1050 (plate V, col. XIV) and of the Kalacuri Karṇa of Tripura, dated A. D. 1042 (plate V, col. XV), both from the eastern part of Central India, and the plates of the Caulukya Bhima I of Gujarāt, dated A. D. 1029 (plate V, col. XVI), give specimens of the northern Nāgarī of the 11th century[246]. Finally, the northern Nāgarī of A. D. 1100-1207 is illustrated by the alphabets of a plate of Jayaccandra, the last Rāṣṭrakūṭa (Gāhaḍavāla) king of Kanauj, dated A. D. 1175 (plate V, col. XX), of the plates of the last Caulukya of Gujarāt, Bhīma II., dated A. D. 1199 and 1207 [52] (plate V, col. XXI), of the plate of the Paramāra Udayavarman of Mālva, dated A. D. 1200 (plate V, col. XXII), and of the Ratnapur stone inscription from the reign of the Kalacuri Jājalla of Tripura, dated A. D. 1114 (plate V, col. XXIII)[247].

With the characters of these Nāgarī inscriptions, agree those of the now numerous ancient palm-leaf MSS. from Gujarāt, Rājputāna and the northern Dekhan, the dates of which run certainly from the 11th, and possibly from the 10th century. Cols. XV-XVII of plate VI exhibit their alphabet chiefly according to Leumann's photographs and tracings of the Viśeṣāvaśyakabhāṣyaṭīkā, dated A. D. 1081, together with some supplements from the Royal Asiatic Society's Gaṇaratnamahodadhi, of A. D. 1229[248]. But a number of MSS. from Nepāl, belonging to the 11th and 12th centuries, show the northern Nāgarī of the preceding century. And col. XIII of plate VI offers a specimen from No. 866, the oldest Cambridge MS. of this class, which is dated A. D. 1008[249]. Of the same type is the alphabet of plate VI, col. XIV, taken from the reproduction of col. 1 of Wylie's copy of the Vajracchedikā in *Anecdota Oxoniensia, Aryan Series*, 1, 1, plate 4.

§ 24.—DETAILS OF THE CHANGES IN THE ACUTE-ANGLED AND THE NĀGARĪ ALPHABETS[250].

A.—*The Mātṛkās.*

Among the numerous changes, which the letters of the acute-angled and Nāgarī scripts undergo in course of time, the following more important ones, affecting the Mātṛkās or radical signs, deserve special mention :—

(1) The signs for *E*, *gha*, *ca*, *tha*, *dha*, *pa*, *ba*, *ma*, *ya*, *la*, *va*, *ṣa* and *sa*, develop gradually,—the later the more distinctly,—shorter or longer tails, which first slant off towards the right below the bottom-line of the letters, but later, in the Nāgarī, become vertical strokes, except in the case of *E*. [53] From the 10th century similar pendent lines appear in the middle of *cha* (plate V, 16, II, III, &c.) and of *ḍha* (plate V, 23, II), of *pha* (plate V, III, &c) and of *ha* (plate V, 42, II-IV, &c.), which the Nāgarī, too, retains in *cha* and *ha* and converts into a medial vertical in the case of *pha*. In the acute-angled script, *kha*, *ga*, *tha*, *dha*, and *śa* frequently show on the right a small horn-like protuberance or an elongation of the vertical, which, owing to the flattening of the tops, the Nāgarī again discards except in the case of *dha*. Both the last mentioned peculiarities are due to the circumstance that the writers drew the left and right portions of the letters separately and neglected to join carefully the two halves[251]. In course of time these irregularities became characteristic features of most of the letters.

(2) In consequence of the elongation of the ends of the wedges and of the use of long straight top-strokes, the heads of *A*, *Ā*, *gha*, *pa*, *pha*, *ma*, *ya*, *ṣa* and *sa* are gradually closed, both in the acute-angled and the Nāgarī scripts[252].

(3) The lower portion of the left half of *A* and *Ā* almost invariably consists of a curve, open towards the left, which first appears occasionally in the Kuṣāna inscriptions (see above, § 19, B, 1) and later regularly on the Uccakalpa plates (plate IV, 1, IX). It is preserved in the Bālbodh of the Marāṭhās and is common in the Bombay editions of Sanskrit works. In other late specimens of the Nāgarī, it is replaced by two slanting strokes (plate V, 1, 2, XVI), to which a third, a remnant of an earlier wedge at the foot of the vertical, is added lower down. This form is the parent of the *A*, *Ā*, used in the Benares and Calcutta prints. Up to the 8th century, the long *Ā* is invariably differentiated by the addition of a curve to the right end of *A*. Later, its mark is a downward stroke, which is attached either to the right of the top (e. g., plate IV, 2, XXI) or to the middle (plate IV, 2, XXII) and thus reoccupies the same positions which the corresponding horizontal bar has in the Aśoka edicts[253]. In the MSS., the downstroke at the top is found even earlier (plate VI, 2, VI).

(4) The sign for *I* is mostly derived from the Gupta form of Indor (plate IV, 3, VII) by the substitution of a curve for the third dot (plate IV, 3, XI-XIII ; V, 3, II-IV, &c. ; VI, 3, V-IX). But in addition there is (plate V, 3, V, XII, XIII, &c. ; VI, 3, XII-XV) a derivative from the *I* of the Uccakalpa plates (IV, 3, IX), in which the upper dot is replaced by a straight line ; and this *I* is the parent of the modern Devanāgarī *I*, in which the two lower dots have been changed into curves and finally have been connected. In Jaina MSS., the *I* with two dots above and a curve below occurs occasionally as late as the 15th and 16th centuries. The unique early forms of the long *Ī* (plate VI, 4, V, VII), as well as their later development (plate VI, 4, XV), which has followed the analogy of *I*, deserve attention.

(5) *U* and *Ū* invariably show at the lower end a tail, drawn towards the left, which in course of time is developed more and more fully.

(6) The curve of *Ṛ*, attached to the right of the *ra*, becomes very shallow and long in the Horiuzi palm-leaves (plate VI, 7, V), and this shallow curve is the precursor of the vertical line of the later palm-leaf MSS. of Western India (plate VI, 7, XV-XVII). In the Cambridge MS. No. 1049 (plate VI, 7, VII) and in No. 1691, the *ṛ*-curve is attached to the lower end of the *ra*.

(7) Among the signs for *Ṝ*, *Ḷ* and *Ḹ*, which are first traceable in the MSS. of this period (plate VI, 8-10, V, VII, X), the long *Ṝ* is clearly formed by the addition of a second *ṛ*-curve to the short *Ṛ*. In the Cambridge MSS. Nos. 1049 and 1691, *Ḷ* is represented by a cursive southern *la* (see plate VII, 34, VI-IX), just as the oldest medial *ḷ* in *kḷ* (VII, 42, XIV) is identical with another form of *la* ; and the long *Ḹ* is derived from the short vowel by the addition of a second *la*, turned in the opposite direction. In the *Ḷ* and *Ḹ* of the Horiuzi palm-leaves (plate VI, 9, 10, V), the *la* has been turned round towards the left, and respectively one and two *ṛ*-curves have been attached to the foot. And the combination *l (a)-ṛ* remains [54] also in the Nāgarī both of the palm-leaves from Western India (plate VI, 9, 10, XV) and of our days, the reason being no doubt the pronunciation *lṛ*, which is customary both there and in other parts of India. These paleographical facts agree with the tradition of the Chinese Buddhists who, as S. Lévi has discovered,[254], ascribe the invention of the signs for the liquid vowels to a South-

Indian, either to Śarvavarman, the minister of the Andhra king Sātavāhana, or to the great Buddhist teacher Nāgārjuna.

(8) *E* and *AI* invariably turn the base of the triangle upwards, and this innovation is found already in the inscriptions with transitional forms (plate IV, 5, X, XI).

(9) *Ka* shows almost invariably[255] on the left a loop, caused by the connection of the end of the bent cross-bar with the *Serif* or wedge at the foot of the vertical, except in combinations with the subscribed vowels *u* and *ṛ* (see, e.g., plate IV, 7, XIV; V, 10, III; VI, 15, XVI, XVII) or with other consonants (see, e.g., plate IV, 41, XVI; V, 43, II, III; VI, 49, V, XV, XVIII). In the Nāgari inscriptions, the looped form occurs, however, not rarely also in the latter cases (see, e.g., plate IV, 7, XX. XXII; V, 43, VII, X-XIII).

(10) The loop or traingle of *kha*, which represents the ancient circle (plate II, 10, VI, and above, §3, A, 19), stands, in all the greatly varying forms of the letters, at the left of the verticals. The very considerable differences in the shape of the left limb are partly due to the flattening of the top of the letter and still more to the various ornamental changes of the wedge, which first was added to the lower end of the ancient hook.

(11) The dot to the right of *ṅa*, which is so characteristic in the modern Devanāgarī letter, appears already on the Benares copper-plate of Karṇa of A. D. 1042 in the word *jaṅgama* (line 11, end)[256], while our plates offer only an example from a much later document (see plate V, 14, XIX). The dot may possibly have been derived from the protuberance, which is often found at the end of the top-stroke of the letter (see, e.g., plate V, 14, V, VI, VIII).

(12) The central bar of *ja* first is made to slant downwards (plate IV, 14, XXI-XXIII, &c.) and then changed into a vertical (V, 17, XIII, &c.; VI, 22, XII, &c.). At the same time, the upper bar becomes the top-stroke of the letter, and the lowest is gradually converted into a double curve.

(13) The right limb of the independent *ña* of the Horiuzi palm-leaves (VI, 24, V) is turned upwards, and the same form occurs occasionally in ligatures. But in the latter the sign is usually laid on its side, its angles are converted into curves and the right limb is attached to the end of the greatly shortened vertical. Hence it often looks like *ṇa* (see plate IV, 16, XI, &c.; V, 19, IV, V, &c.). In the Nāgari of the 11th and later centuries, the subscript *ña* is attached to the left limb of *ja* (plate V, 19, XII-XIV; VI, 24, XVI), and the cursive *jña* of the modern Devanāgarī, which the Hindus now consider to be a Mātṛkā, is due to a simplification of this form.

(14) Since the 6th century, a wedge is often placed above the lingual *ṭa* (plate IV, 17, XVII; V, 20, II, VI; VI, 25, VI); and in the Nāgarī a horizontal line with a short vertical or slanting stroke appears in the place of the wedge (plate IV, 17, XXI, XXII; V, 20, XIII, &c.; VI, 25, XV)

(15) Similar additions appear above the lingual *ṭha* since the 10th century (plate V, 21, X, &c.; VI, 26, XV).

(16) Since the 9th century, the round-backed lingual *ḍa* of the southern alphabets, ending with a curve open to the left, comes into use (plate V, 22, II, VIII, &c.).

(17) The suppression of the original base-stroke of the lingual *ṇa* occurs in ligatures (*ṇḍa*, plate IV, 21, XIX) since the 7th century, and in the uncombined sign since the 8th century (plate V, 24, III); compare also above, § 22, B, 10, and plate IV, 21, III. The sign soon after assumes the modern form and consists of a straight top-stroke with three lines hanging down from it (plate V, 24, VII, &c.; VI, 29, XV, &c.)

(18) The modern form of *ta* with the vertical on the right, which occurs already in the Aśoka edicts, reappears in the 8th century (plate IV, 22, XXI) and becomes the regular one in the 10th century.

(19) The modern form of *tha*, which has been derived from the notched one of the 7th century (plate IV, 23, XVII), is found already in the inscriptions of the same period (plate IV, 23, XVIII, &c.).

(20) [55] In the 7th century, the lower end of *da* is more clearly defined by a *Serif* (plate IV, 24, XVII, &c.), which soon after is changed into the characteristic tail of the modern letter.

(21) Already in the 7th century, the right side of *na* becomes occasionally a vertical, to the left of which the loop is attached (plate IV, 26, XVIII, XIX); compare also below, §30.

(22) On the transformation of *pha* by the development of a central vertical (see above, under 1), the curve of aspiration is attached first to the top of the new sign (plate IV, 28, XXII; V, 31, III, &c.). But in the 11th century it sinks lower down (plate V, 31, XII), and it occupies already in the 12th century the position which it has in the modern Devanāgarī letter (plate V, 31, XX-XXIII). Retrograde archaic forms, like those in plate V, 31, II, XIV, are, however, not rare, Their occurrence has probably to be explained by the influence of the popular cursive alphabets.

(23) As *va* was very generally pronounced *ba*, the ancient sign for *ba* was lost in Northern, Central and Western India, and it was replaced by *va* in the inscriptions of the 7th and later centuries (plate IV, 29, XX; V, 32, II, &c.). In the MSS. the substitution occurs even earlier (plate VI, 37, V, VI). A new *ba*, consisting of *va* with a dot in the centre of the loop, occurs since the 11th century (plate V, 32, XVI), and this form is the parent of the modern Devanāgarī letter.

(24) The left limb of *bha*, mostly an inverted wedge with the point towards the right, is frequently changed into a triangle, open at the apex, from which the lower portion of the original vertical hangs down (plate IV, 30, XIX, &c.; V, 33, II, &c.). The modern Devanāgarī *bha* appears in the 12th century (plate V, 33, XV, &c.) and seems to be derived from the form with the wedge, for which latter a *Serif* was substituted.

(25) Since the 8th century· *ma* usually has on the left a cursive loop (plate IV, 31, XX, XXI), which in the MSS. is mostly filled in with ink (plate VI, 39, XV-XVII),

(26) Both the MSS., and most inscripitions, with the exception of one from Udaypur (above, note 212) and some from Nepāl (note 220), offer exclusively the looped or the bipartite *ya*, which latter occurs already in the inscriptions of the Kuṣāna period,[257] and has been derived from the looped form.[258] In the Nepalese inscriptions of the 7th century, which show the eastern *ṣa*,[259] we find a tripartite *ya* with a small circle at

the top of the first upstroke (plate IV, 32, XVII); the Udaypur inscription has both the ordinary tripartite *ya* of the Gupta period, and also the bipartite letter.

(27) The right extremity of the wedge at the lower end of *ra* is often greatly elongated in the inscriptions of the 7th and later centuries (plate IV, 33, XVIII-XXI, &c.), and sometimes only the outlines of the wedge are marked. These forms are the precursors of the modern tailed *ra*.

(28) Since the 7th century, we find a cursive *śa* (plate IV, 36, XVIII; 42, XIX; V, 39, II, III, &c.; VI, 44, XV-XVII), the left half of which has been turned into a loop with a litttle tail on the right.

B.—*Medial vowels and so forth.*

(1) Medial *ā, e, o, au*, as well as one of the Mātrās of *ai*, are placed very frequently above the line, and are then, particularly in the stone inscriptions, treated more or less ornamentally (see, e.g., plate IV, cols. XIII-XVIII). More rarely medial *i* and *ī* are treated in the same way.

(2) The tails of the curves of medial *i* and *ī* are regularly drawn down low, respectively to the left and the right of the Mātṛkā, while the differences in the curves at the top disappear. These forms lead up to the *i* and *ī* of the mordern Devanāgari.

(3) Medial *ū* is expressed very frequently by the initial *Ū* of the period (plate IV, 30, XII, XIV, XVI, XX; VI, 44, VI). [56] But an older form, found, e. g., in *pū* (IV, 27, VI), is also common and appears to be the parent of the modern *ū*, which occurs already in the western plam-leaf MSS. (see *pū*, plate VI, 35, XVI).

(4) Since the 7th century[260]—first on the Banskherā plate of Harṣa,—the Jihvāmūlīya is occasionally expressed by a cursive sign, consisting of a loop under the wedge of *ka* (plate V, 47, III).

(5) Since the 7th century, the Upadhmānīya is occasionally expressed by a curve open above, with curled ends and sometimes with a dot in the centre. This sign is attached to the left side of the Mātṛkā (plate IV, 46, XXIII; V, 48, VII). It seems to be derived from a form like that in plate VII, 46, IV.

(6) In the older inscriptions, the Virāma is still frequently placed above the vowelless consonant, for which invariably a final form is used; and it receives a tail, which is drawn downwards to the right of the Mātṛkā (see, e.g., plate IV, 22, XIV). But even more commonly it stands below the consonant, and it occurs in this position already in the inscriptions with transitional forms (plate IV, 22, XI)[261].

C.—*The ligatures.*

(1) Both in the inscriptions and in the MSS. of the 6th and later centuries, we find occasionally ligatures, in which the second consonant is placed to the right of the first, instead of below it (see, e.g., plate IV, 45, XI; V, 47, II; VI, 51, VI).[262]

(2) For the stone inscriptions of the acute-angled alphabet, the subscript *ya* frequently is made ornamental and drawn far to the left. Since the 7th century, and occassionally even earlier, the right-hand upstroke of *ya* is drawn up as far as the upper line of the whole sign (see, e.g., plate IV, 46, VIII, XIX; 43, 45, XIII; VI, 51, VI).

(3) *Ra*, being the first part of a compound consonant, usually stands above the line and is expressed by a wedge, or by an angle or a curve open to the right. But in *rma* the left side of *ma* is shortened, and the top of the wedge, which is placed on this shortened lines, does not protrude above the upper line (plate VI, 49, VI). Similar depressions of the superscribed *ra* are found in connection with other consonants in the Aphsaḍ inscription[263], on Harasa's copper-plates, and in some MSS. (plate VI, 51, XIII, XIV). Until the 9th century, *rya* is often expressed by a full *ra* with a subscribed *ya* (see, e.g., plate IV, 44, XVIII ; 45, VII ; and compare EI. 3, 103).

§ 25—THE ŚĀRADĀ ALPHABET : PLATES V AND VI.

A.—The Śāradā script[264], which is easily recognised as a descendant of the western Gupta alphabet, appears since about A. D. 800 in Kashmīr and in the north-eastern Pañjāb (Kāngra and Chambā). The oldest known Śāradā inscriptions are the two Baijnāth Praśastis from Kīragrāma (Kāngra), dated A.D. 804 ; see plate V, col. I. Not much later are the coins of the Varma dynasty of Kashmir, where the Śāradā forms are likewise fully developed[265]. And it is not improbable that the Bakhshāli MS., found in the Yusufzai district (plate VI, Col. VIII), belongs to the same or even a somewhat earlier period[266]. The third specimen of the Śāradā in plate VI, col. IX, which ultimately is derived from Burkhard's plate I, in his edition of the Kashmīrian Śākuntala[267], dates perhaps only from, the 16th or 17th century ; it has been given merely because at present no reproductions of more ancient MSS. are accessible[268]. In consequence of the frequent emigrations of the travel-loving Kashmīrian Pandits, Śāradā MSS. are found in many towns of North-Western India and further east in Benares, and marginal glosses in Śāradā characters are found even in ancient Nāgrī MSS. from Western India[269]. A [57] modern cursive variety of the Śāradā is the so-called Ṭakkari or Ṭākari[270] of the Dogrās in Jammū and the neighbourhood, which of late has been imported also into Kashmīr.

B.—A general characteristic of the Śāradā of all periods is found in the stiff, thick strokes which give the characters an uncouth appearance and a certain resemblance to those of the Kuṣāṇa period. The following signs show, already in the earliest period, peculiar developments :—

(1) The *I*, which consists of two dots, placed side by side, and (compare the *I* of the Bower MS.) a *ra*-like figure below, which represents the other two dots (plate V, 4, I ; VI, 4, IX).

(2) The quadrangular *ca* (plate V, 15, I ; VI, 20, VIII, IX).

(3) The lingual *ḍa*, which shows in the middle a loop, instead of an acute angle, and a wedge at the end (plate V, 22, I ; VI, 27, VIII, IX).

(4) The dental *ta*, which, being derived from a looped form, has lost its left half, while the right has been converted into a curve (plate V, 25, I ; VI, 30, VIII, IX).

(5) The dental *dha*, which is flattened at the top and is below so broad that it resembles a Devanāgari *pa*.

(6) The *va*, which, owing to the connection of the left side of the curve with the top-stroke, closely resembles *dha* (plate V, 38, I ; VI, 43, VIII, IX).

(7) The quadrangular *śa*, which exactly resembles a Nāgarī *sa* (plate V, 39, I; VI, 44, VIII, IX).

(8) The angular medial *r* (plate V, 43, I; VI, 43, VIII), and the detached *o*, which stands by itself above the line (plate V, 24, I; VI, 31, IX), and without doubt is derived from the Gupta *o* (plate IV, 31, IV).

(9) The *ra*, which, as a first part of ligatures, is inserted into the left side of the second letter, just as in the Aphsad inscription[271].

The other letters of the earlier documents differ very little from those of the western Gupta alphabet, and the changes, which are found, all occur also in the acute-angled script. The constant use of the bipartite *ya*, of the *ṇa* with the suppressed base-stroke (see above, § 24, A, 17), of the *i* and *ī*, drawn down respectively to the left and the right of the consonant (§ 24, B, 2), and of the simplified Jihvāmūlīya (plate V, 47, I), indicates that the separation of the Śāradā from the Gupta alphabet did not take place before the 7th century.

In the later Śāradā (plate VI, col. IX), further abnormal developments are noticeable in *U*, *E*, *AI*, *O*, *AU*, *ja*, *ña*, *bha*, *rtha* (which latter occurs also in plate VI, col. VIII), and owing to the use of long top-strokes the heads of several letters, such as *A*, *I* and *ya*, are closed.

§26.—EASTERN VARIETIES OF THE NĀGARĪ ALPHABET AND THE ARROW-HEAD SCRIPT.

A.—*Proto-Bengālī : Plates V and VI.*

Towards the end of the 11th century, the Nāgarī inscriptions of Eastern India shew such distinct traces of changes leading upto the modern Bengālī writing, and these changes become so numerous in the 12th century, that it is possible to class their alphabets as Proto-Bengālī. An approximate idea of the development of the Proto-Bengālī may be obtained by comparing the characters of the following documents, represented in our plates :—(1) of the Deopārā Praśasti[272] of about A.D. 1080-90 (plate V, col. XVIII), which includes the Bengālī *E*, *kha*, *ña*, *ta*, *tha*, *ma*, *ra*, *la*, and *sa*; (2) of Vaidyadeva's land-grant[273] of A.D. 1142 (plate V, col. XIX), with the Bengālī *Ṛ*, *E*, *AI*, *kha*, *ga*, *ña*, *ta*, *tha*, *dha*, *ra* and *va*; and (3) of the Cambridge MSS. No. 1699, 1, 2[274], of A. D. 1198-99 (plate VI, col. X), which offers the Bengālī *A*, *Ā*, *U*, *Ṛ*, *Ṝ*, *Ḷ*, *Ḹ*, *E*, *AI*, *AU*, *ka*, *kha*, *ga*, *ta*, *tha*, *na*, *ma*, *ya ra*, *va* and *sa*, as well as transitional forms of *gha*, *ña*, *ṇa*, and *śa*.

Only a few among the Proto-Bengālī letters are new local formations. The great majority occurs already in other older scripts, be it in exactly the same or in similar shape. [58] Thus, its *Ṛ*, *Ṝ*, *Ḷ* and *Ḹ* agree closely with the corresponding characters of the Horiuzi MS. (plate VI, 7-10, V), its *Ū* with that of the oldest MS. from Nepāl (plate VI, 6, VII; compare also the Śāradā, VI, 6, IX), and its *AU* with that of the Bower MS. (plate VI, 14, I, II). Its signs for *A*, *Ā*, *ka*, *na*, *ma*, *ya*, *va*, *ṣa*, and *sa* occur repeatedly in various alphabets of the 8th-10th centuries, given in plates IV, V. Its *kha*, opened on the right, finds an analogy in that of the Bower MS. (plate VI, 16, I), and its *tha*, likewise opened on the right, somewhat resembles that of plate V, 26, IX. Finally, the *ga* and *ṇa* with the verticals, rising on the right above the line, have precursors in the letters of the 9th and 10th centuries with horn-like protuberances (plate V, 12, 24, II-IV, VI ; compare also above, § 24, A, 1). Even the *ra*, resembling *va* (plate V, 36, XIX ; VI, 41, 49, X), may easily be recognised as due to a slightly abnormal development of the wedge at the end of the letter, for which, forms from Western and Central India in plate V, 36, XIII, XIV, offer more or less close analogies. Only the *E* and *AI*, open on the left, and the peculiar *ña* in *ñca* (plate V, 19, XVIII) and in *jñā* (plate VI, 24, X), appear to be purely local new formations. And this may be true also of the *ta* (plate V, 25, XVIII, XIX ; VI, 30, X), which, however, does not differ much from the Śāradā sign and from the final *t* of some other alphabets.

The most striking and important among the peculiarities of the Proto-Bengālī, discarded in the modern Bengālī script, are the small triangles with the rounded lower side and the "Nepalese hooks", which are attached to the left of the tops of various letters. The triangle is found in *kṣi* (plate V, 47, XVIII) and in very many letters of plate V, col. XIX ; while the hook occurs in the *ka* and *ta* of plate V, 25 and 43, XVIII[275]. If further we compare the Tarpan-Dighi inscription of Lakṣmaṇasena [276], where the triangles and hooks frequently appear alternately in connection with the same letters, it becomes evident that the "Nepaless hook" is a cursive substitute for the triangle. The triangle itself is a modification of the top-stroke with a semi-circle below, occasionally met with in ornamental inscriptions from Nothern and Central India, as, e.g., in Vināyakapāla's plate (letters with this peculiarity have not been given in plate IV, col. XXIII) and in the Cāndella inscription in Cunningham's *Archaeological Reports*, Vol. 10, plate 33, No. 3. This last mentioned form again is connected with, and gives the outlines of, the thick top-strokes, rounded off at both ends, which are not rare in ornamental MSS. like that figured by Bendall, *Catalogue of Sanskrit Buddhist MSS. from Nepāl*, plate 2, Nos. 1, 2, and in the alphabet of plate VI, col. XIV (see particularly lines 5, 7, 15, 30, 34, 37, 49).

Among the abnormal single signs, not received into the modern Bengāli, the following deserve special remarks :—

(1) The forms of *I* in plate V, 3, XVIII, and VI, 3, X, are cursive developments of the ancient *I* in plate IV, 3, IX, &c. But the *I* and *Ī* of plate V, 3, 4, XIX, appear to be southern forms ; compare plate VII, 3, IV-VI.

(2) The curious *ṭa* of plate V, 20, XIX, seems to have been produced by an abnormally strong development of a "Nepalese hook" with a *Serif* at the end, placed above the ancient round *ṭa*, which is represented by the second lower curve on the left ; compare the *ṭa* of col. XVIII, and that of the Cambridge MS. No. 1693 (Bendall, op. cit., plate 4).

(3) The *na* of plate V, 29, XIX, without a connecting stroke between the loop and the vertical, is due to the strongly developed predilection for cursive forms, which is visible also in other letters of Vaidyadeva's inscription, such as *A*, *Ā*, *śa* and the ligature *tkr* (plate V, 47, XIX).

(4) The triangular medial *u*, for instance of *ku* (plate V, 10, XIX), which appears also in Lakṣmaṇasena's Tarpan-Dighi grant and other eastern inscriptions, gives outline of the older wedge-shaped form, found, e. g., in *thu* (plate V, 26, XVIII) and in *ṣu* (plate VI, 45, II).

(5) The Anusvāra of *vaṃ* (plate V, 38, XIX) and of *kaṃ* (plate VI, 15, X) has been placed on the line, as in the Old-Kanarese (see below, § 29, C, 5) and the modern Grantha, and a Virāma stands below it.

(6) In the *Om* of plate V, 9, XVIII, we have the oldest example of the occurrence of the modern Anunāsika. In this case, it shows a little circle instead of the more usual dot, which is found in the *Om* of plate VI, 13, XI. Both forms are rather frequent in the eastern inscriptions of the 12th century[277], whereas in the west[278] they are more rare and are confined to the word *Om*. The Anunāsika, which I have not found in any Indian inscriptipon older than the 11th century, probably is an intentional modification of the Anusvāra, invented because in Vedic MSS. the Anunāsika must be substituted for an Anusvāra followed by liquid consonants, sibilants and *ha*.

(7) [59] The Visarga of *vaḥ* (plate V, 38, XVIII) carries a wedge at the top, which addition appears also in other ornamental scripts (see, e. g., plate VI, 30, XIV); in the *ḥ* of plate VI, 51, X (compare also VI, 41, XI, and the Gayā inscription), it has been changed cursively into a form resembling our figure 8. In the Gayā inscription (IA. 10, 342), as well as in MSS. of this period[279], it receives also a small tail (compare *tāḥ*, plate VI, 30, XIV).

B.—*The Nepalese hooked characters : Plate VI.*

According to Bendall's careful examination of the MSS. from Nepāl[280], the hooked characters first occur in the 12th century and disappear towards the end of the 15th. The facts, stated above, which prove the occurrence of the "Nepalese hooks" in Bengal inscriptions of the 12th century and explain their origin, leave no doubt that the introduction of this modification of the top-strokes is due to the influence of Bengal, which, as Bendall has recognised[281], makes itself felt also in other points.

The first of the two specimens of this character in plate VI, col. XI, which is derived from the Cambridge MS. No. 1691, of A. D. 1179[282], shows in the majority of the letters the forms of the Horiuzi Palm-leaves and of the Cambridge MS. No. 1049 (cols. V-VII), with a few small modifications, such as might be expected in a much later document. Irrespective of the hooks, special Bengālī peculiarities are observable only in *I*, *Ī*, *E* and *AI*. Generally speaking, these remarks hold good also for the second specimen in plate VI, col. XII, from the the British Museum MS., Oriental No. 1439, of A. D. 1286[283]. But in this script the Bengāli influence is visible in *E*, *ṇa*, *dha*, and *śa* (compare the transitional forms of V, 39, XVIII, XIX), while its *I* is very archaic.[284]

Nepāl and Tibet seem to have preserved a number of other, mostly ornamental, alphabets of Eastern India,[285], hand-drawn tables of which have been given by B. Hodgson (*Asiatic Reseaches,* Vol. 16) and by Śarat Chandra Dās (J. ASB., Vol. 57, plates 1 to 7). But up to present time no reliable materials are available, on which a paleographical examinatfon of these scripts could be based.

C.—*The arrow-head alphabet : Plate VI.*

The arrow-head alphabet, plate VI, cols. XVIII, XIX, which C. Bendall, its discoverer[286], is inclined to identify with Berūni's *bhaikṣukī lipi,* appears to be confined to Eastern India. It, of course, has no connection with the Nāgarī, but, as Bendall points out in his very careful description, is the immediate offspring of an ancient form of the Brāhmī. It would seem that the *A*, *Ā*, *ka*, *ña*, *ra* and perhaps also the *jha* of the present alphabet have curves at the lower end. This peculiarity, as well as the peculiar *E*, noted by Bendall (compare plate VIII, 8, VIII) and the absence of a difference between *ṛ* and *ra*, seem to indicate that the present alphabet belonged to the southern scripts, for which these points are characteristic (compare plate III, cols. X-XX, and plates VII, VIII). Its pointed *kha*, *ga*, and *śa* likewise occur in southern alphabets (see plate III, 8, VII; VII, 9, XI, XIV; VII, 11, XVII; 36, IV, XVI, XX). And the forms of *ṇa*, *ta* and *na* perhaps point rather to the south-west than to the south (compare plate VII, cols. I, II, &c.). Only in the case of the looped *sa* it is possible to think of northern (Gupta) influence; but the possibility that it is an independent new formation is not excluded. An inscription in the same alphabet, and shewing wedges instead of arrow-heads at the top of the letters, has been discussed by Bendall in IA. 19, 77 f.

V. THE SOUTHERN ALPHABETS.

§ 27.—*Definition and varieties.*

[60] With Burnell and Fleet, I understand by the term "southern alphabets" the scripts of plates VII and VIII[287], which, developed out of the characters of the Andhra period, have been generally used since about A.D. 350 in the territories south of the Vindhya, and most of which still survive in the modern alphabets of the Dravidian districts.

Their most important common characteristic are :—

(1) The retention of the ancient forms, open at the top, of *gha*, *pa*, *pha*, *ṣa* and *sa* of the old *ma*, and of the tripartite *ya* which is looped only occasionally, especially in the Grantha.

(2) The retention of the long stroke on the right of *la*, which however is mostly bent towards the left.

(3) The *ḍa* with the round back.

(4) The curves, originally open at the top, at the ends of the long verticles of *A*, *Ā*, *ka*, *ña*, and *ra*, as well as of the subscript *ra* and of medial *u* and *ū*.

(5) The medial *ṛ* with a curled curve on the left, with occasional exceptions occurring in *kṛ*.

According to other peculiarities, the southern alphabets may be divided into the following varieties[288] :—

(1) The western variety, which, being strongly influenced by the northern alphabets, is the ruling script between about A.D. 400 and about A.D. 900 in Kāṭhiāvāḍ, Gujarāt, the western portion of the Marāṭhā districts, i.e. the Collectorates of Nāsik, Khāndesh and Sātārā, in the part of Haidarābād (Ajaṇṭā) contiguous to Khāndesh and in the Koṅkaṇ, and which, during the 5th century occasionally occurs also in Rājputāna and the Central Indian Agency, but altogether disappears in the 9th century in consequence of the inroads of the Nāgarī alphabet (see above, § 21).

(2) The Central-Indian script, which in its simplest form closely agrees with the western variety, but in its more developed form, the so-called "box-headed alphabet", shows greater differences, and which from the end of the 4th century is common in northern Haidarābād, the Central Provinces and parts of the Central-Indian Agency (Bundelkhaṇḍ), but appears also occasionally further south in the Bombay Presidency and even in Maisūr.

(3) The script of the Kanarese and Telugu districts of the Dekhaṇ,—i.e. of the southern portion of the Bombay Presidency (the southern Marāṭhā States, Sholāpur, Bijāpur, Beḷgaum, Dhārwār and Kārwār), of the southern territory of Haidarābād (roughly speaking south of Bidar), of Maisūr, and of the north-east portion of the Madras Presidency (Vizagapatam, Godāvarī, Kistna, Karnūl, Bellary, Anantpur, Cuddapah, Nellore),—which appears first in the Kadamba inscriptions of the 5th and 6th centuries, and after a long development leads to the very similar and temporarily identical Kanarese and Telugu round-hand.

(4) The later Kaliṅga alphabet of the north-eastern coast of the Madras Presidency between Cicacole and the frontier of Orissa (Gañjām), which is strongly mixed with northern letters and in later times also with Grantha and Kanarese-Telugu characters, and which occurs in inscriptions of the 7th-12th centuries.

(5) The Grantha alphabet of the eastern coast of Madras, South of Pulikat (North and South Arcot, Salem, Trichinopoli, Madura and Tinnevelli), which first appears in the ancient Sanskrit inscriptions of the Pallava dynasties, and survives in the modern Grantha and its varieties, the Malayāḷam and the Tuḷu.

The Tamil alphabet of the same districts and of the western coast of Madras (Malabar) poobably is derived from a northern script, imported in the 4th or 5th century, but greatly modified by the influence of the Grantha. A cursive variety of the Tamil alphabet is found in Vaṭṭeḷuttu (the "round-hand", Burnell) or Cera-Pāṇḍya (Aultzsch)[289], which is known through inscriptions from the western coast and the extreme south of the Peninsula, and according to Burnell [61] has fallen into disuse only in recent times[290]. Though these two alphabets come from a different source, they have been included in this chapter, because they occur in the same districts as the other five.

§ 28.—THE WESTERN SCRIPT AND THE SCRIPT OF CENTRAL INDIA: PLATES VII AND VIII

A.—*The western script.*

The western variety of the southern alphabets is found in the inscriptions of the Imperial Guptas and their vassals since the time of Candragupta II[291], of the kings of Valabhī[292], of the Gurjaras of Broach[293], of some of the Calukyas of Bādāmi (Pulakeśin II and Vijayabhaṭṭārikā), and of Nāsik and Gujarāt and their vassals[294], of the Traikūṭakas[295], of the Aśmakas (?) of Khāndesh[296], and of the Rāṣṭrakūṭas of Gujarāt[297], as well as in numerous votive inscriptions in the caves of Kaṇheri, Nāsik and Ajaṇṭā[298]. Ordinarily, its characters no doubt were written with ink, just like those of the northern alphabets (see above, § 21). This is made highly probable by the use of wedges on the tops of the letters during the Gupta period (see plate VII, cols. I-III) and by the thick, frequently knob-like, heads of the signs of the Valabhī, Gurjara and Rāṣṭrakūṭa grants (plate VII, cols. IV-IX, and plate VIII, col. I), both of which ornaments can only be drawn with ink. Another argument is furnished by the fact that all the copper-plates from Gujarāt have been cut according to the ordinary size of the Bhūrja leaves (Burnell), on which it is not possible to write with a *stilus*.

The finds of nearly or quite contemporaneous inscriptions with northern characters in Rājputāna, the Central-Indian Agency[299], and Valabhī, as well as the Nāgarī signatures of the Gurjara princes[300], prove that northern scripts were being used simultaneously with this southern alphabet. And this circumstance is no doubt the cause of its showing traces of northern peculiarities in the following letters :—(1) in the *kha* with a large loop and a small hook (plate VII, 9, I-IX ; VIII, 12, I); instead of which the true southern form appears only very rarely[301] ; (2) in the *ca*, rounded off on the right (plate VII, 13, I-IX ; VIII, 16, I) ; (3) in the ancient *ta* without a loop (plate VII, 22, I-IX ; VIII, 25, I) ; (4) in the narrow *dha* (plate VII, 25, I-IX ; VIII, 28, I ; compare plate IV, 25, I-III) ; (5) in the looped *na* (plate VII, 26, I-IX ; VIII, 29, I), which agrees more exactly with the northern forms of plate IV, 26, than with the southern one of VII, 26, XIII (compare below, § 29, A) ; (6) In the Mātrās often placed above the line in medial *e* (plate VII, 26, V), *ai* (plate VII, 10, IV) and *o* (plate VIII, 35, I), which latter, however, has a peculiar looped form in *lo* (plate VII, 34, III, IV) ; (7) in the medial *au*, consisting of three strokes above the line (VII, 25, V ; 36, III) ; and compare plate IV, 7, IV) ; (8) in the subscript *ña*, which occasionally, as in plate VII, 42, VII, shows the northern cursive form. The inscriptions Nos. 17 and 62 of Fleet's *Gupta Inscriptions* (CII. 3), plates 10, 38, B, which are not represented in plate VII, show, [62] besides, the northern *A* and *ka* without the curve at the foot. A *ka* of this description occurs also sometimes in the Valabhī inscriptions (plate VII, 8, V).

Irrespective of these northern peculiarities, which throughout remain almost unchanged, the characters of this script show three stages in their development, that of the 5th century (plate VII, cols. I-III), that of the 6th and 7th centuries (cols. IV-VI, VIII), and that of the 8th (col. IX) and 9th centuries (plate VIII, col. I) which last is very markedly cursive.

Among the single letters the following deserve special remarks :—

(1) The *I* (plate VII, 3, IV, ff. ; VIII, 3, I), which here, as in most southern alphabets, consists of a curved line with a notch in the centre and of two dots below, and which appears to be a modification of a form like that in plate IV, 3, IX.

(2) The *Ī* (plate VII, 3, I ; VIII, 4, I), which, like that of the Bower MS. (plate VI, 4, I), has been developed by the transformation of two dots into a line, but in addition has the curved tail, characteristic of the southern alphabets.

(3) The *E*, which usually consists of a triangle with the apex at the top, and is irregularly broadened on the left (plate VII, 6, I ; and compare *AI* in VII, 6, VII), and which from the end of the 6th century frequently, especially in Gurjara inscriptions, is opened at the top (plate VII, 6, VI) and finally resembles a northern *la* (plate VIII, 8, I).

(4) The *ḍa*, which in its oldest form (plate VII, 19, II), as mostly in the southern alphabets, is undistinguishable from *da*, but from the 6th century develops a little tail (plate VII, 19, IV-IX), or, in some inscriptions of the 8th and 9th centuries, a loop at the end (plate VII, 43, VII; plate VIII, 22, I).

(5) The *ṭha* with a ringlet on the base-line (plate VII, 23, III, IV, VI) instead of the cross-bar (plate VII, 23, I, II), developed out of the ancient dot, or since the end of the 6th century with the southern notch in the base (plate VII, 23, VII-IX; plate VIII, 26, I)[302].

(6) The *la* with the diminutive main portion of the original sign and the enormous tail (plate VII, 34, VI, VIII), which latter since the 7th century frequently becomes the sole representative of the letter (plate VII, 34, VII, IX).

(7) The *śa*, which shows regularly in the Gurjara inscriptions (plate VIII, 39, I) and the Nāsik Calukya inscription[303], and occasionally in the Valabhī inscriptions[304], a cursive combination of the cross-bar with the vertical on the right, which occurs also in the north[305].

(8) The *sa*, which occasionally shows (plate VII, 38, V) a cursive combination of the left limb with the *Serif* occurring also in southern scripts (plate VIII, 41, XI).

(9) A number of cursive forms in ligatures, thus :—(*a*) The prefixed *ña* which often loses the hook on the right and looks like *ṇa* (compare also plate V, 19, V, VII). (*b*) The prefixed *na*, which especially before *ta*, *tha*, *dha* and *na* (see the *nta* of *anumantavyaḥ*, plate VII, 42, V) consists of a horizontal or bent stroke and looks like *ta*[306]. (*c*) The subscript *ka*, which occasionally, as in *ṣka* (plate VII, 46, VIII), is looped on the left (compare IA. 11, 305). (*d*) The subscript *ca* of *ñca* (plate VII, 41, VIII, IX), which since the 6th century remains open on the right and bears the hook of *ña* on its base. (*e*) The subscript *ṇa*, which already since early times is merely indicated by a loop (see *rṇṇa*, plate VII, 41, IV). (*f*) The subscript *tha*, which, as in other southern alphabets (compare, e.g., plate VII, 45, XX), is changed to a double curve open on the right (plate VII, 45, IV; plate VIII, 49, I).

B.—*The script of Central India.*

The Central-Indian script is found fully developed in the inscriptions of Samudragupta at Eraṇ and of Candragupta II at Udayagiri[307], on the copper-plates of the kings of Śarabhapura[308], of the Vākāṭakas[309], and of Tīvara king of Kosala[310], and in two early Kadamba inscriptions[311]. In all these documents, the heads of the letters bear small squares, which are either hollow (plate VII, col. XI) or filled in (pl. VII, col. X). These squares, to which on account of their resemblances to small boxes the script owes the name "box-headed", are, like the wedges, artificial developments of the *Serifs*. The solid, filled in, squares probably have been invented by writers who [63] used ink, and the hollow ones by persons writing with a *stilus*, who feared to tear their palm-leaves. Both varieties of "box-heads" occur occasionally or constantly in other districts and in connection with other alphabets (see, e.g., the Valabhī inscription of plate VII, col. V, the archaic Kadamba inscription of plate VII, col. XII, the Pallava inscription of plate VII, col. XX), and even in Nos. 21 and 21, A, of the Campā inscriptions from Further India[312]. But the very peculiar appearance of the Central-Indian inscriptions of this class is due to the more or less rigorous modification of the letters by the contraction of their breadth and the conversion of all curves into angular strokes. This is best visible in the grants, figured in EI. 3, 260, and in Fleet's *Gupta Inscriptions* (CII. 3), Nos. 40, 41, 56, 81, plates 26, 27, 35, 45, among which No. 56 is represented in col. XI of our plate VII, while col. X offers the less carefully modified characters of F.GI (CII. 3), No. 55, plate 34. Both these inscriptions were issued in the same year from the *Dharmādhikaraṇa* of the *Vākāṭaka* king Pravarasena II.

Traces of the influence of the northern alphabets are visible in this script just as in the western variety, and particularly in the letters *ta*, *dha*, *na*, and in the Mātrās of medial *e*, *ai* and *o*, which in F.GI (CII. 3), No. 81, plate 45 (not in our plate), shew the peculiar tailed northern form of the 7th and 8th centuries. But in the ligatures (see, for instance, *nta*, plate VII, 43, X), we meet repeatedly with the looped *ta* and with the *na* without the loop, and even an independent looped *ta* appears exceptionally[313] in the word *snātānām* (No. 55, line 7; No. 56, line 6). Medial *au* has the tripartite western and northern form in F. GI (CII. 3), Nos. 2, 3, 40, 81, plates 2, A, B, 25, 45, but the southern bipartite form (see *dau*, plate VII, 24, XI) in the Vākāṭaka inscriptions. The *kha*, which has a big hook and small loop, and the oblong *ca* with the vertical on the right, likewise agree with the southern forms. But F. GI (CII. 3, No. 2, line 17, offers once, in *śulkā*, the northern *ka* without the curve at the foot.

The other letters of this script frequently show greater or smaller variations. Our plate offers a few in the case of *Ā*, *ja*, *tha*, *ba* and *la*. More have been pointed out by Fleet and Kielhorn in their editions of the inscriptions in F.GI (CII. 3) and in EI. 3. I may add to Fleet's remarks, that his Nos. 40, 41 and 81 have the angular form of *ma* of the later Kanarese-Telugu alphabet (see below, § 29, B, 6).

§ 29.—THE KANARESE AND TELUGU ALPHABET: PLATES VII AND VIII.

A.—*The archaic variety.*

[64] The archaic variety of this script is found :—(*a*) In the west, in the inscriptions of the Kadambas of Vaijayanti or Banavāsi (plate VII, cols. XII, XIII), and of the early Calukyas of Vātāpi or Bādāmi, e.g. of Kīrtivarman I, and Maṅgaleśa (plate VII, col. XIV), Pulakeśin II, and Vikramāditya I (sometimes). (*b*) In the east, on the Śālaṅkāyana plates, and on those of the first two Calukyas of Veṅgi, Viṣṇuvardhana I and Jayasiṃha I (plate VII, col. XVII[314]). The date of the Śālaṅkāyana plates, which used to be assigned to the 4th century[315], is uncertain[316]. The Kadamba grants probably belong partly to 5th and partly to the the 6th centuries; for, Kākusthavarman, who issued the oldest known record, was the contemporary of one of the Imperial Guptas, probably of Samudragupta[317], and his descendants all ruled before the overthrow of the Kadamba kingdom by Kīrtivarman I, between A.D. 566-67 and 596-97. The archaic Calukya inscriptions fall between A.D. 578 and about 660[318].

During this period, the characters of the western and eastern documents do not differ much. The alphabet of the Śālaṅkāyana plates[319] agrees very closely with that of plate VII, col. XIII; and in the first half of the 7th century the letters of the Calukya inscriptions from Vātāpi and from Veṅgi show an almost perfect resemblance[320]. But the more considerable differences between cols. XII and XIII, which both are derived from grants of the Kadamba Mṛgeśavarman issued within a period of only five years, have to be explained by the assumption that the letters of col. XIII, with which nearly all the other Kadamba inscriptions agree, imitate writing with ink, and those of col. XII, writing with the *stilus*. This explanation is suggested by the thinness of the signs of col. XII, and by the much greater thickness of those in col. XIII, and by the wedges and solid squares at their heads (compare above, §28, B).

The letters of the older documents of this period remain very similar to those of the Andhra inscriptions of plate III, the so-called "cave-characters." In the Śālaṅkāyana grant, and in those of the Kadambas Kākusthavarman, Śāntivarman, Mṛgeśavarman and Ravivarman, we find only few, and by no means constant, traces of the development of the later characteristic round forms. Thus, col. XII no doubt offers rather far advanced signs for *A* and *ra*, but at the same time a more archaic *Ā*, and the facsimile frequently shows even an angular *ra* with a not very long upward stroke. In the grants of the last Kadamba king Harivarman and in those of the Calukyas between A.D. 578 and 660, the *A*, *Ā*, *ka* and *ra*, characteristic of the next stage of development, occur not rarely, but never constantly. Thus col. XIV, derived from the Bādāmi inscription of Kīrtivarman I and Maṅgaleśa, has the *ka* closed on the left. But this form is the only one used there, and it never appears on Maṅgaleśa's copper-plate, nor on the Haidarābād plates of his successor Pulakeśin II[321]. Further, this *ka*, as well as the closed *ra* of 33, col. XV, occur on the Nerūr plates of Pulakeśin II[322]. Finally, the Aihoḷe stone inscription, of the time of Pulakeśin II[323], has exclusively the older *ka* and *ra*, but occasionally the later *A* of col. XV. This vacillation indicates that between A.D. 578 and 660, and perhaps even earlier, the round-hand forms of the middle Kanarese alphabet existed, but that they either had not completely displaced the older ones, or that they were not yet considered as really suitable for inscriptions, though the clerks occasionally introduced them by mistake into the official documents (compare above, § 3, page 20 f.).

Among the other signs, the following may be noted especially :—

(1) The *ṇa* (plate VII, 21, XII-XIV, XVII) which is never looped, but looks as if it were cursively developed form a looped from similar to that of col. I, ff.

(2) The *ta*, which keeps the old form of the western inscriptions without a loop in 22, XIII, but shows in cols. XII, XIV, XVII, a cursive development from the looped *ta* of cols. XX-XXIII, which likewise is not rare in Kadamba and Calukya inscriptions of this period.

(3) The tailed *da* (24, XIV, XVII) agreeing exactly with the western form [65] of *ḍa* (19, IV-IX).

(4) The *na*, which sometimes has the looped form (26, XIII), and more frequently that without the loop (26, XII, XIV-XVII); the latter being, however, apparently derived from the looped one.

(5) The very exceptionally looped *ya* (in *yā*, 45, XIV), which thus is identical with the much older northern form.

(6) The medial vowels :—(*a*) *ū* in *pū* (27, XIII), a cursive substitute for the *ū* of *yū* (32, VI), *cū* (13, IV), &c. ; (*b*) the subscript *ṛ* of *kṛ* (8, XII, XVII ; 41, XIV), somewhat resembling a northern *ṛ* (which latter actually occurs once on the seal figured in IA. 6, 24 in *Mṛgeśa*), but probably independently derived from a not uncommon *ṛ* in the shape of an unconnected semicircle before *ka* ; (*c*) the exceedingly rare *ḷ* of *kḷ* (42, XIV), which, differing from the northern subscript *ḷ* (plate VI, 35, XVII), but agreeing with the northern initial sign of the Cambridge MS., consists merely of a cursive *la* ; (*d*) the Mātrā of *e* (in *ṇe*, 21, XII), of *ai* (in *cai*, 13, XII ; and *vai*, 35, XIII), and of *o* and *au* (in *thau*, 23, XII), which, except in connection with *le* (see *le*, 34, XII, and *lo*, 34, XIII, XVII), frequently stands at the foot of the consonant ; (*e*) the *au* (in *pau*, 27, XII, XIV), the right-hand portion of which invariably and in all southern alphabets consists of a hook, formed by a cursive combination of the second Mātrā with the *ā*-stroke (compare *yau*, plate III, 31, VI).

B —*The middle variety.*

This second variety is found from about A. D. 650 to about A. D. 950 :—(*a*) In the West in the inscriptions of the Calukyas of Vātāpi or Bādāmi, of their successors the Rāṣṭrakūṭas of Mānyakheṭa (in cases when they did not use the Nāgarī, see above, § 23), of the Gaṅgas of Maisūr, and of some smaller dynasties ; (*b*) in the east, on the copper-plates of the Calukyas of Veṅgi and of their vassals. During this period, some marked differences are observable in the *ductus* between the several classes of documents. The copper-plates of the Westerm Calukyas (plate VII, col. XVI)[324] mostly show carelessly drawn cursive signs sloping towards the right, and their stone inscriptions (plate VII, col. XV) upright, carefully made, letters, which especially in the ligatures are abnormally large. With the characters of the latter agree those of the inscriptions of the Rāṣṭrakūṭas (plate VIII, cols. II, III),[325] with the exception of the sign-manual on the Baroda copper-plate of Dhruva II.[326] In this royal signature and in the inscriptions of the Calukyas of Veṅgi (plate VIII, cols. IV, V), the letters are broader and shorter, and in this respect resemble very closely the Old-Kanarese.[327]

In addition to the above-mentioned rounded forms of *A*, *Ā*, *ka* and *ra*, which become constant during this period, the following letters deserve special remarks :—

(1) The very rare *Ṛ* (plate VII, 5, XVI ; compare also the earlier letter in the facsimile at IA. 6, 23, end), which seems to be a modification of the northern form of plate VI, 7, I, II.

(2) The strongly cursive *kha* (plate VIII, 12, III-V), which is identical with the Old-Kanarese letter, and which according to Fleet[328] never occurs before about A. D. 800, but actually appears in the cognate Pallava inscriptions (plate VII, 9, XXIII ; compare below, § 31, B, 4) already since the 7th century.

(3) The *ca*, which from the 9th century begins to open in *ñca* (plate VII, 41, XIX ; plate VIII, 19, III, IV).

(4) The *da* (plate VIII, 27, II, IV, V) the tail of which begins to turn upwards since the 9th century.

(5) The *ba*, opened above (plate VIII, 32, V), which according to Fleet[329] first occurs about A. D. 850.

(6) The *ma* (plate VII, 31, XVII; VIII, 34, II-V), the upper part of which is drawn towards the right and placed nearly on the same level as the lower one, and which thus becomes the precursor of the Old-Kanarese *ma*.

(7) The abnormal cursive *la* (plate VII, 34, XVI), which elsewhere appears only as the second part of ligatures (as in *ślo*, plate VII, 44, XVIII).

(8) The Mātrās, which occasionally stand below the consonant (as in *dhe*, plate VIII, 28, V).

(9) The vertical Virāma, above final *m* (plate VII, 41, XVIII; plate VIII, 46, V) and final *n* (plate VIII, 45, V).

(10) The Dravidian *ṛa* (plate VII, 45, XV, XVIII; 46, XXI; plate VIII, 47, II, III) [66] and *ḷa* (plate VII, 46, XV, XVIII; plate VIII, 4?, II, V), which first appear in the 7th century. The first of them, *ṛa*, may possiably represent two round *ra*, and *ḷa* may be a modification of a *ḷ*ɪ like that in plate VII, 40, XIV, XVI. The occurrence of these signs proves that the Kanarese languge had a literature already in the 7th century.

C.—*The Old-Kanarese alphabet.*

The third and last variety of the Kanarese-Telugu alphabet, which Burnell calls "the transitional" and Fleet more appropriately "Old-Kanarese", does not differ much from the modern Kanarese and Telugu scripts. In the east, it first appears in the Veṅgi inscriptions of the 11th century; in the west, a little earlier, in a Gaṅga inscription of A. D. 978 and in a not much later Calukya inscription[330]. Some of its characteristics, like the opening of the loop of *ma* and of the head of *va*, appear however in the sign-manual of Dhruva II, on the Baroda plates, mentioned above under B. The specimens of this script[331] in plate VIII, among which cols. VI, and VII date from the 11th century, col. VIII, from the 12th, and col. IX (according to Hultzsch, Telugu) from the 14th, show the gradual progress very distinctly.

One of the most characteristic marks of the Old-Kanarese consists in the angles over all Mātṛkās which do not bear superscribed vowel-sings. These angles, which in col. VI resemble those of the modern Telugu and in cols. VII, VIII, those of the modern Kanarese, probably are cursive representatives of wedges, and have been invented because the latter did not suit the writing with the *stilus*. Since the 6th century, they occur more or less frequently in single inscriptions from other districts, such as Guhasena's grant of A. D. 559-69 (plate VII, col. IV) and Ravikīrti's Aihoḷe Praśasti[332], sometimes together with wedges. But it is only in this alphabet that they become a constant distinctive feature.

The most important among the changes in the several signs are :—

(1) The opening of the heads of *E* (plate VIII, 8, VI, VIII), of *ca* (16, VI-IX), of *bha* (33, VI-IX, which in col. IX becomes identical with *ba* by the connection of the two

base-strokes), and of *va* (38, VII-IX), as well as of the loop of *ma* (34, VI, VIII) and of the right limb of *cha* (17, VI-IX; compare also col. V).

(2) The cursive looped forms of *A*, *Ā* (1, 2, VII-IX), and of *I*, *Ī* (3, 4, VI-IX; compare their precursors in 3, II, and 4, III, V), and of *śa* (39, VII-IX), the central cross-bar of which is connected with the curved end of the right side

(3) The conversion of the long drawn loops of *ka* (11, VI-IX) and of *ra* (36, VI-IX), into much smaller circles.

(4) The cursive rounding off of the angles of *ṇa* (24, VI-IX), *na* (29, VI-IX), and *sa* (41, VI-IX).

(5) The development of new loops or ringlets to the right of the top of *Ṛ* (7, IX), *ṅa* (15, VIII, IX) and *ja* (18, VI-IX; compare col. V).

(6) The exclusive employment of the medial *u* turning upwards on the right (see, for instance, *pu*, 30, IX), which in earlier times is restricted to *gu*, *tu*, *bhu* and *śu*, but later appears also in *su* (plate VIII, 41, II, III).

(7) Finally, the appearance of the Anusvāra on the line (see *raṃ*, 36, VIII), which cannot be a survival from ancient times, but must be an innovation intended to make the lines more equal (compare above, § 26, A, 5)[333].

§ 30.—THE LATER KALIṄGA SCRIPT: PLATES VII AND VIII.

[67] This script has been found hitherto only on the copper-plates of the Gaṅga kings of Kaliṅganagara, the modern Kaliṅgapattanam in Gañjām, which in olden times was the residence of the Ceta king Khāravela and his successors (see § 18 above). The dates of these documents run from the year 87 of the Gāṅgeya era. Though its exact beginning has not yet been determined, Fleet has shown that the oldest Gaṅga grants probably belong to the 7th century[334].

The signs of these documents resemble, up to the Gāṅgeya year 183, partly the letters of the Central-Indian script (above, §28, B) and partly those of the western variety, which exhibits the medial *au*, of the Ajaṇṭā inscriptions (above, § 28, A), and they show only a few peculiar forms. A specimen of the Kaliṅga script of the latter kind has been given in plate VII, col. XIX, from the Cicacole grant of the Gāṅgeya year 148, in which only the Grantha-like *Ā* (2, XIX), and the *ga* (10, XIX) and *śa* (36, XIX) with curves on the left, differ greatly from the corresponding Valabhī letters. The alphabet of the Acyutapuram plates[335] of the Gāṅgeya year 87, which exhibits angular forms with solid box-heads, closely resembles the Central-Indian writing; but its *na* is identical with that of the modern Nāgarī. The Cicacole plates[336] of the Gāṅgeya year 128 show in general the same type; but they offer the ordinary looped *na* of the north and west, and the looped *ta* of the archaic Grantha (22, XX ff.). Finally, the Cicacole plates[337] of Gāṅgeya year 183 come close to the script of plate VII, col. X; but their *na* is again that of the late Nāgarī, and their medial *ā* mostly stands above the line, as in various northern and also Grantha documents of the 7th and 8th centuries.

In the grants of the 3rd and 4th centuries of the Gāṅgeya era, and in a late undated inscription, the mixture of the characters is much greater, and the same letter is often expressed by greatly differing signs. In plate VIII, col. X, from the Cicacole plates of the Gāṅgeya year 51, that is 251[338], and in col. XI, from the Vizagapatam plates of the year 254, and in col. XII, from the Alamaṇḍa plates of the year 304, we find a northern *A*, *Ā* (1, 2, X-XII), *I* (3, XI), *U* (5, X), *ka* (44, XI, XII), *kha* (12, XI), *ṅga* (15, X), *ṅka* (15, XII), *ja* (18, XII), *ña* (in *jñā*, 19, X), *ḍā* (22, XII), *ṇa* (24, XI, XII), *dha* (28, 45, XI), *na* (48, X), and *pra* (47, XII). The other letters are of southern origin, and belong partly to the middle Kanarese, partly to the middle Grantha, or are peculiar developments. The restricted space available in plate VIII has made it impossible to enter all the variants for each letter. But the three different forms of *ja* (18, 46, and 47, X) show how very great the variations are.

Still stronger are the mixture and variations in the Cicacole plates of the Gāṅgeya year 351[339] and in the undated grant of Vajrahasta from the 11th century (Kielhorn)[340], neither of which is represented in our plate. In the first-named document each letter has, according to Fleet, at leat two, but sometimes three or four forms. The majority of the signs belong to the southern Nāgarī. But Old-Kanarese and late Grantha signs likewise occur. In Vajrahasta's grant there are, according to Kielhorn's calculation, 320 Nāgari letters and 410 southern ones of different types, and each letter again has at least two and sometimes [68] four or more forms. Kielhorn points out that the writer has shown a certain art in the grouping of the variants ; and he is no doubt right in hinting that the mixture is due to the vanity of royal scribes, who wished to show that they were acquainted with a number of alphabets. For the same reason, the writer of the Cicacole plates of the Gāṅgeya year 183 has used three different systems of numeral notation in expressing the date (see below, §34). The kingdom of the Gaṅgas of Kaliṅga lay between the districts in which the Nāgarī and the Kanarese-Telugu scripts were used, and it was not far from the territory of the Grantha. Its population was probably mixed, and used all these scripts[341], as well as, in earlier times, those employed in the older western and Central-Indian inscriptions. The professional clerks and writers of course had to master all the alphabets.

§ 31.—THE GRANTHA ALPHABET : PLATES VII AND VIII.

A.—*The archaic variety.*

For the history of the Sanskrit alphabets in the Tamil districts during the period after A.D. 350, we have only the Sanskrit inscriptions of the Pallavas, Coḷas and Pāṇḍyas from the eastern coast, among which only those of the first-named dynasty can lay claim to a higher antiquity. Corresponding inscriptions from the western coast are hitherto wanting. For this reason, and because only a small number of the eastern documents have been published with good facsimiles, it is as yet impossible to give a complete view of the gradual development of the letters.

The most archaic forms of the Sanskrit scripts of the Tamil districts, which usually are classed as "Grantha", are found on the copper-plates of the Pallava kings of Palakkada and (? or) Daśanapura[342] (plate VII, cols. XX, XXI) from the 5th or the 6th century (?), with which the ancient inscriptions, Nos. 1 to 16, of the Dharmarājaratha (plate VII, col. XXII)[343] closely agree. These inscriptions, together with a few others[344], exhibit what may be called the archaic Grantha, the latest example of which occurs in the Bādāmi inscription, incised, according to Fleet's newest researches[345], by the Pallava Narasiṃha I, during his expedition against the Calukya Pulakeśin II (A.D. 609 and about 642) in the second quarter of the 7th century; and it seems to have gone out soon after, as the Kūram plates of Narsiṃha's son Parameśvara I show letters of a much more advanced type. It is met with also in the stone inscription from Jambu in Java; see IA. 4, 356.

The characters of the archaic Grantha in general agree with those of the archaic Kanarese-Telugu (see above, § 29, A), but shew a few peculiarities which remain constant in the later varieties, thus :—

(1) The *tha*, the central dot of which is converted into a loop, attached to the right side (plate VII, 23, XXI); compare the *tha* of col. XX, where the straight stroke of the Kanarese-Telugu script appears.

(2) The *śa* with the cross-bar converted into a curve or loop and attached to the right side (plate VII, 36, XX-XXII, 45, XXII); compare also the cursive *śa* of the western script, mentioned above, § 28, A, 7.

(3) The *ṣa* with the cross-bar treated similarly (plate VII, 37, XX); compare the *ṣa* of col. XXI, which shows the older form.

The characters of plate VII, cols. XX, XXI, show no closer connection with those of the Prākṛt inscriptions of the Pallavas, discussed above in § 20, D.

B.—*The middle variety.*

The earliest inscription of the much more advanced forms of the second variety or the middle Grantha, is found on the Kūram copper-plates (plate VII, col. XXIV) of the reign of Parameśvara I, the adversary of the Western Calukya Vikramāditya I (A.D. 655-680)[346]. [69] Compared with this document, which appears to offer a real clerk's script, the monumental inscription of the Kailāsanātha temple (plate VII, col. XXIII, built according to Fleet[347] by Narasiṃha II, the son of Parameśvara I, is retrograde, and shows more archaic forms for several paleographically important letters. On the other hand, the Kaśākūḍi copper-plates (plate VIII, col. XIII), incised in the time of Nandivarman who succeeded Mahendra III, the second son of Narasiṃha II, and warred with the Western Calukya Vikramāditya II (A.D. 733-749)[348], agree more closely with the Kūram plates, and offer, besides some archaic forms, also much more advanced ones.

The most important innovations, either constantly or occasionally observable in this second variety of the Grantha, are :—

(1) The development of a second vertical in *A*, *Ā*, *ka* and *ra* (plate VII, 1, 2, 8, 33, XXIII, XXIV; plate VIII, 1, 2, 11, 36, XIII), as well as in medial *u* and *ū* (plate VII, 31, 38,

XXIV ; plate VIII, 34, 40, XIII), out of the ancient hook ; compare the transitional forms in the facsimiles at IA. 9, 100 ; 102.

(2) The connection of one of the dots of *I* with the upper curved line (plate VII, 3, XXIII, XXIV ; plate VIII, 3, XIII, *a*, *b*).

(3) The opening of the top of *E* (plate VII, 5, XXIV), which however shows closed up-forms in col. XXIII, and in plate VIII, 8, XIII.

(4) The development of a loop to the left of the foot of *kha*, and the opening up of the right side of the letter (plate VII, 9, XXIII), as in the Kanarese-Telugu script (see above, § 29, B, 2).

(5) The upward turn of the *Serif* at the left-hand lines of *ga* and *śa* (plate VII, 10, 36, XXIV ; plate VIII, 13, 39, XIII ; not in plate VII, col. XXIII).

(6) The opening up of the loops of *cha* (plate VIII, 17, XIII), and perhaps also in the indistinct *cha* of the Kūram plates, i, line 5.

(7) The transposition of the vertical of *ja* to the right end of the top-bar, and the conversion of the central bar into a loop connected with the lowest bar (plate VII, 15, XXIV ; plate VIII, 15, XXIV ; plate VIII, 18, XIII ; not in plate VII, col. XXIII).

(8) The incipient opening up of the tops of *dha* and *tha* (plate VII, 23, 25, XXIII, XXIV ; plate VIII, 26, 28, XIII).

(9) The opening up of the top of *ba*, and the transposition of the original top-line to the left of the left-hand vertical (plate VII, 29, XXIV ; plate VIII, 32, XIII ; not in plate VII, col. XXIII).

(10) The adoption of the later northern *bha* (see above, §24, A, 24), or the development of an exactly similar sign (plate VII, 30, XXIV ; plate VIII, 33, XIII ; not in plate VII, col. XXIII).

(11) The combination of the left-hand vertical of *sa* with the left end of the old side-limb, and of the right end of the side-limb with the base-stroke (plate VII, 38, XXIV ; a transitional form in col. XXII, and a different cursive form in plate VIII, 41, XIII).

(12) The frequent separation of medial *ā*, *e*, *ai*, *o*, *au*, from the Mātṛkā (constant in plate VIII, col. XIII), as well as the use of the *ā* standing above the line, as in the northern alphabet of this period and in the Central-Indian script (compare plate VII, 17, 19, 21, 31-33, XXIII ; 8, 24, XXIV).

(13) The expression of the Virāma (as in the Kanarese-Telugu script) by a vertical stroke above, or in the Kaśākūḍi plate also to the right of, the final consonant (plate VII, 41, XXIII ; plate VIII, 47, XIII ; and compare the facsimiles).

(14) The transposition of the Anusvāra to the right of the Mātṛkā (plate VII, 38, XXIV) below the level of the top-line, as in the Kanarese-Telugu script.

(15) The occasional development of small angles, open above, at the tops of the verticals, for the left part of which a dot usually appears in plate VIII, col. XIII.

The fully-developed and very constant characteristics of the alphabet of the Kūram plates make it probable that they have not arisen within the period of twenty to thirty years, which lies between the issue of the Kūram grant and the incision of the much more archaic Bādāmi inscription of Narasiṃha I (see above, under A). Very likely the Kūram alphabet had a longer history.

C.—*The Transitional Grantha.*

The series of the published datable Pallava inscriptions of the 8th century ends for the present with the Kaśākūḍi plates; and facsimiles of document of the next following centuries [70] are not accessible to me. I am, therefore, unable to exactly fix the time when the third or transitional variety of the Grantha, Burnell's Coḷa or middle Grantha, came into use, which is found in the inscriptions from the reign of the Bāṇa king Vikramāditya[349] about A. D. 1150 (plate VIII, col. XIV) and of Sundara-Pāṇḍya,[350] A. D. 1250 (plate VIII, col. XV), as well as in other documents.[351] It would however appear, both from the Grantha signs occurring in the Gaṅga inscriptions (plate VIII, cols. XI, XII and from Burnell's Coḷa-Grantha alphabet of A. D. 1080[352], that the new developments originated partly towards the end of the 8th century and partly in the 9th and 10th, about the same time when the Old-Kanarese script (above, § 29, C) was formed.

The most important changes, which the transitional Grantha shows, are as follows :—

(1) The suppression of the last remaining dot of *I* (plate VIII, 3, XIV, XV ; compare 3, XIII, *a*).

(2) The formation of a still more cursive *E* (8, XIV) out of the Kūram letter (plate VII, 6, XXIV).

(3) The formation of a still more cursive *kha* (plate VIII, 12, XIV, XV), closely resembling the later Kanarese-Telugu sign (plate VIII, 12, III ff.), out of the letter of plate VII, 9, XXIII.

(4) The development of a single or double curve to the left of *gha* (plate VIII, 14, XIV, XV).

(5) The opening up of the top of *ca*, and the conversion of its left side into an acute angle (plate VIII, 16, XIV, XV).

(6) The addition of a curve to the right end of *ḍa* (plate VIII, 22, XIV, XV).

(7) The development of an additional loop in *ṇa* (plate VIII, 24, XIV, XV), in accordance with the practice of the Tamil alphabet (see below, §32, A).

(8) The complete opening up of the tops of *tha* and *dha* (plate VIII, 26, 28, XIV, XV).

(9) The development of a curve at the left side of *pa* (plate VIII, 30, XIV, XV).

(10) The closing up of the top of *ma* (plate VIII, 34, XIV, XV), found already in the Gaṅga inscription of about A D. 775 (plate VIII, 46, XI).

(11) The suppression of the circle or loop on the right side of *ya* (plate VIII, 35, XIV, XV), whereby the letter obtains a very archaic appearance.

(12) The opening up of the top of *va*, and the addition of a curve to its left side (plate VIII, 38, XIV, XV).

(13) The complete separation of medial *ā*, *e*, *ai*, *o* from the Mātṛkās, and the formation of a separate sign for the second half of *au*, consisting of two small curves with a vertical on the right.

It is worthy of note that the later alphabet of col. XV has some more archaic signs than the earlier one of col. XIV. The reason no doubt is that the latter imitates the hand of the clerks of the royal office, while the former shows the monumental forms, suited for a public building. All the Grantha inscriptions imitate characters written with a *stilus*.

§ 32.—THE TAMIL AND VAṬṬEḶUTTU ALPHABETS: PLATE VIII.

A.—*The Tamil.*

The Tamil, as well as its southern and western cursive variety, the Vaṭṭeḻuttu or "round-hand," differs from the Sanskrit alphabet by the absence not only of the ligatures, but also of the signs for the aspirates, for the *mediae* (expressed by the corresponding *tenues*), for the sibilants (among which the palatal one is expressed by *ca*), for the spirant *ha*, for the Anusvāra and for the Visarga, as well as by the development of new letters for final *n*, and for *ṟa*, *ḷa* and *ḻa*, which latter three characters do not resemble those for the corresponding sounds in the Kanarese-Telugu script. The great simplicity of the alphabet fully agrees with the theories of the Tamil grammarians, and is explained by the peculiar phonetics of the Tamil language. Like all the older Dravidian dialects, the Tamil possesses no aspirates and no spirant. Further, it has no *ja*, and only one sibilant, which, according to Caldwell, lies between *śa*, *ṣa* and *ca*, and which, if doubled, becomes a distinct *cca*. [71] The use of separate signs for the *tenues* and *mediae* was unnecessary on account of their mutual convertibility. The Tamil uses in the beginning of words only *tenues*, and in the middle only double *tenues* or single *mediae*. Hence, all words and affixes beginning with gutturals, linguals, dentals and labials, have double forms[353]. A knowledge of these simple rules makes mistakes, regarding the real phonetic value of *ka*, *ṭa*, *ta* and *pa*, impossible. The use of ligatures probably has been discarded because the Tamil allows even in loan-words no other combinations of consonants but repetitions of the same sound, and because it seemed more convenient to use in these cases the Virāma[354].

The occurrence of signs for the Dravidian liquids, which, though the sounds correspond with those of the older Kanarese and Telugu, differ from the characters of the Kanarese-Telugu script, indicates that the Tamil alphabet is independent of the latter and has been derived from a different source. Hultzsch's important discovery of the Kūram plates[355], with a large section in the Tamil script and language of the 7th century, confirms this inference. The Tamil alphabet of these plates agrees only in part with their Grantha, and many of its letters offer characteristics of the northern alphabets.

Specific Grantha forms occur in *U* (plate VIII, 5, XVI ; compare plate VII, 4, XXIV) ; in *O* (plate VIII, 9, XVI ; compare col. XV) ; in *ṭa* (plate VIII, 25-28, XVI ; compare plate VII, 22, XXIV) ; in *ṇa* (plate VIII, 29, XVI ; compare plate VII, 26, XXIV) ; in *ya* (plate VIII, 35, XVI ; compare plate VII, 32, XXIV) ; in medial *u* in *ku* (plate VIII, 14, XVI ; compare 44, XIII) ; in medial *e* (in *ṭe*, plate VIII, 28, XVI ; compare *khe*, plate VII, 9, XXIV) ; and in the vertical Virāma, which mostly stands above the vowelless consonant but to the right of *n* and *r* (compare *ṅ*, plate VIII, 15, XVI ; *m*, 34 ; *ḷ*, 43 ; *n*, 49). The Tamil *ai* (for instance, *ṇai*, plate VIII, 29, XVI) appears to be a peculiar derivative from the Grantha *ai*, the two Mātrās having been placed, not one above the other, but one behind the other.

Unmodified or only slightly modified northern forms appear in *A* and *Ā* (plate VIII, 1, 2, XVI), with the single vertical without a curve at the end (compare plate IV, 1, 2, I ff.), and with the loop on the left, which is found in recently discovered inscriptions from Swāt as well as in the Grantha; in *ka* (plate VIII, 11-14, XVI; compare plate IV, 7, I ff.); in *ca* (plate VIII, 16-18, XVI; compare plate III, 11, III); in *ṭa* (plate VIII, 20-22, XVI; compare plate IV, 17, VII, VIII); in *pa* (plate VIII, 30-33, XVI; compare plate IV, 27, I ff.); in *ra* (plate VIII, 36, XVI; compare plate IV, 33, I ff.); in *la* (plate VIII, 37, XVI; compare plate IV, 34, VII ff.); in the medial *u* of *pu, mu, yu, vu* (plate VIII, 32, 40, XVI; compare plate IV, 27, II); and of *ru* (plate VIII, 36, XVI; compare plate IV, 33, III); and in the medial *ū* of *ḷū* and *ḻū* (plate VIII, 44, 46, XVI; compare *pū*, plate IV, 27, IV).

The *ṅ* (plate VIII, 15, XVI) is more strongly modified, as it has been formed out of the angular northern *ṅa* (plate IV, 11, I ff.) by the addition of a stroke rising upwards on the right; and the *ma* (plate VIII, 34, XVI) is probably a cursive derivative from the so-called Gupta *ma* (plate IV, 31, I ff.).

The signs for the Dravidian liquids, too, may be considered as developments of northern signs. The upper portion of the *ḷa* (plate VIII, 43, 44, XVI) looks like a small cursive northern *la*, to which a long vertical, descending downwards, has been added on the right. The *ṟa* (plate VIII, 47, 48, XVI) may consist of a small slanting northern *ra* and a hook added to the top. And the *ḻa* (plate VIII, 45, 46, XVI) is perhaps derived from a northern *ḷa* (plate IV, 40, II), the end of the horizontal line being looped and connected with the little pendent stroke below; compare also the looped *ḷa* (read erroneously *ḍha*) in the Amarāvatī inscription, J. RAS. 1891, plate at p. 142.

The origin of the remaining signs is doubtful. Some, such as *va* (plate VIII, 38-40, XVI) and medial *ā* (see *kā*, plate VIII, 12, XVI), occur both in northern and in southern scripts. Others are modifications of letters common to the north and the south. The final *n* (plate VIII, 49, XVI) is evidently the result of a slight transformation of both the northern and the southern *ṇa* with two hooks [72] (plate III, 20, V, XX; plate IV, 21, VII f.; plate VII, 21, IV ff.); and from this comes the Tamil *ṉa* (plate VIII, 24, XVI) by the addition of another curve. The parent of the peculiar *E* (plate VIII, 8, XVI) may be either that of plate IV, 5, X ff., or that of plate VII, 5, XXIII. Similarly, the angular medial *u* in *tu* (plate VIII, 27, XVI) and in *ṟu* (plate VIII, 48, XVI) is due to a peculiar modification of the curve, rising upwards on the right, which is found in connection both with northern and with southern letters (see *śu*, plate IV, 36, III, XVII and plate VII, 36, II, IV). Finally, the greatly cursive *I* (plate VIII, 3, XVI) appears to be the result of a peculiar combination of three curves, which replaced the ancient dots. But an *I* of this kind has hitherto not been traced.

This analysis of the Tamil alphabet of the 7th century makes it probable that it is derived from a northern alphabet of the 4th or 5th century, which in the course of time was strongly influenced by the Grantha, used in the same districts for writing Sanskrit.

The next oldest specimen of the Tamil script, which is found in the Kaśākūḍi plate[356] of about A. D. 740 (not represented in plate VIII), shows no essential change except in the adoption of the later Tamil *ma*.

But the inscriptions of the 10th, 11th and later centuries[357] (plate VIII, cols. XVII-XX) offer a new variety, which is more strongly modified through the influence of the Grantha.

The ṭa, pa and va have now the peculiar Grantha forms. Besides, in the 11th century begins the development of the little strokes, hanging down on the left of the tops of ka, ṅa, ca, ta and na. In the 15th century (plate VIII, cols. XIX, XX) these pendants are fully formed, and ka shows a loop on the left. It is worthy of note that in the later Tamil inscriptions the use of the Virāma (Pulli) first becomes rarer and finally ceases,[358] while in the quite modern writing the Virāma is again marked by a dot.

B.—*The Vaṭṭeḻuttu.*

Among the Vaṭṭeḻuttu inscriptions, the Śāsanas of Bhāskara-Ravivarman in favour of the Jews (pl. VIII, cols. XXI, XXII) and of the Syrians of Kocin,[359] as well as the Tirunelli copper-plates of the same king[360], have been published with facsimiles. Trusting to rather weak arguments, Burnell ascribes the first-named two documents to the 8th century.[361] But the Grantha letters occurring in the Śāsana of the Jews belong to the third and latest variety of that alphabet, and the Nāgarī śā or śī (probably for śrīḥ) at the end of the document, to which Hultzsch has called attention,[362] resembles the northern forms of the 10th and 11th centuries (compare plate V, 39, 47, VIII ; 48, X).

From a paleographical point of view, the Vaṭṭeḻuttu may be described as a cursive script, which bears the same relation to the Tamil as the modern northern alphabets of the clerks and merchants to their originals, e.g., the Moḍī of the Marāṭhās to the Bālbodh and the Ṭākarī of the Dogrās to the Śāradā.[363] With the exception of the I, probably borrowed from the Grantha, all its letters are made with a single stroke from the left to the right, and are mostly inclined towards the left. Several among them, such as the ṅa (plate VIII, 15, XXI) with the curve and hook on the left, the va with the open top and the hook on the left (plate VIII, 38, XXI, XXII ; compare cols. XVII-XX) and the round ṛa (plate VIII, 45, 46, XXI, XXII ; compare 47, XVII-XX), show the characteristics of the second variety of the Tamil of the 11th and later centuries. And with the usage of the later Tamil inscriptions agrees the constant omission of the Virāma. Some other characters, such as the round ṭa (plate VIII, 20-23, XXI, XXII ; compare col. XVI), the ma with the curve on the right (plate VIII, 34, XXI, XXII ; compare col. XVI), and the ya with the loop on the left (plate VIII, 35, XXI, XXII ; compare col. XVI), seem to go back to the forms of the earlier Tamil. And three, the rounded U (plate VIII, 5, XXI), the pointed E (plate VIII, 8, XXI and the ṉa with a single notch (plate VII, 26, XXI, XXII), possibly show characteristics dating from a still earlier period. Perhaps it may be assumed that the "round-hand" arose already before the 7th century, but was modified in the course of time by the further development of the Tamil and the Grantha scripts. Owing to the small [73] number of the accessible inscriptions, this conjecture is however by no means certain.

The transformation of the Vaṭṭeḻuttu ka (plate VIII, 11-14, XXI, XXII), which seems to be derived from a looped form, is analogous to that of the figure 4 in the decimal system of numeral notation (compare plate IX, B, 4, V-VII, and IX). The curious ṭa (plate VIII, 25-28, XXI, XXII) has been developtd by the change of the loop of the

Tamil letter (compare cols. XVII, XVIII) into a notch and the prolongation of the tail up to the head. The still more extraordinary *na* (plate VIII, 29, XXI) may be explained as a cursive derivative of the later Tamil *na* with the stroke hanging down from the top.

VI. NUMERAL NOTATION.

§33.—THE NUMERALS OF THE KHAROṢṬHĪ : PLATE I[364].

In the Kharoṣṭhī inscriptions of the Śakas, of Gondopherres, and of the Kuṣānas, from the 1st century B.C. and the 1st and 2nd centuries A.D., as well as in other probably later documents, we find a system of numeral notation (plate I, col. XIV)[365] which Dowson first explained with the help of the Taxila copper-plate[366].

Its fundamental signs are : -(*a*) One, two and three vertical strokes for 1, 2, 3. (*b*) An inclined cross for 4. (*c*) A sign, similar to the Kharoṣṭhi *A*, for 10. (*d*) A double curve, looking like a cursive combination of two 10 (BAYLEY), for 20. (*e*) A sign, resembling a Brāhmī *ta* or *tra*, for 100, to the right of which stands a vertical stroke, whereby the whole becomes equivalent to IC.

The numbers lying between these elements are expressed by groups, in which the additional ones invariably are placed on the left. Thus, for 5 we have 4 (+) 1 ; for 6, 4 (+) 2 ; for 8, 4 (+) 4 ; for 50, 20 (+) 20 (+) 10 ; for 60, 20 (+) 20 (+) 20 ; for 70, 20 (+) 20 (+) 20 (+) 10. Groups formed of the signs for 10 (+) 1 to 10 (+) 9, and 20 (+) 1 to 20 (+) 9, and so forth, are used to express the numerals 11 to 19, and 21 to 29, &c.

The higher numerals beyond 100 are expressed according to the same principle ; thus, 103 is 100 (+) 3 or IC III. The sign for 200 consists of 100, preceded on the right by two vertical strokes. And the highest known number is IIC XX XX XX X IV, which means 274[367].

The few numeral signs in the Aśoka edicts of Shāhbāzgarhī and Mansehra (plate I, col. XIII)[368] show that in the 3rd century B.C. the Kharoṣṭhī system of numeral notation differed from the later one at least in one important point. Both in Shāhbāzgarhi, where the signs for 1, 2, 4, 5 occur, and in Mansehra, which offers 1, 2, 5, the inclined cross for 4 is absent, and 4 is expressed by four parallel vertical strokes, and 5 by five. It is as yet not ascertainable, how the other signs looked in the 3rd century B.C.

Burnell and others[369] have stated long ago that the Kharoṣṭhī numerals are of Semitic origin. And it may now be added that probably they have been borrowed from the Aramaeans, and that, with the exception of the cross-shaped 4, they have been introduced together with the Aramaic letters. According to [74] Euting's table of the ancient Aramaic numerals[370], 1 to 10 are marked, as in the Aśoka edicts, by vertical strokes, which however, contrary to the Indian practice, are divided into groups of three. The Kharoṣṭhī 10 comes close to that of the Teima inscription,  , and the 20 resembles the sign of the Satrap coins,  , which is also found in the papyrus Blacas [371] (5th century B. C.), and somewhat modified in the papyrus Vaticanus. Both the Aramaeans and the Phoenicians used the signs for 10 and 20 in the same manner as the Hindus, in order to express 30, 40, and so forth.

For the Kharoṣṭhī 100, Euting's table offers no corresponding Aramaic sign, and that given in his edition of the Saqqarah inscription[372] is, as he informs me, not certain. Hence, there remain only the Phoenician symbols, ꟾo, þ, which are suitable for comparison. But the close relationship of Phoenician and Aramaic writing makes it not improbable that the latter, too, possessed in earlier times a 100, standing upright. The Kharoṣṭhī practice of prefixing the signs for 1 and 2 to the 100 is found in all the Semitic systems of numeral notation.

The inclined cross, used to express the 4 in the later Kharoṣṭhī inscriptions, is found only in Nabataean inscriptions incised after the beginning of our era, and is used there only rarely for the expression of the higher units. The late occurrence of the sign both in Indian and in Semitic inscriptions makes it probable that both the Hindus and the Semites independently invented this cursive combination of the original four strokes.

§34.—THE NUMERALS OF THE BRĀHMĪ: PLATE IX.

A.—*The ancient letter-numerals*[373].

In the Brāhmī inscriptions and coin-legends we find a peculiar system of numeral notation, the explanation of which is chiefly due to J. Stevenson, E. Thomas, A. Cunningham, Bhāū Dājī and Bhagvānlāl Indrājī[374]. Up to the year A. D. 594-95 it is used exclusively, and later together with the decimal system[375]. It appears also exclusively in the Bower MS. and in the other MSS. from Kashgar[376], as well as together with the Decimal system,—chiefly in the pagination,—in the old MSS. of the Jainas of Western India and of the Bauddhas of Nepāl as late as the 16th century[377]. And the Malayāḷam MSS. have preserved it to the present day[378].

In this system, 1 to 3 are expressed by horizontal strokes or cursive combinations of such; 4 to 9, 10 to 90, 100, and 1000, each by a separate sign (usually a Mātṛkā or a ligature); the intermediate and the higher numbers by groups or ligatures of the fundamental signs. In order to express figures consisting of tens and units, or of hundreds, tens and units, and so forth, the symbols for the smaller numbers are placed either unconnected to the right of, or vertically below, the higher ones. The first principle is followed in all inscriptions and on most coins, the second on a few coins[379] and in the pagination of all manuscripts. In order to express 200 and 2000, one short stroke is added to the right of 100 and 1000. Similarly, 300 and 3000 are formed by the addition of two strokes to the same elements. [75] Ligatures of 100 and 1000 with the signs for 4 to 9 and 4 to 70, stood for 400 to 900 and 4000 to 70000 (the highest known figure), and the smaller figures are connected with the right side of the larger ones.

The Jaina MSS. offer, however, an exception in the case of 400. In the pagination of their MSS., both the Jainas and the Bauddhas use mostly the decimal figures for 1 to 3 (plate IX, A, cols. XIX-XXVI), more rarely the Akṣaras *E* (*eka*), *dvi*, *tri*, or *sva* (1), *sti* (2), *śrī* (3)[380], the three syllables of the well-known Maṅgala, with which written documents frequently begin. Occasionally the same documents combine the naught and other figures of the decimal system[381] with the ancient numeral symbols. Similar mixtures occur also in some late inscriptions. Thus, the year 183 of Devendravarman's Cicacole plates is given first in words and next expressed by the symbol for 100, the decimal 8, and the syllable *lo*, i.e. *loka*=3 (see below, § 35, A), while the day of the month, 20, is given only in decimal figures[382].

In the MSS., the signs of this system are always distinct letters or syallables of that alphabet in which the manuscript is written. They are however not always the same. Very frequently they are slightly differentiated, probably in order to distinguish the signs with numeral values from those with letter values. In other cases there are very considerable variants, which appear to have been caused by misreadings of older signs or dialectic differences in pronunciation. The fact that these symbols really are letters is also acknowledged by the name *akṣarapalli*, which the Jainas occasionally give to this system, in order to distinguish it from the decimal notation, the *aṅkapalli*[383]. A remark of the Jaina commentator Malayagiri[384] (12th century), who calls the sign for 4 the *ṅkaśabda*, "the word *ṅka*," indicates that he really pronounced, not *catuḥ*, but *ṅka*.

The phonetical values of the symbols in plate IX, A, cols. XIX-XXVI[385], and of some others, given by Bendall (B.), Bhagvānlāl Indrājī (Bh.), Kielhorn (K.), Leumann (L.), and Peterson (P., see note 377 above), are :—

4=*ṅka* (XIX; compare L., p. 1); with intentional differentiation, *rṅka* (L., p. 1) and *rṅkā* (XXV); with *ṇa* for *ṅa* and additions, *ṇka* (XXVI; B., Bh.), *rṇka* (XXIV; compare K.), or *pka* (XX, XXI), or *hka* (XXIII; B.).

5=*tṛ* (XIX, XXI, XXV, XXVI; B., Bh., K.); with intentional differentiation, *rtṛ* (Bh., K.); with a mistaken interpretation of the top-stroke as *ā*, *rtṛā* (XXIV); with a misinterpretation of the curved *ta* (compare the sign of B.'s No. 1464), also *hṛ* (compare the sign of B.'s No. 1645 ff.) or *hva* (*XXIII*).

6=*phra* (XIX, XXI, XXVI[386]; B., Bh.) or *phu* (K.); and with intentional differentiation, *rphu* or *rphru* (XXIV; K.); with a misinterpretation of an old *pha*, also *ghra* (XXII); and with dialectic softening of the *tenuis*, *bhra* (XXIII; compare B., p. LIV).

7=*gra* (XIX, XXI, XXVI; Bh.) or *grā* (XXV; B., Bh., K.); with intentional differentiation and misinterpretation of the *ra*-stroke, *rggā* (XXIV; P.); with misinterpretation of *ga*, *bhra* (XX; compare B., p. LIV) or *n̄a* (XXIII; compare B., p. LIV).

8=*hra* (XIX, XXI, XXIII, XXVI; B., Bh.; partly with irregular addition of the *ra*-stroke to the hook of *ha*) or *hrā* (XXV; B., Bh., K.); and with intentional differentiation, *rhra* (K.) or *rhrā* (XXIV; K.).

9=*O* (XIX, XXI, XXIII, XXIV, XXVI; B. Bh.) or *Oṃ* (XXV; K.).

10=*ṅṛ* (XIX), formed out of the ancient *ṭhā* (cols. IV-VI) through the opening of the circle of *ṭha*; or *ḍā* (XX, XXIII; B., Bh.), the Nepalese representative of older *ḷa* (cols. X, XI; compare IA. 6, 47), which likewise is a derivative from *ṭhā*; or especially in

Nāgarī MSS., *ḷ* (XXI, XXV, XXVI ; Bh., K.), through a misinterpretation of *ḷa* ; and with intentional differentiation, *rḷ* (XXIV ; K.).

20=*tha*[387] or *thā* (XIX-XXI, XXIII, XXIV, XXVI ; B., Bh., K.) ; or with intentional differentiation, *rtha* and *rthā* (XXV ; K.).

30=*la* or *lā* (XIX-XXI, XXIII, XXIV, XXVI ; B., Bh., K., P.) ; or with intentional
[76] differentiation, *rla* and *rlā* (XXV ; K.).

40=*pta* and *ptā* (XX, XXI, XXIII, XXIV, XXVI ; B., Bh., K.) ; or with intentional differentiation, *rpta* and *rptā* (XXV ; K.).

50=Anunāsika (? Bhagvānlāl), but corresponding only in col. XXIV, to an actually traceable form of this nasal (IA. 6, 47) ; occasionally turned round (XX ; B. : XXIII ; K.).

60=*cu*, frequent in Nepalese MSS. (XX, XXI, XXIII), or *thu*, regular in Nāgarī MSS. (XXV, XXVI ; Bh., K.) ; and with intentional differentiation, *rthu*[388] (XXIV ; K.).

70=*cū*, frequent in Nepalese MSS. (XX, XXI, XXIII : B., Bh.) or *thū*, regular in Nāgarī MSS. (XXV, XXVI) ; and with intentional differentiation, *rthū* (XXIV ; K.).

80=Upadhmānīya with one central bar (XXIII, XXVI ; B., Bh. : compare plate IV, 46, III), or later modified forms of that sign (XXI, XXIV ; Bh., K.), which appear also in MSS. (K.) and in inscriptions (plate IV, 46, XXIII).

90=Upadhmānīya, with two cross-shaped bars (XXI, XXIII, XXVI ; compare plate VII, 46, V, VI), and cursive forms of that sign (XXIV), or perhaps Jihvāmūlīya (XXV ; Bh.,) derived from the *ma*-like sign of plate VII, 46, III, XIII.

100=*su* in Nāgarī MSS. (XXIV, XXV ; Bh., K.) ; or *A* in Nepalese MSS., owing to a misinterpretation of *su* (XX, XXIII. B., Bh.,) ; or *lu* in Nepalese and Bengālī MSS., the result of another misinterpretation (XXI, XXVI ; B., Bh.).

200=*sū* in Nāgarī MSS. (XXIV, XXV ; Bh., K.), or *Ā* in Nepalese MSS. (XX, XXIII ; B., Bh.), or *lū* in Nepalese and Bengālī MSS. (XXVI ; Bh., B.).

300=*sū-ā* in Nāgarī MSS. (XXIV, XXV ; Bh. : read *stā* by K.), or *Ā-ā* in Nepalese MSS. (XX).

400=*sū-o* (XXV ; read *sto* by K.) in Nāgarī MSS.

In the inscriptions, the phonetical values of the signs often differ from those in the MSS. and vary very considerably, and almost every one of the vertical and horizontal columns (plate IX, A, I-XVIII)[389] shows at least some, occasionally a great many, cursive or intentionally modified forms, which possess hardly any resemblance to letters :—

4=*ka* (I), *ki* (III, in 400, 4000 ; IV, A ; V, A ; VI, B), *kri* (V, B ; IX, A), *pka* (III, A ; VI, A ; VIII, A ; IX, B), *ṅka* (X, A), *lka* (facsimile IA. 5, 154), *yka*.

5=*tra*, mostly with irregular addition of the *ra* stroke to the vertical of *ta* (V, A ; VIII, A, B ; IX, B ; X, A ; XV, A), *trā* (VII, A), *tu* (IX, A), *nu* (IV, B), *na*, *nā* (XI, A, B), *tr* (XIII A), *hr* (XIII, B ; XIV, A ; XVII, A), *hra* (XVI, A), together with two cursive signs without phonetic value in V, A, B.

6=*ja*, *sa*[390] (I, II ; compare plate II, 15, III ; 39, VII), *phra* (III, in 6000 ; IV, V), *phrā* (IX, XI), *phā* (XIII), *pha* (XIV), together with four cursive signs (VI-VIII, XV), among which the first is probably derived from *ja*, the second from *sa*, and the other two from *phra*.

7=*gra* or *gu* (III-VI, IX-XI, XIII, XV), *ga* (VII) with a cursive sign (XII) derived from a *gra* like that in XIII.

8=*hra* with irregular addition of the *ra*-stroke to the end of *ha* (IV, A, B ; VI, A), *ha* (VI, B), *hā* (VII, A ; X), *hrā* (XI, XVII, XVIII) or in eastern inscriptions *pu* (VIII, B ; XV, A ; XVI) probably a cursive derivative from *hra*, together with five cursive signs without phonetic value (V, A ; VIII, A ; IX, A, B ; XV, B), among which the second and the fifth are derived from *pu*, the first from *hra*, the third from *hrā*, and the fourth from *hā*.

9=*O* ; really occuring letter-forms in col. V (compare plate IV, 6, IX), in col. VI (compare *AU*, plate VII, 7, X), in col. IX (compare plate VI, 13, I), in cols. XI, XII (compare plate V, 47, IX), in col. XIV (compare plate V, 9, XV), in col. XVII (compare plate VI, 13, V ff.), different from the most ancient form (III, IV) in cols. VII, and XIII, cursive in cols. X and XVI.

10=*ṭhū*[391] (III, in 10000 ; IV, A, B ; V, A ; VI, A), hence a cursive sign, derived by the opening of the circle of *ṭha* (V, B ; VI, B ; VII, A ; VIII, IX), which later is converted into *a* (X, XI, A, B), or into *rya* (XVI, A), or, as in the MSS., into *ḷ* (XIII, A, B ; XVII, A), or into *kha* and *ce* (XV, A, B).

20=*ṭha* (III, in 20000 ; XV), or, as in the MSS., *tha*, *thā*, of the type of the period.

30=*la*, as in the MSS. ; occasionally with small modification.

40=*pta*, as in the MSS., for which occasionally a cursive cross (V, A) or a *sa* through a transposition of the *ta* (V, B ; XI, B ; XV).

50=[77] Anunāsika (? Bhagvānlāl), as in the MSS., facing either the right or the left, occasionally with small modification.

60=*pu* (IX), together with four different cursive signs without phonetic value.

70=*pū* (IV-VI ; IX, XI, A), or *prā* (XII), together with a cursive cross (VII) and another cursive sign (XI, B), both possibly derived from *pū*.

80=Upadhmānīya with a diagonal bar, and cursive forms of the Upadhmānīya exactly as in the MSS.

90=Upadhmānīya with the central cross, as in the MSS.

100=either *su* (I, in 200 ; III ; IX, A, B ; X ; XIII, in 300 ; XIII, in 400 ; XIV, in 400), for which, through a misreading, appears *A* in the Nepāl inscriptions of the 7th and 8th centuries (XIII, A, B ; XIV, in 300), and *lu* in eastern inscriptions [392] of the 6th and later centuries (X, in 200 ; XVIII, in 200), or *śu* (probably owing to the dialectic permutation of *śa* and *sa*) in the western[393] and Kaliṅga inscriptions (IV ; V ; XI ; XII in 400 ; XV, A, B) for which, through a misreading, *O*, (XVII, A, B) appears in late northern inscriptions.

200 and 300 are formed by the addition of respectively one and two horizontal bars, to the right of *akṣara* for 100 ; but in the Rūpnāth sign (I) by the prolongation of the vertical of *sa*. A distinct *ū*, as in the MSS., appears only in the 200 of col. XVIII.

400=*su-ki* (III), or *su-pka* (X ; XIII ; XIV), but *śu-pka* (XI). 500=*śu-tra* (IV). 600=*śu-phra* (XII). 700=*su-gra* (III).

1000=*ro* (III), or *cu* (probable in IV, distinct in XV, in 8000), or *dhu* (IV, in 2000 ; IV, in 70000). 2000 and 3000=*dhu* with one or two horizontal strokes (IV).

4000=*ro-ki* (III), or *dhu-ki* (IV). 6000=*ro-phara* (III). 8000=*dhu-hra* (IV), or *cu-pu* (XVI).

10000=*ro-ṭhū* (III). 20000=*ro-ṭha* (III). 70000=*dhu* with the cursive sign for 70.

The above details show :—(1) That the inscriptions of all periods, even the Aśoka edicts in the case of 100, differ from the MSS. by offering, side by side with distinct letters, numerous cursive or intentionally modified forms, and that, in the case of 50 and 60, just the older inscriptions show no real Akṣaras.

(2) That, excepting 7, 9, 30, 40, 80, 90, the phonetical value of the letters varies already since the earliest times, and that in many cases, as in those of 6, 10, 60, 70, 100, 1000, the variations are very considerable.

(3) That occasionally, as in the case of 10, 60, 70, the distinct letters, used in the later inscriptions and the MSS., are derived in various ways from cursive signs without a phonetical value.

These facts, as well as the incompleteness of our knowledge of the most ancient forms, make an explanation of the origin of the system for the present very difficult. Bhagvānlāl Indrāji, who first attempted the solution of the problem, conjectured that the numeral symbols of the Brāhmi are of Indian origin, and due to a peculiar use of the Mātṛkās and certain ligatures for numeral notation. But he declared himself unable to find the key of the system. In 1877, I agreed with him, and Kern[394] likewise concurred, but explained the 4 and 5 as combinations of four and five strokes, arranged in the form of letters. But Burnell differed entirely. He denied that the older "cave-numerals", with the exception of rare cases, resemble letters, and dwelt strongly on the impossibility of finding a principle, according to which the Akṣaras of the MSS. have been converted into numerals. He further pointed out the general agreement of the principles of the Indian system with those of the Demotic notation of the Egyptians. From this fact, as well as from the resemblance [78] of the Demotic signs for 1 to 9 to the corresponding Indian symbols, he inferred that the "cave-numerals" have been borrowed from Egypt, and after further modifications have been converted into Akṣaras. Finally, E.C. Bayley tried to show in his lengthy essay, quoted above, that, though the principles of the Indian system have been derived from the hieroglyphic notation of the Egyptians, the majority of the Indian symbols have been borrowed from Phoenician, Bactrian, and Akkadian figures or letters, while for a few a foreign origin is not demonstrable.

Bayley's explanation offers great difficulties, *inter alia* by the assumption that the Hindus borrowed from four or five different, partly very ancient and partly more modern, sources. But the comparative table of the Egyptian and Indian signs given in his paper, and his remarks about the agreement of their methods in marking the hundreds, induce me to give up Bhagvānlāl's hypothesis, and to adopt, with certain modifications, the view of Burnell, with whom also Barth concurs[395]. It seems to me probable that the Brāhma numeral symbols are derived from the Egyptian Hieratic figures, and that the Hindus effected their transformation into Akṣaras, because they were already accustomed to express numerals by words (compare below, § 35, A).

This derivation, the details of which, however, still present difficulties and cannot be called certain, has been given in Appendix II to the 2nd edition of my *Indian Studies* No. III. But two other important points may be considered as certain :—(1) That the varying forms in the Aśoka edicts show these numerals to have had a longer history in the 3rd century B.C. ; and (2) that the signs have been developed by Brahmanical schoolmen, since they include two forms of the Upadhmānīya, which without doubt has been invented by the teachers of the Śikṣā.

B.—*The Decimal Notation.*

For the decimal notation, now occasionally called *aṅkapalli*, the Hindus used originally the *aṅkas* or the units of the ancient system, together with the cipher or naught[396], which originally consisted of the *śūnyabindu*, the dot (marking a blank, see below, § 35, E), called by abbreviated names *śūny* and *bindu* (see BW.). Very likely this system is an invention of the Hindu mathematicians and astronomers, made with the help of the Abacus (Burnell, Bayley). If Hoernle's very probable estimate of the antiquity of the arithmetical treatise, contained in the Bakhshāli MS., is correct[397], its invention dates from the beginning of our era or even earlier. For, in that work the decimal notation is used throughout. At all events, it was known to Varāhamihira (6th century A.D.), who employs the word *aṅka*, "the decimal figures", in order to express the numeral 9 (*Pañcasiddhāntikā*, 18, 33 ; compare below, § 35, A). Its most important element, the cipher or naught, is mentioned in Subandhu's *Vāsavadattā*, which Bāṇa (about A.D. 620) praises as a famous book. Subandhu compares the stars with "ciphers (*śūnyabindavaḥ*) which the Creator, while calculating (the value of) the universe, on account of the absolute worthlessness of the Saṃsāra marked with his chalk, the crescent of the moon, all over the firmament which the darkness made similar to a skin blackened with ink."[398] The cipher, known to Subandhu, of course consisted of a dot, like that of the Bakhshāli MS. (plate IX, B, col. IX).

The earliest epigraphic instance of the use of the decimal notation occurs in the Gurjara inscription of the Cedi year 346, or A.D. 595[399], where the signs (plate IX, B, col. I) are identical with the numeral symbols of the country and of the period (compare the Valabhi column of plate IX, A)[400]. The same remark applies to the 2 in the date of the month of the Cicacole plate mentioned on page 98 above, in which document we find also the later circular cipher and [79] a decimal 8 in the shape of a cursive sign derived from *pu*. Another inscription of the 8th century, the Sāmāngaḍ plates of Śakasaṃvat 675, or A.D. 754, offers only strongly modified cursive signs (plate IX, B, col. II).

In the specimens[401] (plate IX, B, cols. III-VIII, XIII) from inscriptions of the 9th and later centuries, when the use of the decimal figures is the rule, we have likewise only cursive signs, which in the 11th and 12th centuries (compare cols. VII, VIII, and XIII) show local differences in the west, east and south. But all their figures have been derived either directly from the letter-numerals of the older system, or from letters with the same phonetic value. The last remark applies to the 9 of cols. III, V, VI ff., which is identical with the signs for *O* used in later inscriptions in the word *Oṃ* (compare, e.g., IA. 6, 191 ff., Nos. 3-6).

Among the specimens from MSS. (plate IX, B, cols. IX-XII), the decimal figures of the Bakhshāli MS., show the ancient letter-numerals for 4 and 9.

The Tamil numerals, which greatly differ from the usual ones and preserve the old signs for 10, 100 and 1000, have been given by Burnell, ESIP. plate 23 (compare *ib.* page 68). Those from Kābul are contained in the table accompanying E. C. Bayley's paper, *Numismatic Chronicle*, 3rd Series, 2, 128 ff.

§35.—NUMERAL NOTATION BY WORDS AND LETTERS.

A.—*The word-numerals.*

[80] In many manuals of astronomy, mathematics and metrics, as well as in the dates of inscriptions and of MSS., the numerals are expressed by the names of things, beings or ideas, which, naturally or in accordance with the teaching of the Śāstras, connote numbers. The earliest traces of this custom have been discovered by A. Weber in the *Śrautasūtras* of Kātyāyana and Lāṭyāyana[402]. A few examples are found in the Vedic Jyotiṣa and in the arithmetic of the Bakhshāli MS. More numerous instances occur in Piṅgala's manual of metrics, and from about A.D. 500 we find, first in Varāhamihira's *Pañcasiddhāntikā*, a system of this description, which, gradually becoming more and more perfect, extends to the cipher or nought, and to nearly all the numbers between 1 and 49. During this latter period any synonym may be used for the words expressing numbers, and in some cases the same word may be used for different numbers. If the words are compounds, they may be represented by their first or second part.

This system of numeral notation, of course, has been invented in order to facilitate the composition of metrical handbooks of astronomy and so forth. The most important words, used to express numbers, are as follows[403] :—

The cipher, 0, is expressed by (*a*) *Śūnya* (Var., Ber.), "a void"[404] ; (*b*) *ambara, ākāśa*, &c., "the (empty) space of heaven" (Var., Ber., Bro.), *ananta* (Bro.).

1 is expressed by (*a*) *rūpa* (Jyo., Bakh., Piṅg., Var.) "one piece" ; (*b*) *indu, śaśin, śītaraśmi*, &c. (Var., Ber., Bro.), or abbreviated into *raśmi* (Ber.), "the moon" ; (*c*) *bhū, mahī* &c. (Var., Ber., Bro., Bur.), "the earth" ; (*d*) *ādi* (Ber.), "beginning" ; (*e*) *pitāmaha* (Ber.), "Brahman" ; (*f*) *nāyaka* (Bro.), "the hero" (of a play) ; (*g*) *tanu* (Bro.), "the body".

2 is expressed by (*a*) *yama, yamala* (Var., Ber.), "twins" ; (*b*) *aśvin, dasra* (Var., Ber.), "the two Aśvins" ; (*c*) *Pakṣa* (Var., Ber.), "the two wings, or the halves of the body" ; (*d*) *kara*, &c. (Var., Bur.), "the hands" ; (*e*) *nayana*, &c. (Var., Ber., Bur.), "the eyes" ; (*f*) *bāhu* (Bro.), "the arms" ; (*g*) *karṇa* (Bro.), "the ears" ; (*h*) *kuṭumba* (Bro.), "the family", i.e., husband and wife ; (*i*) *ravicandrau* (Ber.), "sun and moon".

3 is expressed by (*a*) *agni, hotṛ*[405], &c. (Var., Ber., Bro., Bur.), "the sacrificial fires" ; (*b*) *rāmāḥ* (Var., Bro.), "the three Rāmas" (of epic poetry) ; (*c*) *guṇa* (Var.), *triguṇa* (Ber.), "the qualities of matter" ; (*d*) *trijagat, loka* (Ber.), "the three worlds" ; (*e*) *trikāla* (Ber.), "the three times" ; (*f*) *trigata*[406] (Ber.), "sounds, &c., with three meanings" ; (*g*) *sahodarāḥ* (Bro.), "the three uterine brothers" ;[407] (*h*) *trinetra*, &c. (Bro.), "the three eyes of Śiva".

4 is expressed by (*a*) *aya*, *āya* (Jyo.) *kṛta*[408] (Var., Ber.), "the (four) dice"; (*b*) *veda*, *śruti* (Piṅg., Var., Ber.), "the Vedas"; (*c*) *abdhi*, *jaladhi*, &c. (Piṅg., Var., Ber., Bur.), abbreviated *jala* (Var.), *dadhi* (Ber.), "the oceans;" (*d*) *diś* (Ber.), "the cardinal points"; (*e*) *yuga* (Bro.), "the (four) ages of "the world"; (*f*) *bandhu* (Bro.), "the (four) brothers";[409] (*g*) *koṣṭha* (Bro.), (?); (*h*) *varṇa* (manuscript), "the (four) principal castes".

5 is expressed by (*a*) *indriya*, &c. (Piṅg., Var., Bur.), "the organs of sense"; [81] (*b*) *artha*, *viṣaya*, &c. (Var., Ber.), "the objects of the senses"; (*c*) *bhūta* (Piṅg., Var., Ber.), "the elements"; (*d*) *iṣu*, &c. (Var., Ber., Bur.), "the arrows of Kāma"; (*e*) *Pāṇḍava* (Ber.), abbreviated *(pāṇḍu) suta*, *putra* (Bro.), "the (five) Pāṇḍu sons"; (*f*) *prāṇa* (Bro.); "the vital airs"; (*g*) *ratna*[410] (Ber.) "the (five) jewels".

6 is expressed by (*a*) *rasa* (Bakh., Piṅg., Var., Ber.), "the (six) flavours"; (*b*) *ṛtu* (Piṅg., Var., Ber.), "the seasons"; (*c*) *aṅga* (Ber.), "the auxiliary sciences of Vedic studies"; (*d*) *māsārdha* (Ber.), "one half of the (twelve) months"; (*e*) *darśana*, &c. (Bro.), "the (six) philosophical systems"; (*f*) *rāga* (Bro.), "the (six principal tunes"; (*g*) *ari* (Bro.), "the (internal) foes (of men)"; (*h*) *kāya*[411] (inscription), "the bodies" (?)

7 is expressed by (*a*) *ṛṣi*, *muni* (Piṅg., Var.), "the (seven) seers"; or by *atri*, the first among them (Bro.); (*b*) *svara* (Piṅg., Var., Bro.), "the notes" (of the octave); (*c*) *aśva* (Var., Bro.), "the horses" (of the sun); (*d*) *aga*, &c. (Var., Ber., Bur.), "the (primeval) mountains"; (*e*) *dhātu* (Bro.), "the elements" (of the body); (*f*) *chandas* (Bro.), "the (classes of the) metres"; (*g*) *dhī* (Ber.), (?); (*h*) *kalatra* (Bro.), (?).

8 is expressed by (*a*) *anuṣṭubh* (Piṅg.), a metre with octosyllabic Pādas or lines; (*b*) *vasu* (Piṅg., Var.), "the Vasu gods"; (*c*) *ahi*, &c. (Ber., Bur.), "the (eight classes of) snakes"; (*d*) *gaja*, &c. (Ber., Bur.), "the elephants (guarding the eight points of the horizon)"; (*e*) *maṅgala*, *bhūti* (Ber., Bro.), "the (eight kinds of) auspicious things"[412]; (*f*) *siddhi* (manuscript), "the supernatural powers",

9 is expressed by (*a*) *aṅka* (Var., Bro.), "the decimal figures": (*b*) *nanda* (Var., Ber.), "the (nine) Nandas"; (*c*) *chidra*, &c. (Ber.), "the cavities of the body"; (*d*) *go*, *graha* (Ber., Bro., Bur.), "the planets"; (*e*) *nidhi* (Bur.), "the treasures (of Kubera)"; (*f*) *pavana* (Ber.), (?).

10 is expressed by (*a*) *diśah*, &c. (Piṅg., Var., Ber.). "the (ten) points of the horizon"; (*b*) *rāvaṇaśiras* (Ber.), "the heads of Rāvaṇa"; (*c*) *avatāra* (Bro.), "the incarnations (of Viṣṇu)"; (*d*) *karman* (Ber.), "the (ten (Gṛhya)-ceremonies"; (*e*) *khendu* (Ber.), cipher (0) and moon (1), i.e. 10.[413]

11 is expressed by (*a*) *rudra* (Piṅg., Var., Ber.), "the (eleven) Rudras", or by *īśa*, *śiva*, &c. (Var., Ber.), the first of the eleven Rudras; (*b*, *c*) *akṣauhiṇī*, *lābha* (Bro.), (?).

12 is expressed by (*a*) *āditya*, *arka*, &c. (Piṅg., Var., Ber.), "the (twelve) sun-gods"; or "suns";, (*b*) *vyaya* (Bro.), (?).

13 is expressed by (*a*) *viśvedevāḥ*, abbreviated *viśva* (Var., Ber.), "the (thirteen) all-gods[414]"; or by *kāma*, the most famous among them (Bro.); (*b*) *atijagatī* (Var.), a metre with thirteen syllables in each Pāda; (*c*) *aghoṣa* (Jagaḍūcarita),[415] "the surd consonants".

14 is expressed by (*a*) *manu* (Var., Ber.), "the (fourteen) Manus"; (*b*) *indra* (Var., Ber.), "the (fourteen) Indras"; (*c*) *loka* (Bro.), "the (fourteen) worlds".

15 is expressed by (*a*) *tithi* (Var., Ber.), "the lunar days (of a half-month)"; (*b*) *ahan* (Bro.), "the solar days (of a half-month)"; (*c*) *pakṣa* (Bro.), "half a month (fifteen days)".

16 is expressed by (*a*) *aṣṭi* (Var., Ber.), a metre with sixteen syllables in the Pāda; (*b*) *bhūpa*, &c. (Var., Ber.), "the (famous sixteen) kings,"[416] (*c*) *kalā* (Bro.), "the digits of the moon".

17 to 19 are expressed by *atyaṣṭi* (Ber.), *dhṛti*, *atidhṛti* (Var., Ber.), metres with seventeen to nineteen syllables in the Pāda.

20 is expressed by (*a*) *kṛti* (Var., Ber.), a metre with twenty syllables in the Pāda; (*b*) *nakha* (Var., Ber.), "the nails (of the hands and feet)."

21 is expressed by (*a*) *utkṛti* (Ber.,)[417]; (*b*) *Svarga* (Bro.), "heaven."

22 is expressed by *jāti* (Bro.), (?).

24 is expressed by *jina* (Var., Ber.), "the (twenty-four Tirthaṃkaras of the Jainas."

25 is expressed by *tattva* (Ber.), "principles of the Sāṃkhya philosophy."

26 is expressed by *utkṛti* (Var.), a metre with twenty-six syllables in the Pāda.

27 is expressed by *bhasamūha* (Jyo.), *nakṣatra* (Bro.), "the lunar mansions".

32 is expressed by *danta*, &c. (Var., Bro.), "the teeth".

33 is expressed by *sura*, &c. (Var., Bro.) "the gods".

40 is expressed by *naraka* (Var., *Pañcasiddhāntikā*, 4, 6), "the hells".

49 is expressed by *tāna* (Bro.), "the notes".

[82] In the Jyotiṣa and in the arithmetic of the Bakhshāli MS., only single words are used to indicate numbers.

In Piṅgala's and other metrical manuals, the words with numeral meanings often form (sometimes together with ordinary numerals) Dvandva compounds, which must be dissolved by "or". Thus, *vedartusamudrāḥ* means "4 or 6 or 4".

In the works of Varāhamihira and other astronomers, we find, in addition, longer Dvandva compounds, consisting of such word-numerals (be it alone, or associated with ordinary numerals), which have to be dissolved by "and", and then yield long rows of figures to be read from the right to the left[418]. Thus, in the *Pañcasiddhāntikā*, 4, 44, we have :—

0		0		4		4		1		
kha	—	*kha*	—	*veda*	—	*samudra*	—	*śītaraśmayaḥ*	=	14400;

and in 9, 9 of the same work, we have :—

0		0		16		2		
kha	—	*kh*	—	*āṣṭi*	—	*yamāḥ*	=	21600

Such Dvandva compounds, which presuppose the existence of the decimal notation, are used also for the dates of inscriptions. Dates expressed in this manner, are found in the Kamboja and Campā inscriptions of the 7th century[419]. In Java they occur in the 8th century[420]. And about the same time appears the first trace of such a notation in an Indian document, the Cicacole copper-plate inscription mentioned on page 98 above, where *lo*=3, is an abbreviation of *loka*. Next follow the dates of the Kaḍab plates of A. D. 813[421], and of the Dholpur stone inscription of A. D. 842[422], which are expressed in word-numerals; and, in the next century, the plates issued by the Eastern Calukya Amma II in A. D. 945[423]. In later times the epigraphic instances become more frequent, and the ancient palm-leaf MSS. of the Jainas[424], as well as the later paper MSS., offer a good many. The notations of this kind have been caused sometimes by the vanity of the clerks and copyists, who wished to prove their acquaintance with the methods of the astronomers, and perhaps still more frequently by metrical reasons in the case of dates given in verse.

B.—*Numeral notation by letters.*

Two system of numeral notation, according to Burnell originally South-Indian, which both employ the phonetically arranged characters of the alphabet, have still to be described, as they are not without interest for paleography. In the first system[425], only the vowelless consonants have any importance, and their numeral values are :—

k kh g gh ṅ c ch j jh ñ = 1 2 3 4 5 6 7 8 9 0

ṭ ṭh ḍ ḍh ṇ t th d dh n = 1 2 3 4 5 6 7 8 9 0

p ph b bh m .. .. = 1 2 3 4 5

y r l v ś ṣ s h ḷ .. = 1 2 3 4 5 6 7 8 9

The consonants are, however, not used by themselves, but for the formation of chronograms, containing any vowels and also compound consonants, of which the last element alone has numerical value. In the figures, resulting from those chronograms, the units invariably stand on the left, and the whole sum has to be turned round. An interesting instance of this notation, probably the most ancient hitherto discovered, occurs at the end of Ṣaḍguruśiṣya's commentary on the *Sarvānukramaṇī* (Macdonell, page 168), where the chronogram, according to Kielhorn's undoubtedly correct emendation, is[426] :—

2 3 = 1 = 5 6 5 = 1

khago = *ntyān* = *meṣam* = *āpa.*

As the author himself adds, this has the value of 1565132. And this figure corresponds, as the author likewise says, to the number of the days elapsed since the beginning of the Kaliyuga, and yields the vernal equinox, 24th March, A. D. 1184, as the date of the completion of the work. The equinox is indicated also by the verbal meaning of the chronogram :—"(Coming) from the last (sign of the Zodiac), the sun reached Aries".

The second system to be considered[427], which is still used in Ceylon, Siam and Burma for the pagination of MSS., and according to Burnell formerly also [83] occurred in Southern India, utilises the Brahmanical *Bārākhaḍī* (see page 16 above). According to Burnell, the Akṣaras *ka* to *ḷa* are equivalent to 1 to 34; *kā* to *ḷā*=35 to 68; *ki* to *ḷi*=69 to 102; and so on. But in the Pali MSS. of the Viennese Court Library from Burma, I find *ka* to *kaḥ*=1 to 12; *kha* to *khaḥ*=13 to 24; and so on: and in those from Ceylon, where the *Bārākhaḍī* includes the vowels *ṛ*, *ṝ*, *ḷ* and *ḹ*, *ka* to *kaḥ*=1 to 16, and *kha* to *khaḥ*=17 to 32, whereby a somewhat different employment of the Akṣaras results[428]. Fausböll has kindly informed me that the last two methods alone (not that mentioned by Burnell) are used in the Pali MSS. known to him. And he adds that, after the exhaustion of the whole *Bārākhaḍī*, the Ceylonese MSS. begin again with 2 *ka*, 2 *kā*, and so on, and further that the pagination of Siamese MSS. agrees exactly with those from Burma.

VII. THE EXTERNAL ARRANGEMENT OF INSCRIPTIONS AND MANUSCRIPTS.

§36.—THE LINES, GROUPING OF WORDS, INTERPUNCTUATION, AND OTHER DETAILS.

A.—The lines.

Already in the earliest inscriptions incised on smoothed stones, the Hindus have tried to form regular straight lines and to make the upper ends of the Mātṛkās of equal height. Aśoka's masons, however, have rarely succeeded, even in the pillar edicts and in the rock edicts of Girnār, Dhauli and Jaugada, to keep the line in more than a few consecutive words, mostly those of one group (see below, under B). But in other documents of the same period, as in the Ghasundi stone inscription (see page 49 above), the later[429] and still valid principle has been more carefully observed, according to which only the vowel-signs, the superscribed *ra* and similar additions may protrude above the upper line. This regularity probably has been attained by marking the upper line with chalk, as is still done, or by other mechanical appliances.

The lines of the MSS. are always very regular, even in the oldest specimens, such as the Dhammapada from Khotan, and probably have been made with the help of a ruler (see below, § 37, J). In the ancient palm-leaf MSS. and in many later ones on paper, the ends of the lines are marked by vertical double strokes, running across the whole breadth of the leaves. In the MSS., the lines always run horizontally, and from the top to the bottom; and this is also the case in most inscriptions. But there are a few inscriptions which have to be read from below[430].

Vertical lines sometimes occur on coins, especially on those of the Kuṣānas and the Guptas[431]. The cause of the latter arrangement of the letters was probably the want of space.

B.—*The Grouping of Words.*

[84] In addition to the still usual method of writing the words continuously without a break, up to the end of a line, of a verse, half-verse or other division, we find already in some of the oldest documents, such as certain Aśoka edicts[432], instances of the separation of single words, or of groups of words which belong together, either according to their sense or according to the clerk's manner of reading. A similar grouping of the words occurs also in some prose inscriptions of the Andhras and the Western Kṣatrapas at Nāsik ; compare Nos. 5, 11A, B, and 13. In the carefully written

metrical inscriptions of the later times, the Pādas or the half-verses occasionally are separated by blank spaces[433], and each line contains a half-verse or a verse[434].

Similarly, in the Kharoṣṭhī Dhammapada from Khotan, each line contains one Gāthā, and the Pādas are divided off by blanks. In other old MSS., as the Bower MS., single words and groups of words are often written separately, apparently without any certain principle.

In inscriptions, the Maṅgala, especially when it is the word *siddham*, often stands by itself on the margin[435].

C.—*Interpunctuation*[436].

Signs of interpunctuation are not found in the Kharoṣṭhī inscriptions. But the Dhammapada from Khotan offers at the end of each verse a circular mark, often made negligently, but resembling the modern cipher[437]. At the end of a Vagga appears a sign, which is found at the end of various inscriptions, e.g. F.GI (CII. 3), No. 71, plate 41A, and which probably is intended to represent a lotus.

In connection with the Brāhmī, signs of interpunctuation occur since the earliest times, and the signs employed are the following:—

(1) A single vertical stroke (*daṇḍa*) is used (irregularly and sometimes wrongly) in some Aśoka edicts[438] for the separation of single words or of groups. In later times it serves to separate prose from verse[439], or occurs at the end of portions of sentences[440], of sentences[441], of half-verses[442] or verses[443], and occasionally even marks the end of documents[444]. In the inscriptions of the Eastern Calukyas[445] the *daṇḍa* has occasionally a small horizontal top-bar ; thus, T.

(2) A double vertical stroke, ‖ appears in the Junnar inscriptions Nos. 24-29 after numerals, and once after the name of the donor. Later it occurs at the end of sentences[446], half-verses[447], verses[448], larger prose sections and documents[449]. From the 5th century, a hook is often added to the top of the first stroke ; thus ʕl [450]. Or both strokes receive such additions ; thus, ɪɪ [451]. Curves and hooks are added also to the foot of one of the strokes or of both[452]. From the end of the 8th century, a bar is attached on the left, to the middle of the first stroke ; thus, ⊣l [453]. In the inscriptions of the Eastern Calukyas, bars stand at the top of the strokes ; thus, TT : and a Kaliṅga inscription has similarly ʅT [454].

(3) A triple vertical stroke marks occasionally the end of inscriptions[455].

(4) A single short horizontal stroke, placed on the left below the first sign of the last line, marks in the Aśoka edicts of Dhauli and Jaugada the end of an edict. From the 2nd century B. C.[456] to the 7th century A. D., this sign, which is often curved or bears a hook at one of its ends, serves the same purposes as the single vertical stroke[457].

(5) A double horizontal stroke, often bent, appears from the 1st to the 8th century A. D. in the place of the double vertical[458]. The Kuṣāna inscriptions and some later ones offer in its stead a double dot[459], which looks exactly like a Visarga.

(6) A double vertical, followed by a horizontal stroke, occasionally marks the end of inscriptions[460].

(7) A crescent-like stroke, > , marks the ends of the Aśoka edicts at Kālsī, Nos. I-XI.

(8) A crescent-like stroke with a bar in the middle, ϶ , stands twice in Kuṣāṇa inscriptions after the Maṅgala *siddham*[461].

Besides, numeral figures alone occasionally mark the ends of verses, see, e.g., F.GI (CII. 3), Nos. 1, 2, and similarly Maṅgala-symbols (see below, under D) stand at the end of inscriptions or of sections of the text, especially in ancient MSS, such as the Bower MS.

Finally, it is necessary to call attention to the frames surrounding the Aśoka edicts in the Girnār version, the Jaugada separate edicts, and the Dhauli separate edict No. I.

What the inscriptions teach us regarding the history of the Indian interpunctuation may be briefly summed up, as follows. During the earliest period up to the beginning of our era, only single strokes, either straight or curved, are used, and their use is rare. After the beginning of our era, we find more complicated signs. [85] But up to the 5th century their use remains irregular. From that time onwards, we have, especially in the Praśastis on stone, more regular systems of interpunctuation. And the Māndāsor Praśasti of A.D. 473-74, F.GI (CII.3), No. 18, plate 11, first proves the existence of the still valid principle, which requires one stroke after a half-verse and two strokes at the end of a verse. But up to the 8th century there are various copper-plates and stone inscriptions, especially from Southern India, without any interpunctuation[462]. Its methodical development is due to the Brahmanical schoolmen. In the offices, interpunctuation apparently never became a favourite. As a comparison of the documents of one and the same dynasty easily shows, the degree of regularity with which the signs are used, depends not upon the age of the Śāsanas, but on individual qualities of the writers, their learning and their carefulness.

D.—*Maṅgalas and ornamentation.*

In accordance with the ancient Brahmanical maxim, which requires a Maṅgala, a benediction or an auspicious word, at the beginning, in the middle and at the end of a composition in order to insure its completion and preservation, sacred symbols of auspicious import are found at the beginning and the end of two Aśoka edicts[463] and of many inscriptions of the next four centuries[464]. The most common Maṅgala-symbols, employed in this way, are the well-known Svastika, the trident or the so-called Triratna symbol resting on the Dharmacakra, and the conventional representation of a Caitya tree[465]. But there are also others, the names of which are as yet unknown. Once[466] the Svastika appears after the word *siddham*.

In later times, we find also Maṅgala-symbols with greatly modified forms, partly in the texts at the end of larger sections and partly at the end of documents or literary works. A very common sign of this description is a large circle with a smaller one, or with one or several dots in the middle[467]. This may be a conventional representation either of the

Dharmacakra which is still distinctly visible in front of F. GI (CII. 3), No. 63, plate 39, A, or of the lotus, which likewise occurs. As a circle with a dot, ⊙ , corresponds to the ancient *tha*, other signs, closely resembling or identical with later forms of *tha*, are used as substitutes[468]. And the modern MSS. finally offer the well-known छ, which corresponds to one of the medieval forms of *tha*, but is now read *cha*.

Since the 5th century, we find also new symbols, consisting of highly ornamental forms of the ancient *O* of the word *Oṃ* (plate IV, 6, XVIII ; plate V, 47, IX), which latter is a great Maṅgala. They are used both at the beginning and at the end of inscriptions and occasionally even on the margin of copper-plates[469].

Many of the sculptures, found in connection with stone inscriptions, appear to have the same meaning as the Maṅgala-symbols just mentioned. Of this kind are, e.g., several of the relievos above Bhagvānlāl's Nepāl inscriptions[470], such as the Śaṅkhas (No. 3), the lotuses (Nos. 5, 15), the bull Nandi (Nos. 7, 12), the fish (No. 9), the sun-wheel and the stars (No. 10). It is however possible that the lotus of No. 15 may refer also to the donation of a silver lotus, the dedication of which the inscription records. Again, the sun-wheel and the stars of No. 10 may also be intended to indicate the wish, often expressed explicitly in words, that the donation, to which the inscription refers, may last "as long as sun and stars endure".

Similar illustrations of the contents of the inscriptions and symbolical representations of the wishes[471] and of other matters expressed in them, are not rare. Corresponding engravings on the copper-plates are less common. But on these the royal coat of arms is sometimes engraved below or by the side of the text, instead of on a separate seal, and the stone inscriptions, too, occasionally exhibit such devices[472]. Among the MSS., those of the Nepalese Buddhists and of the Jainas of Gujarāt are often richly ornamented and perfectly illustrated[573]. Specimens of illuminated Brahmanical MSS. are, however, not wanting.

E.—*Corrections, Omissions and Abbreviations*[474].

In the earliest inscriptions, as in the Aśoka edicts (see, e.g., Kālsī edict XII, line 31) erroneous passages [86] are simply scored out. Later, dots or short strokes above or below the line are used to indicate clerical errors. The same signs occur in MSS., where however, in late times the *delenda* are covered with turmeric or a yellow paste. On the copper-plates, they are frequently beaten out with a hammer, and the corrections are then engraved on the smoothed spot. We possess even entire palimpsests of this kind[475].

In the Aśoka edicts and other early inscriptions, letters and words, left out by mistake, are added above or below the line without any indication of the place to which they belong[476], or they are also entered in the interstices between the letters. In the later inscriptions and the MSS., the spot of the omission is indicated by a small upright or inclined cross, the so-called *kākapada* or *haṃsapada*, and the addenda are given either in the margin [477] or between the lines.

A Svastika is sometimes put instead of the cross[478]. In South-Indian MSS., the cross is used also to indicate intentional omissions, made in Sūtras with commentaries[479]. Elsewhere, intentional omissions, or such as have been caused by defects in the original of the copy, are marked by dots on the line or by short strokes above the line[480]. The modern sign for the elision of an initial *A*, the so-called Avagraha, has been traced first on the Barodā copper-plate of the Rāṣṭrakūṭa king Dhruva, dated A. D. 834-35[481]. A *kuṇḍala*, "ring", or a Svastika, served to mark unintelligible passages; see *Kashmīr Report*, 71 and Kielhorn, *Mahābhāṣya*, 2, 10, note.

In Western India, abbreviations are found first in an inscription of the Andhra king Siri-Puḻumāyi (Nāsik, No. 15) of about A. D. 150, and in the nearly contemporaneous one of Sirisena- or Sakasena-Māḍhariputa (Kanheri, No. 14). In the north-west, they are very common in the inscriptions of the Kuṣāṇa period. The commonest instances are:— *saṃva, sava, saṃ* and *sa* for *saṃvatsara*; *gri, gṛ* or *gi* for *grīṣmāḥ* or *gimhānaṃ*; *va* for *varṣāḥ*; *he* for *hemantaḥ*; *pa* for *pakhe*; and *diva* or *di* for *divasa*; and they are only found when the dates are expressed by figures. In this connection, they are used regularly in the later inscriptions and even in our days. But in these later times we find usually *saṃvat*, which sometimes even is inflected[482], before the dates of the years; but, before the dates of the month falling in the bright half, *śu* or *su di* for *śuddha*- or *śukla-pakṣa-dina*, or in Kashmir *śu* or *su ti* (*tithi*), and before those falling in the dark half, *ba* or *va di* for *bahula*- or *vahula-pakṣa-dina*, or in Kashmīr *ba ti*.

From the 6th century, the inscriptions of Western India offer here and there abbreviations of other words, such as *dū* for *dūtaka*, *dvi* for *dvitīya*[483].

Later, especially since the 11th century, abbreviations of titles and the names of tribes, castes and so forth become very common. In the MSS. they are noticeable since the earliest times. Thus, the Khotan Dhammapada (Paris fragment) has, at the end of a Vagga, *ga 30* for *gāthā 30*; and in the Bower MS., plate II, *ślo* for *śloka* and *pā pāda* often occur in connection with figures at the end of a section. In the inscripions and MSS. of the 12th century we find with names, not with dates, the small circle or *bindu*[484], which is still used to indicate abbreviations; e.g., ठ° for *ṭhakkara*. The same sign is used in Prākṛt MSS. to indicate the omission of one or several letters that can be easily supplied; e.g., *a°ṭabhavaṃ*, for *aṭṭabhavaṃ*, *di°ṭhā* for *diṭṭhā*[485].

F.—*Pagination.*

The Hindus number only the leaves (*pattra*), not the pages (*pṛṣṭhā*), of their MSS.; and in the Dravidian districts the figure stands on the first page of each leaf, in all other parts of India on the second (*sāṅkapṛṣṭhā*)[486]. The same rule holds good in the case of copper-plates, the sheets of which sometimes (but rarely) are numbered[487].

G.—*Seals.*

According to the law-books[488], all Śāsanas [87] must bear the royal seal. Consequently, seals, welded to the plates or to the rings connecting the plates, or attached to them by pins, are found with the majority of the grants. They show the royal coat of arms (mostly the representation of an animal or of a deity), or, in addition to such emblems, a shorter or longer inscription, giving the name of the king or of the founder of the dynasty, or the whole pedigree, and sometimes merely an inscription[489].

VIII. WRITING MATERIALS, LIBRARIES AND WRITERS.

§ 37.—WRITING MATERIALS[490]

A.—*Birch-bark.*

[88] The inner bark of the *Bhūrja*-tree (Baetula Bhojpattr), which the Himālaya produces in great quantity, probably is alluded to already by Q. Curtius (see above, page 20) as a writing material used by the Hindus at the time of Alexander's invasion, and later it is frequently named as such in Northern Buddhist and Brahmanical Sanskrit works[491]. It is even called *lekhana*, the "writing material", and written documents go by the name of *bhūrja*. According to Berūnī[492], pieces, one ell in length and one span in breadth, were prepared for use by rubbing them with oil and polishing them. The art of the preparation has however been lost in Kashmīr, when the introduction of paper during the Moghal period furnished a more convenient material[493]. But a not inconsiderable number of old birch-bark MSS. still exist in the libraries of of the Kashmīr Pandits. According to a statement made to me by Bhāū Dāji, birch-bark MSS. occur also in Orissa, and amulets, written on Bhūrja, are still used throughout all the Aryan districts of India[494]. The use of the *bhūrjapattra* of course began in the north-west; but it seems to have spread in early times, as the copper-plates of Central, Eastern and Western India appear to have been cut according to the size of the Bhūrja, which in Kashmir mostly corresponds to our quarto (Burnell). As stated in many classical Sanskrit works and by Berūnī, all letters were written on Bhūrja at least in Northern, Central, Eastern and Western India.

The oldest documents on Bhūrja, which have been found, are the Kharoṣṭhī Dhammapada from Khotan, and the inscribed "twists", tied up with threads, which Masson discovered in the Stūpas of Afghanistan (see above, page 34, and note 100). Next come the fragments from the Godfrey Collection and the Bower MS., the leaves of which have been cut according to the size of palm-leaves, and, like these, are pierced in the middle in order to pass a string through, intended to hold them together[495]. Next in age is the Bakhshāli MS., and then follow after a considerable interval the birch-bark MSS. from Kashmir in the libraries of Poona, London, Oxford, Vienna, Berlin, &c., none of which probably dates earlier than the 15th century.

B.—*Cotton cloth.*

The use of well-beaten cotton cloth is mentioned by Nearchos (see above, page 20), and some metrical Smṛtis, as well as some inscriptions of the Andhra period state that official and private documents were written on *paṭa*, *paṭikā* or *kārpāsika paṭa*[496]. According to Burnell, and Rice (*Mysore and Coorg Gazetteer*, 1877, 1. 403), the Kanarese traders still use for their books of business a kind of cloth, called *kaḍatam*, which is covered with a paste of tamarind-seed and afterwards blackened with charcoal. The letters are written with chalk or steatite pencils, and the writing is white or black. In the Bṛhajjñānakoṣa at Jesalmir, I found a silk band with the list of the Jaina Sūtras, written with ink. Recently Peterson (*Fifth Report.* 113) has discovered at Aṇhilvāḍ Pāṭaṇ a MS., dated Vikrama-Saṃvat 1418 (A.D. 1361-62), which is written on cloth.

C.—*Wooden Boards.*

The passage of the *Vinayapiṭaka* (see above, page 19), which forbids "the incising" of precepts for religious suicide, bears witness to a very early use of wooden boards or bamboo chips as writing materials. Equally, the Jātakas, and also later works, mention the writing board, used in the elementary schools. Chips of bamboo (*śalākā*), with the name of the bearers served as passports for Buddhist monks (Burnouf, *Introd. à l'histoire du Bouddhisme*, 259, note). An inscription from the time of the Western Kṣatrapa Nahapāna[497] speaks of boards (*phalaka*) in the guildhall, on which agreements regarding loans were placarded, and Kātyāyana prescribes that plaints are to be entered on boards with *pāṇḍulekha*, i.e., with chalk[498]. Daṇḍin narrates, in the *Daśakumāracarita*, that Apahāravarman wrote his declaration, addressed to the sleeping princess, on a varnished board[499]. MSS. on varnished boards, which are common in Burma, have hitherto not been discovered in India proper ; but there are indications that the Hindus, too, used boards for literary purposes. Winternitz informs me that the Bodleian Library possesses a MS. on wooden boards, which comes from Assam. [89] And Rājendralāl Mitra asserts, in Gough's *Papers*, p. 18, that in the North-West Provinces poor people copy religious works with chalk on black boards.

D.—*Leaves.*

According to the Canon of the Southern Buddhists (see above. page 20), leaves (*paṇṇa*) were in ancient times the most common writing material. Though the texts[500] do not mention the plants which furnished these leaves, it is not doubtful that they came then, as in later times, chiefly from the large-leaved palm-trees, the *tāḍa* or *tāla* (Borassus flabelliformis) and the *tāḍī* or *tālī* (Corypha umbraculifera, or C. taliera), which, originally indigenous in the Dekhaṇ, are found at present even in the Pañjāb. The earliest witness[501] for the general use of palm-leaves throughout the whole of India is Hiuen Tsiang (7th century). But we possess clear proof that they were used even in north-west India during much earlier times. The Horiuzi palm-leaf MS certainly goes back to the 6th century, and some fragments in the recently discovered Godfrey Collection from Kashgar belong, as Hoernle has shown on the paleogrphical evidence, at least to the 4th century, and are older than the Bower MS[502]. Again, the *bhūrjapattra* leaves of the Bower MS. are cut according to the size of palm-leaves, and that is also the case with the Taxila copper-plate (see above, page, 41) which certainly is not later then the 1st century A.D. As the coppersmith then chose a palm-leaf for his model, it follows that palm-leaves must have been commonly used for writing, even in the Pañjāb. A Buddhist tradition, preserved in the *Life of Hiuen Tsiang*[503], asserts that the Canon was written on palm-leaves at the first Council held immediately after Buddha's death. And the story regarding Saṃghabhadra's "dotted MS. of the Vinaya", published by Takakusu in J.RAS. 1896, 436 f., shows that this tradition is at least two centuries older ; one inference, which may be drawn from it, is, that about A. D. 400 the Buddhists believed palm-leaves to have been used for writing since immemorial times.

According to Rājendralāl Mitra[504], the palm-leaves, to be used for writing, are first dried, next boiled or soaked in water, then again dried, and finally polished with stones or conch-shells and cut to the proper size. It agrees with this statement, that the leaves of the ancient MSS. from Nepāl and Western India frequently show traces of an artificial preparation. Their length varies between one and three feet, and their breadth between one and a quarter and four inches[505]. Against this, Burnell[506] asserts that the people of Southern India take no trouble with the preparation, and mostly even neglect to trim the leaves properly. The last assertion is not borne out by the appearance of the South-Indian MSS. known to me, though it is no doubt true of the leaves used by clerks and men of business in offices and for letters.

The Horiuzi MS., and the fragments in the Godfrey Collection, as well as the numerous palm-leaf MSS. of the 9th and later centuries from Nepāl, Bengal, Rājputāna, Gujarāt and the northern Dekhaṇ prove that since ancient times the palm-leaves were written on with ink all over Northern, Eastern, Central and Western India. Since the introductian of paper, they are no longer used in these districts, except in Bengal for MSS. of the Caṇḍīpāṭha[507].

In the Dravidian districts and in Orissa, the letters were, and still are, incised with a *stilus* and afterwards blackened with soot or charcoal. The oldest MS., found in the south, dates according to Burnell[508] from A. D. 1428.

All palm-leaf MSS. are pierced either with one hole, usually in the middle, more rarely, in specimens from Kashgar, on the left, or with two holes on the left and the right, through which strings (*sūtra* or *śarayantraka*)[509] are passed in order to keep the leaves together.

In Southern India, raw palm-leaves were, and still are, commonly used for letters, for private and official documents, as well as in the indigenous schools. For the latter purpose they are also employed in Bengal[510]. According to Adams[511], the pupils of the *tolls* write also with lamp-soot on the large Banānā and Sāl leaves.

E.—Animal Substances.

D'Alwis[512] asserts that Buddhist works mention skins among the writing materials, but neglects to quote the passages. It is possible to infer from the passage of the *Vāsavadattā*, quoted above (§ 31, B) that in Subandhu's time skins were used for writing. But the fact that leather is ritually impure makes the inference hazardous. And hitherto no MS. on leather has turned up in India, though pieces of leather from Kashgar, inscribed with Indian characters, are said to exist in the Petersburg collections. A blank piece of parchment [90] lay among the MSS. ofthe Jesalmir Bṛhajjñānakoṣa.

Manuscripts on thin plates of ivory occur in Burma, and the British Museum possesses two specimens.[513]

F.—*Metals.*

The Jātakas[514] state repeatedly that the important family records of rich merchants, and verses and moral maxims, were engraved on gold plates, and Burnell[515] mentions that they were used for royal letters and for land-grants. A gold plate with a votive inscription in Kharoṣṭhī has been found in a Stūpa at Gāṅgu near the ruins of Taxila[516]. Specimens of small MSS. and official documents on silver likewise are preserved[517], and among them is one from the ancient Stūpa at Bhaṭṭiprolu. In the British Museum there are also MSS. on gilt and silver plated palm-leaves.

It is a matter of course that the precious metals were used only in rare and exceptional cases. But, as the exceedingly numerous finds prove., copper-plates (*tāmrapaṭa, tāmrapattra, tāmraśāsana*, abbreviated *tāmra*) were since ancient times the favourite material for engraving various kinds of documents which were intended to last, and especially land-grants, to the donees of which they served as title-deeds.

According to Fahian (about A.D. 400), the Buddhist monasteries possessed grants engraved on copper, the oldest of which dated from Buddha's time[518]. Though this statement requires confirmation, the Sohgaura plate (see above, page 49) teaches us that during the Maurya period official decrees were committed to copper. Another Buddhist tradition, preserved by Hiuen Tsiang[519], asserts that Kaniṣka caused the sacred books to be engraved on sheets of copper. And a similar story, which Burnell declares to be untrustworthy, is told regarding Sāyaṇa's commentaries on the Vedas[520]. But it is undeniable that copper has been used also for the preservation of literary works, as plates with such contents have been found at Tripatty, and specimens from Burma, and Ceylon (some of which are gilt) are now in the British Museum[521]. Photographs of quite modern copper-plates with lists of goods in Gurumukhī and Nāgarī, sent from Kashgar to St. Petersburg, have reached me through the kindness of S. von Oldenberg.

As regards the technical preparation, the oldest *tāmraśāsana* known, the Sohgaura copper-plate (see above, page 49), has been cast in a mould of sand, into which the letters and the emblems above them had been previously scratched with a *stilus* or a pointed piece of wood. Hence both the letters and the emblems appear on the plate in relievo. All other copper-plates have been fashioned with the hammer, and many among them show distinct traces of the blows. Their thickness and size vary very considerably. Some are very thin sheets, which could be bent double and weigh only a few ounces; others are exceedingly massive and are eight or nine pounds in weight or even heavier[522]. Their size is partly determined by the nature of the writing material commonly used in the districts where they were issued, and partly by the extent of the document to be engraved, the size of the clerk's writing, and so forth. The smiths always imitated the originals given them. If these were written on palm-leaves, the plates were made narrow and long. If the material was birch-bark, the plates became much broader, often almost square. Of the first description are all the copper-plates from Southern India, with the exception of those of the Yādavas of Vijayanagara, which imitate stone *stelae*[523]. To the second class belong all the Śāsanas issued further north, with the exception of the Taxila plate, which, a stated already, is the size of a palm-leaf. A comparison of the numerous plates of the Valabhi kings shows very clearly how their size gradually grows with the increasing length of the Praśasti.

If, as is mostly the case, several plates were required for one document, they were usually connected by copper rings passed through round holes in the plates. The single ring is usually found in Śāsanas from Southern India, and then the hole is usually made in the left side of the plate. If there are two rings, the holes go through the lower part of the first plate, the upper part of the second, and so on alternately. The rings correspond to the threads which keep the palm leaves together, and they make of many *tāmraśāsanas* small volumes[524], which can be opened quite conveniently. The lines run always, except in the Vijayanagara plates, [91] parallel to the broadest side of the plate. The letters have mostly been incised with a chisel, rarely with a graver (compare above, page 35). In order to protect the writing, the rims of the plates are usually thickened, and slightly raised[525], and the first side of the first plate, as well as the second side of the last, is left blank. The copper seals attached to the plates seem to have been cast, and their inscriptions and emblems are raised on a counter-sunk surface. According to Bāṇa[526], the state seal of king Harṣa was made of gold.

Various copper statues show votive inscriptions on their bases. A single inscription on iron, that on the iron pillar of Meharaulī, near Delhi[527], has become known. The British Museum possesses a Buddhist MS. on tin[528].

G.—*Stone and Brick.*

Stones of the most various kinds, rough and artificially smoothed blocks of basalt or trap, as well as artistically carved columns of standstone, or even prisms of crystal, have been since the most ancient times the most common materials for making documents, as Aśoka expresses himself, *ciraṭhitika*, "such as to endure for a long time". And it is indifferent whether the documents are official or private, whether they contain royal proclamations, treaties between kings, or agreements between private individuals, grants and donations or poetical effusions. There are even some instances of the incision of larger literary works; large fragments of plays by the Cāhamāna king Vigraha IV, and by his poet-laureate Somadeva, have been found at Ajmīr[529], and a large Jaina Sthalapurāṇa in a number of Sargas, impressions of which (unpublished) I owe to Führer and G. H. Ojha, exists in Bijholli (Rājputāna).

Bricks, showing single or a few letters, have been known for some time, as specimens have been found by Cunningham[530], Führer and others in various parts of India, and even in Burma. But recently a set has been discovered in the North-West Provinces by Hoey, on which Budhhist Sūtras are inscribed, the characters having apparently been scratched on the moist clay, before it was baked[531].

H.—*Paper.*

During the period to which this work refers, paper was hardly known or at least little used in India, as its introduction is only due to the Muhammadans. Rājendralāl Mitra[532], however, asserts that a "letter-writer" by king Bhoja of Dhārā proves its use in Mālva during the 11th century. The oldest paper MS. in Gujarāt is said to date from A.D. 1223-24[533].

Paper MSS. dated Vikrama-Saṃvat 1384 and 1394 (A.D. 1327-28 and 1337-38), the leaves of which are cut according to the size of palm-leaves, have been discovered by Peterson at Aṇbilvāḍ Pāṭan[534]. It is very doubtful if any of the ancient MSS. from Kashgar, which are written on a peculiar paper, covered with a layer of gypsum, are of Indian origin ; Hoernle believes that all of them were written in Central Asia[535].

I.—*Ink.*

The oldest undoubtedly Indian term for ink is *maṣi* or *maṣī* freequently spolt *masi* or *masī*. The word, which occurs as a *varia lectio* already in a Gṛhyasūtra, is derived from the verb *maṣ* (*hiṃsāyām*), and means etymologically "powder[536]." Further, it serves to denote several kinds of pulverised charcoal, which were mixed with water, gum, sugar and so forth, and used for the preparation of ink[537]. Burnell is mistaken when he asserts that in Classical Sanskrit Literature *maṣī*, "ink" occurs only in the late works ; it was known to Bāṇa (about A. D. 620) and to his predecessor Subandhu[538].

Benfey, Hincks and Weber have derived *melā*, another word for "ink", for the Greek μέλας. But it is, no doubt, the feminine (viz., *maṣī*) of the common Prākṛt adjective *maīla*, "dirty, black" which cannot have been borrowed from the Greeks[539]. *Melā*, likewise, was known to Subandhu, who uses the denominative *melānandāyate*, "becomes an inkstand"[540]. The Koṣas offer for "inkstand" also *melāmandā*, *melāndhu*, *melāndhukā* and *maṣimaṇi*, and the Purāṇas *maṣīpātra*, *maṣībhāṇḍa* and *maṣīkūpikā*[541].

The statements of Nearchos and Q. Curtius (see above, page 20) according to which the Hindus wrote on cotton cloth and on the inner bark of trees, i.e. Bhūrja, make it very probable that they used ink already in the 4th century B.C. To the same conclusion points the fact that in some letters of the Aśoka edicts dots are occasionally substituted for loops[542]. The oldest specimen of writing with ink, on the relic-vase of the Stūpa [92] of Andher (see above, page 20) is certainly not later than the 2nd century B. C. From the first centuries A. D. dates the Kharoṣṭhī Dhammapada from Khotan, as well as the twists of Bhūrja and the stone vessels with Kharoṣṭhī letters in ink from the Stūpas of Afghanistan. Somewhat later are the ancient Bhūrja and palm-leaf MSS. with Brāhma characters. Painted inscriptions occur still in the caves of Ajaṇṭā[543].

Coloured ink, which in later times the Jainas especially have used extensively for their MSS[544], is mentioned also in Brahmanical works, e.g., in the sections of the Purāṇas on the donation of MSS[545]. Besides chalk (see above, § 34, B), red lead or minium (*hiṅgula*) was used, already in ancient times, as a substitute for ink[546].

J.—*Pens, pencils, &c.*

The general name of "an instrument for writing" is *lekhanī*, which of course includes the *stilus*, pencils, brushes, reed and wooden pens, and is found already in the epics[547].

The *varṇaka*, mentioned in the *Lalitavistara*, no doubt refers to the little stick without a slit, with which the school-boys still draw the letters on the writing board (see above, page 20). The Koṣas offer the variant *varṇikā*. The *varṇavartikā*, which occurs in the passage of the *Daśakumāracarita* referred to above (see page 113 above, and note 499), must be a brush or coloured pencil, as, according to other passages, the *vartikā* was used for drawing or painting[548]. *Tūlī* or *tūlikā* probably denoted originally "a brush", though it is explained also by the modern *saḷaī*, "graver", a *stilus.*[549]

The most usual name of the reed pen is the word *kalama*, κάλαμος, Calamus, which occurs in all eastern languages; the rarer indigenous Indian name is *iṣīkā* or *īṣikā* literally "reed"[550]. Pieces of reed, bamboo or wood, cut after the manner of our pens, are used in all parts of India where the use of ink prevails,[551] and all the existing ancient MSS. on palm-leaves and Bhūrja probably have been written with such pens[552]. The Sanskrit name of the *stilus* used in Southern India is *śalākā*, in Marāṭhi *saḷaī*.

Regarding the now very generally used "ruler", a piece of wood or cardboard with strings fixed at equal distances, and regarding its probable predecessors, see *Anecdota Oxoniensia, Aryan Series*, 1. 3, 66, and *Anzeiger d. W. Akademie*, 1897 No. VIII, where photographs of two specimens have been given. According to a letter from C. Klemm (April 21, 1897), the Ethnological Museum of Berlin possesses two specimens, one from Calcutta with the inscription *nivedanapattra* and one from Madras called *kiḍugu*.

§38.—THE PRESERVATION OF MANUSCRIPTS AND COPPER-PLATES, AND THE TREATMENT OF LETTERS.

A.—*Manuscripts and Libraries.*

[93] Wooden covers, cut according to the size of the sheets, were placed on the Bhūrja and palm-leaves, which had been drawn on strings, and this is still the custom even with the paper MSS[553]. In Southern India the covers are mostly pierced by holes, through which the long strings are passed. The latter are wound round the covers and knotted. This procedure was usual already in early times[554] and was observed in the case of the old palm-leaf MSS. from Western and Northern India. But in Nepāl the covers of particularly valuable MSS. sometimes are made of embossed metal; the MSS. (*pustaka*) which have been prepared in this manner are usually wrapped up in dyed or even embroidered cloth. Only in the Jaina libraries the palm-leaf MSS. sometimes are kept in small sacks of white cotton cloth, which again are fitted into small boxes of white metal. The collections of MSS., which, frequently are catalogued, and occasionally, in monasteries and in royal courts, are placed under librarians, generally are preserved in boxes of wood or cardboard. Only in Kashmīr, where in accordance with Muhammadan usage the MSS. are bound in leather, they are put on shelves, like our books.

The ancient Indian name of a library, *bhāratībhāṇḍāgāra*, "treasury of the goddess of speech", occurs frequently in Jaina works; more rarely the modern synonym, *sarasvatī-bhāṇḍāgāra*. Such Bhāṇḍāgāras were, and still are, found in the temples[555], colleges (*vidyāmaṭha*), monasteries (*maṭha, upāśraya, vihāra, saṃghārāma*)[556], at the courts of princes and in the houses of many private individuals. The Purāṇas declare it to be the sacred duty of the wealthy to make donations of books to temples and so forth[557]. Equally, such donations are obligatory on the Jaina and Bauddha laymen, and the Praśastis of the old MSS. prove that the obligation was fulfilled in the most liberal manner. A famous royal library of the middle ages was that of king Bhoja of Dhārā (11th century); on the conquest of Mālva, about A. D. 1140, Siddharāja-Jayasiṃha transferred it to Aṇhilvāḍ[558]; there it seems to have been amalgamated with the court library of the Calukyas which is repeatedly mentioned in works of the 13th century. The *bhāratībhāṇḍāgāra* of the Calukya Vīsaladeva or Viśvamalla (A. D. 1242-1262) furnished, according to an unpublished Praśasti, the copy of the Naiṣadhīya, on which Vidyādhara wrote the first commentary of the poem, and the MS. of the *Kāmasūtra*, according to which Yaśodhara composed his *Jayamañjalāṭīkā*[559]. One of the manuscripts of the *Rāmāyaṇa* in the library of the University of Bonn has been derived from a copy of Vīsaladeva's collection[560].

The search for Sanskrit MSS., instituted by the Government of India, has shown that there are still a good many royal libraries in India, and the catalogues of several, such as those of Alwar, Bīkāner, Jammu, Mysore, and Tanjore, has been published. The documents, published in connection with the search, have brought to light also a surprisingly large number of private libraries. And various notes in older Sanskrit works make it apparent that considerable private libraries existed in early times. Thus, Bāṇa (about A. D. 620) tells us that he kept a particular reader (*pustaka-vācaka*), whose manipulation of the MS. of the Vāyupurāṇa he describes in his *Harṣacarita*[561]. *Burnell's* remarks[562], regarding the bad treatment of the MSS. by the Brahmans, do not hold good for the whole of India, perhaps not even for the whole of Southern India. In Gujarāt, Rājputāna and the Marāṭhā country, as well as in Northern and Central India, I have seen, besides some ill-kept collections, very carefully preserved libraries in the possession of Brahmans and Jaina monks. The treatment of the books usually depends only upon the worldly circumstances of the owner[563].

B.—*Copper-plates.*

The way in which private individuals kept their copper-plate grants, seems to have been very peculiar. In many places, e.g., in the ruins of Valabhi, near the modern Valā, they have been found immured in the walls or even in the foundations of the houses of the owners. In many other cases [94] the grants have turned up in those fields to the donation of which they refer, often hidden in small *caches* constructed of bricks.

The finders or poor owners often sell or pledge plates to the Vāṇiās, and this custom explains why they frequently come into the hands of European collectors at great distances from the places of issue. The originals of the grants, according to which the plates were prepared, probably remained in the royal Daftar, the keeper of which, the *akṣapaṭalika*, is frequently mentioned[564].

C.—*The treatment of letters.*

The Jātakas already mention the custom of wrapping up important letters in white cloth and sealing the packet[565]. At present, official or ceremonial letters often are sent in bags of silk or brocade. In the case of ordinary letters on palm-leaves, the proceeding is simpler; the leaves are folded, their ends are split and joined, and the whole is tied up with a thread[566]. It is probable that letters on Bhūrja were treated similarly.

According to Bāṇa[567], the postal runner (*dīrghādhvaga, lekhahāraka*) tied each separately to a strip of cloth and wound this round his head.

§ 39.—WRITERS, ENGRAVERS AND STONE-MASONS.

. Though the oldest Indian alphabet is a creation of the Brahmanical schoolmen (see above, page 33), and though the instruction in writing has remained even in recent times chiefly in the hands of Brahmans, there are yet indications that professional writers, and perhaps even castes of professional writers, existed already at an early period. The oldest name of these men is *lekhaka*, used in the Canon of the Southern Buddhists and the epics (see above, page 19). In the Sāñcī inscription, Stūpa I, No. 143[568], it is clearly used to designate the profession of the donor ; it may, however, be doubted if it means, as I have translated it, "copyist of MSS." or "writer, clerk." In various later inscriptions[569], *lekhaka* undoubtedly denotes the person who prepared the documents to be incised on copper or stone. But in the present day a *lekhak* is always a man who copies MSS., and this profession is usually the resource of poor Brahmans, and sometimes of worn-out clerks (*Kāyasths, Kārkūns*). Such men were, and are, employed also by the Jainas. But many Jaina MSS. have been copied, as their Praśastis show, by monks or novices, and even by nuns. Similarly, we find, among the copyists of the Bauddha MSS. from Nepāl, Bhikṣus, Vajrācāryas and so forth[570].

Another name of the professional writers, which was used already in the 4th century B. C., is the word *lipikara* or *libikara*, discussed above, page 20. In the Koṣas [571] it is given as a synonym of *lekhaka*, and in the *Vāsavadattā*[572] it means "writer" in general. Aśoka uses it in the 14th rock edict as a designation of his clerks. Similarly, Paḍa, who copied the Śiddāpura edicts, calls himself *lipikara*, and in the Sāñcī inscription, Stūpa I, No. 49[573], the donor Subāhita-Gotiputa takes the higher title *rājalipikara*, "a wrtier of the king". In the earlier times, *lipikara* probably was an equivalent for "clerk".

In a number of Valabhī inscriptions of the 7th and 8th centuries, the writer of the documents, who is usually "the minister for alliances and war" (*sandhivigrahādhikṛta*), receives the title *divirapati* or *divīrapati*, and the simple word *divira* occurs even earlier in a Central-Indian inscription of A.D. 521-22[574]. *Divira* or *divīra* is the Persian *debīr*, "writer," which probably became domesticated in Western India during the time of the Sassanians, when [95] the trade and intercourse between Persia and India was greatly developed. *Divira* appears also in the Rājataraṅginī, and in other Kashmirian works of the 11th and 12th centuries. Kṣemendra's *Lokaprakāśa* mentions even various sub-divisions, *gañjadivira*, "bazaar-writers," *grāma-divira*, "village-writers," *nagara-divira*, "town-writers," and *khavāsadivira* (?)[575].

The two works just mentioned, as well as other contemporaneous ones, designate the writers also by the term *kāyastha*, which first occurs in the *Yājñavalkya-Smṛti* 1, 335, and even at present is common in Northern and Eastern India. The Kāyasthas, however, form a strictly separate caste, which, though according to the Brahmanical account it is *mixed with Śūdra blood, yet claims a high rank*[576], and in reality frequently has possessed a great political influence. In the inscriptions, the Kāyasthas occur since the 8th century, first in the Kaṇasva inscription of A. D. 738-39 from Rājputāna[577].

Other designations of the writers in the inscriptions are *karaṇa*[578], *karaṇika*[579] or more rarely *karaṇin*[580], *śāsanika*[581] and *dharmalekhin*[582]. *Karaṇa* is perhaps only a synonym of *kāyastha*[583], as the law-books mention the Karaṇas as one of the mixed castes. The other terms, among which *karaṇika* has to be rendered, according to Kielhorn, by "writer of legal documents (*karaṇa*)," appear to be merely official titles without any reference to caste. The development of the Indian alphabets, and the invention of new forms of the letters, no doubt is due partly to the Brahmans and the Jaina and Bauddha monks, but much more to the professional writers and to the writer castes. The opinion, according to which the modifications have been introduced by the stone-masons and the engravers of the copper-plates, is less probable, because these persons were not suited for such work by their education and their occupation[584].

As the remarks at the end of many inscriptions show, it was customary to make over a Praśasti or Kāvya, which was to be incised on stone, to a professional writer, who prepared a fair copy, and to set the mason (*sūtradhāra*, *śilākūṭa*, *rūpakāra*, *śilpin*) to work according to the latter[585]. This custom was observed also in a case which fell under my personal observation. The mason received a sheet with the fair copy of the document (the Praśasti of a temple) exactly of the size of a stone on which it was to be incised. He first drew the letters on the stone under the supervision of a Pandit, and then incised them. In some exceptional cases, the authors of the poems assert that they have done the work of the masons[586], and in others the masons say that they have made the fair copies of the inscriptions[587].

The statements regarding the preparation of the copper-plate Śāsanas are less accurate and explicit. Usually, the inscriptions mention only the person who drew up or wrote the document. And they mostly name as such either a high official (*amātya*, *sāndhivigrahika*, *rahasika*) or a general (*senāpati*, *balādhikṛta*). Occasionally, they assert that the drafting was done by a stone-mason, a *sūtradhāra*[588] or *tvaṣṭā*[589], who, however, in reality merely engraved the grant. According to Kalhaṇa[590], the Kashmirian kings kept a special official for this work; he bore the title *paṭṭopādhyāya*, "the teacher (charged with the preparation) of title-deeds," and belonged to the *akṣapaṭala* office, which Stein believes to be the Accountant-General's Office, while I take it to be the Record-Office or Court of Rolls (Daftar).

The Śāsanas name only rarely, and in late times, the person by whom the plates were engraved (*utkīrṇa*, *unmīlita*). The engravers mentioned are various artisans, a *pītalakāra*, *lohakāra* or *ayaskāra*[591], i. e., the Kansār or coppersmith of the present day, a *sūtradhāra*[592], "stone-mason," a *hemakāra* or *sunara*[593] (probably equivalent to *soṇāra*), "goldsmith," a *śilpin*[594] or *vijñānika*[595], "an artisan." In the Kaliṅga Śāsanas, we find in their stead an *akṣaśālin*, *ākṣaśālika*, *akhasālin*, or *akhasāle*[596], whereby a member of the goldsmith caste, now called Aksāle[597], is meant.

Finally, the existence of manuals for clerks and writers must be mentioned. We still possess several works of this kind, among which the *Lekhapañcāśikā* gives the rules for drafting not only private letters, but also land-grants and the treaties between kings, while a section of Kṣemendra-Vyāsadāsa's *Lokaprakāśa* shows how the various kinds of bonds, bills of exchange (*huṇḍī*) and so forth ought to be done[598].

CONCLUDING REMARKS

[96] Dr. W. Cartellieri, whose name appears at the bottom of the Plates, is responsible for the drawing and tracing of the letters for which no cuttings from facsimiles were available, as well as for the arrangement and the *retouche* of the cuttings, except in the case of plates VII-IX, which were finished by a young lithographer, Mr. Böhm. I have also to acknowledge Dr. Cartellieri's assistance in the selection of the signs, which in a few cases he has made independently, and in others has been influenced by a revision of my proposals; and I have to thank him for various ingenious remarks on the Indian alphabets, as well as for a collection of the variants in the Aśoka edicts.

If I have been able to illustrate most of the Indian alphabets by cuttings from facsimiles, insted of by hand-drawn signs, I owe this chiefly to my friend Dr. J. Burgess, who during many years has kindly furnished me with separate copies of his excellent reproductions of Indian inscriptions. Some other donors of facsimiles or photographers, Dr. E. Hultzsch, Professor E. Leumann, and Dr. S. von Oldenberg, have already been mentioned in the notes.

ABBREVIATIONS

AR (or) As. Res.	*Asiatic Researches.*
B. ASRSI	Burgess, *Archaeological Survey Reports, Southern India.*
B. ASRWI	Burgess, *Archaeological Survey Reports, Western India.*
B. ESIP	Burnell, *Elements of South-Indian Paleography*, 2nd. ed.
B. IS	Bühler, *Indian Studies.*
BOR	Babylonian and Oriental Records.
BRW	Böthlingk and Roth, *Sanskrit-Wörterbuch.*
BW	Böthlingk, *Sanskrit-Wörterbuch in kürzerer Fassung.*
C. ASR	Cunningham, *Archaeological Survey Reports.*
C. CAI	Cunningham, *Coins of Ancient India.*
C. CIS	Cunningham, *Coins of the Indo-Scythians.*
C. CMI	Cunningham, *Coins of Mediæval India.*
C. IA (CII. 1)	Cunningham, *Inscriptions of Aśoka, (Corpus Inscriptionum Indicarum*, Vol. I*).*
C. MG	Cunningham, *Mohābodhi-Gayā ; i.e, Mahābodhi or the Great Buddhist Temple under the Bodhi Tree at Buddha-Gayā.*
D. WA	*Denkschriften der Wiener Akademie.*
EI	*Epigraphia Indica.*
Ep. Carn.	*Epigraphia Carnatica*, ed. Rice.
E. TSA	Euting, *Tabula Scripturae Aramaicae.*
F. GI (CII. 3)	Fleet, *Gupta Inscriptions*, (*Corpus Inscriptionum Indicarum* Vol III).
IA	*Indian Antiquary.*
IP	*Inscriptions de Piyadasi*, Senart.
J.	*The Jātaka*, ed. Fausböll.
JA	*Journal Asiatique.*
J. AOS	*Journal, American Oriental Society.*
J. ASB	*Journal, Asiatic Society of Bengal.*
J. BBRAS	*Journal, Bombay Branch of the Royal Asiatic Society.*
J. RAS	*Journal, Royal Asiatic Society.*
L. IA	Lassen, *Indische Altertumskunde*, 2nd. ed.
M. Bh	*Mahābhāṣya*, ed. Kielhorn.
M. M. HASL	Max Muller, *History of Ancient Sanskrit Literature.*
M. M. RV	Max Muller *Ṛgveda-Saṃhitā* with *Sāyaṇa's Commentary*, 2nd. ed.
P. IA	Prinsep's *Indian Antiquities*, ed. Thomas.
SBE	*Sacred Books of the East.*
SB. WA	*Sitzungsberichte der Wiener Akademie.*
SII	*South-Indian Inscriptions*, ed. Hultzsch.
S. IP	Senart, *Inscriptions de Piyadasi'.*
S. NEI	Senart, *Notes d, Epigraphie Indienne.*
W. AA	H. H. Wilson, *Ariana Antiqua.*
W. Ind. Str.	Weber, *Indische Streifen.*
W. IS	Weber, *Indische Studien.*
WZKM	*Winner Zeitschrift für die Kunde des Morgenlandes*, i.e., the Vienna Oriental Journal.
ZDMG	*Zeitschrift der Deutschen Morgenländischen Gesselschaft.*

FOOTNOTES
To
Bühler's Indian Paleography

1. B. IS. III. 2, 28-35 ; cf. *Anecdota Oxon., Aryan Series*, I, 3,67 ; B. ESIP. 6 ; A. Ludwig, *Yavanāni ; Sitz. Ber. Böhm. Ges. d. Wiss.* 1893, IX., and the works quoted by Dr. Burnell.

2. SBE. 28, 58f.

3. SBE. 28,804.

4. Siyuki 1,77 (Beal).

5. W. IS. 16,280,399.

6. IA. 6,366, Pl.

7. Moor, *Hindu Pantheon*, Pl. 8, 4 ; AR. 1,248.

8. BOR. 1,59.

9. Sansk. text, 148 (Bibl. Ind.), and the Chinese translation of A. D. 808.

10. *India* 1,171 (Sachau).

11. *loc. cit.* ; a third list, with about 80 mostly very corrupt names, in the *Mahāvastu* 1, 185 (Senart).

12. BOR. 1, 59.

13. Cf. WZKM. 9,66, and B. IS. III, 2,118 f.

14. EI. 2,328, ff.

15. *Mahābhāṣya* 2,290 (Kielhorn).

16. Herodotus, VII, 65,66.

17. B. V. Head, *Cat. of Greek Coins : Attica*, p. XXXI. f., pp. 25-27.

18. W. IS. 16,481.

19. Sansk. Text (Bibl. Ind.) 145 ; Leumann, 127.

20. B. IS. III, 2,80.

21. Siyuki 1,78 (Beal) ; St. Julien, *Mémoires des pèlerins Bouddhiques* 1,72, and note.

22. Siyuki 1,77.

23. B. IS. III, 2,81.

24. B. IS. III, 2,83.

25. B. IS. III, 2, 5f. ; M. M. HASL. 497 ff ; L. IA. 2,1,1008 ff. ; B.ESIP. 1, ff. ; Weber, *Ind. Streifen* 8,848f.

26. SBE. 14, xvii ff.

27. M. M. ṚV. 4. 72.

28. M. M. HASL 521 ff ; Goldstücker, *Mānava Kalpa Sūtra*, Intr. 14 ff. ; W. IS. 5,16 ff. ; M.M. ṚV. 4. 72 ff.

29. Whitney, *Or. and Ling. St.* 82 ; J.AOS. 6,568 ; Benfey, ZDMG. 11,847 ; Böthlingk, *Bull. Pet. Akad.* 1859, 847 ; Pischel and Geldner, *Vedische Studien*, 1, XXIII, XXVI ; J. Dahlmann, *Das Mahābh.* 185 ; against these views, M. M. ṚV. 4. *loc. cit.* ; Letter in Takakusu's trans. of Itsing, X ff. ; W. IS. 5, *loc. cit.*

30. See below, § 5.

31. Jacobi, *Das Rām.* 8 ff.

32. Kirste in B. IS. II. 27 ff.

33. See Below under B.

34. B. IS. III, 2, 7-16 ; Oldenberg, SBE. 18, xxxii ff. ; D' Alwis, *Introd. to Kaccāyana's Gram:* xxvi f., cxv f., 72-103 ; Weber, *Ind. Streifen* 2,387 ff.

35. B. IS. III, 2,7 f.

36. B. IS. III, 2, 8f., 120.

37. B. IS. III, 2, 10, 18.

38. B. IS. III, 2, 10f.

39. B. IS. III, 2, 10, 120.

40. B. IS. III, 2, 120.

41. B. IS. III, 2, 16.

42. B. IS. III, 2, 18ff.

43. Sansk. Text, 148 ; (cf. BOR. 1, 59.)

44. *India* 1, 182 (Sachau).

45. *Sixth Oriental Congress*, 8, 2, 154.

46. B. IS. III, 2, 16 ff ; Oldenberg, *Vinayapiṭaka* 1, xxxiv ff. ; M. Müller, SBE. 10, xxix ff.

47. Cunningham, *Bhilsa Topes*, p. 249, pl. 80, 6.

48. B. IS. III, 21f. ; Westergaard, *Zwei Abhandl.* 88.

49. Strabo, XV, 717.

50. *Hist. Alex.* VIII, 9 ; cf. C. Müller, *Fragm. Hist. Graec.* 2, 421.

51. C. Müller, *op. cit.* 480.

52. *Frag.* 27 ; C. Müller, *op. cit.*, 421 ; Schwanbeck, Megasthenes, p. 50, n. 48 ; M. M. HASL. 515 ; B. ESIP. 1 ; L. IA. II, 2, 724 ; Weber, *Ind. Skizzen* 181 f.

53. B. IS. III, 2, 65-58.

54. B. ASRWI. No. 10, 39, plate.

55. C. MG. pl. 10, 2.

56. See below § 16, C.

57. See below, § 16, B.

58. See below, § 4 A.

59. See below § 16, C.

60. See below § 16, C.

61. See below § 16, D.

62. B. ASRSI. 1, 115.

63. C. CAI. pl. 11, 18, and plate II, col. I, of this work.

64. If according to C. CMI, 27, as Mr. A. V. Smith points out to me, some coins of Mihirakula show inscriptions running from the right to the left, this peculiarity must be ascribed to Sassanian influence.

65. Plate II, cols. XIII—XV.

66. C. CAI. 88 f.

67. C. CAI, pl. 2, 8.

68. WZKM. 9, 65 ; B. IS. III, 2, 118.

69. See below § 8

70. See below § 9, B, 4.

71. B. IS. III, 2, 58-82.

72. R. N. Cust, *Ling. and Or. Essays*, 2nd. Ser., 27-52.

73. C. IA (CII. 1), 51 ff.

74. ZDMG. 10, 389 ff. ; *Ind. Skizzen* 125 ff.

75. ZDMG. 31, 598 ff

76. *The Alphabet*, 2, 314 ff. ; restated with some modifications by F. Müller *Mélanges Harlez* 212 ff.

77. JA. 1885, 268 ff. ; *Revue Sem*. 1895, 228 ff.

78. Mordtmann and D. H. Müller, *Sab. Denkmäler* (in DWA. *Phil Hist. Cl.* 31), p. 108 f.

79. D. H. Müller, *Denkmäler aus Arabien* (DWA. *Phil. Hist. Cl.* 37), p. 15 ff.

80. Cf. Beruni's *India*, 1. 172 (Sachau).

81. AR. 2, plate at p. 400.

82. M. M. HASL 505 ff.

83. See below, § 24, B. 8 : pl IV, 30, XII, XIV ; pl. VII, 30, XII, XX, XXI.

84. B. IS. III, 2, 68-91.

85. According to Benfey, *Indien* 254, the Semitic alphabet came to India from Phoenicia ; accoring to A. Weber, *Ind. Skizzen* 137, either from Phoenicia or from Babylonia.

86. No. 339, Fausböll, 3, 126 ; cf. also Fick, *Die Sociale Gliederung in nordöstl. Indien*, 178 f.

87. SBE. 2, 228 ; 14, 146, 200, 217 ; cf. *Manu* 8, 158 ; 8, 157, 406, and Dahlmann, *Das Mahābhārata*, 176 ff.

88. B. IS. III, 2, 16 ff.

89. Ṛ̥V. 1. 116. 5 ; cf. Oldenberg, *Vedische Religion*, 214.

90. Oldenberg, *op. cit.* 276.

91. J. ASB. 57, 41 f.

92. Cf. Westergaard, *Zwei Abhandlungen* 87 ff.

93. Ṛ̥V. 7.103. 5 ; cf M. M. HASL. 506.

94. cf. Wackernagel, *Altind. Grammatik* 1, lvii.

95. Regarding the name, see §1 above, and B. IS. III, 2, 118 f,

96. P. IA. 1, 178-185 ; 2, 128-148 ; W.AA. 242 ff. ; J. ASB. 28, 714 . C. ASR 1, viii ; *Centenary Review* 2, 69-81 ; C. CIS. 8 ff ; Senart, IP. 1, 22 ff. ; ZDMG. 48, 129 ff.

97. See the next paragraph.

98. B. IS. III, 2, 47-58 ; C. ASR. 2, 82 ff., pl. 59, 63 ; 5, 1 ff., pl. 16, 28 ; W.AA, 55ff ; C. CAI. 31 ff.

99. B IS. III, 2, *loc. cit.* ; The question of the lower limit of the use of the Kharoṣṭhi is difficult on account of the uncertainty regarding the date of Kaniṣka and his two successors, all of whom S. Lévi now places in the 1st. Cent. A D. (JA. 1897, 1, 1 ff.). The limit given above is based on the assumption that Kaniṣka's dates refer to the śaka era or to the 4th. Cent. of the Seleucidan era. I still make use of it, not because I consider it to be unassailable, but for the reasons stated in WZKM., 1, 169. The letters in the inscriptions of Saṃvat 200 and 276 or 286 (Hashtnagar image) look more ancient than those of the Kuṣāna inscriptions. According to a communication from Dr. Th. Bloch, Prof. Hoernle has read dates of the 4th. century of the same unknown Saṃvat on recently found Gandhāra sculptures.

100. W.AA. pl. 3 at p. 54, No. 11 ; similar twists have been found in other Stupas, see *op. cit.* 60, 84, 94, 106 ; but the fragments in the British Museum said to belong to them, show no letters.

101. See Oldenberg, *Predvaritelnae zamjetkao Buddhiiskoi rukopisi, napisannoi pismenami Kharoṣṭhi*, St. Petersburg, 1897, and Senart, *Acad. des Inscrs, Comptes rendus*, 1897, 251 ff.

102. IA. 10, 325.

103. W.AA. 111.

104. B. IS. III, 2, 97 f.

105. B. IS. III, 2, 92 ff.

106. P. IA. 2, 144 ff. ; regarding Kharoṣṭhi legends on late coins running from left to right, see Proc. J. ASB. 1895, 88 f.

107. I. Taylor, *The Alphabet*, 2, 261 f. ; C. Cai. 38.

108. J. RAS. 1895, 865 ff.

109. Clermont-Ganneau, *Revue Archéologique*, 1878-79 ; Ph. Berger, *Hist. de l'Ecrit. dans l'Antiquité*, 214, 218 ff.

110. Weber. *Ind. Skizzen*, 144 f. ; E. Thomas, P. IA. 2, 146 ; C. CAI. 33 ; and below § 9, B, 4.

111. J. Halévy, JA. 1885, 2, 243-261, believes that Kharoṣṭhi to have been derived about B. C. 330 from 16 signs of the Papyri and of a Cicilian coin, and, *Revue Sémitique*, 1895, 372 ff., from the script of the Papyri and of the *ostraka* from Egypt.

112. B. IS. III, 2, 99 ff. : cf. the more or less differing attempts of E. Thomas, P. IA. 2, 147 ; I. Taylor, *The Alphabet*, 2, plate at p. 286 ff. ; J. Halévy, JA. 1885, 2,252 ff., *Revue Sémitique*, 1895, 372 ff.

113. *Preparation of* Plate I :—

1-37, Cols. I-V, and 38, 39, Cols. I-XIII, traced by Dr. Dedekind from Dr. Burgess' impressions of the Aśoka edicts of Shāhbāzgarhī and Mansehra, and reduced to photography.

1-87, Cols. VI, VII, and 88, 89, Col. XIV, drawn by Dr. W. Cartellieri from P. Gardner's autotypes of Indo-Grecian coins.

1-87, Cols, VIII, IX, and 22-25, Col. XIII, traced from Dr. Burgess' impressions of the Mathurā lion capital and the photograph of the Taxila copper- plate of which a collotype has since then been published in EI. 4, 56 (10 & 14, Col, VIII, and 25, Col. XIII).

1-87, Cols. X-XII, and 81-87, Col. XIII, traced or drawn according to Dr. Hoernle's facsimile of the Sue Bihār inscription, supplemented by some signs from the Manikyāla stone and gelatine copies of the Wardak and Bimāran vases by Oldenberg.

26-80, Col. XIII drawn according to P. Gardner's autotypes of the older Kuṣāna coins.

1-20, Cols. XIII, XIV, numerals drawn according to the impressions and facsimiles of the Aśoka edicts and later inscriptions.

Older tables of the Kharoṣṭhī alphabet in P. IS. 2, 166, pl. 11; W. AA. 262; C. IA (CII. 1), pl. 27; P. Gardner, *Cat. I. C. Br. Mus.* p. lxx. f.; Von Sallet, *Nachfolger Alex. d. Gr.* (end); G. H. Ojha, *The Ind. Pal.* pl. 26.

114. Other facsimiles of Kharoṣṭhī inscriptions :— (1) Aśoka edicts in J. RAS. 1850, 158; C. IA (CII. 1), pl. 1, 2; C. ASR. 5, pl. 5; S. IP. 1 (end); IA. 10, 107; (2) Later inscriptions in P. IA. 1, 96 (pl. 6), 144 (pl. 9) 162 (pl 18); W. AA. 54 (pl. 2), 262; C. ASR. 2,124, (pl. 59), 160 (pl. 68); 5, (pl. 16), 28; J. RAS. 1868, 222 (pl. 8), 238 (pl. 4), 250 (pl. 9), 256 (pl. 10), and 1877, 144; J. ASB. 23, 57; 81, 176, 582; 89, 65; IA. 18, 257; S. NEI. Nos. 8 (JA. 1890, 1, pl. 1, No. 2) and 5 (JA. 1894, II, pl 5, Nos. 84, 86): all useless except the last three.

115. Cf. ZDMG. 48, 128 ff, 274 ff.

116. O. Franke, *Nachr. Gott. Ges. d. Wiss.*, 1895, 540, and ZDMG. 50, 608, proposes to read *fa* and *fi* for the signs which I read *spa* and *spi*.

117. The MS. of the Dhammapada shows this same sign both in the terminations of the absolutives in *tva* (*tvā*) and in *atma* (*ātman*), and thus further confirms the explanation proposed.

118. Regarding the characters on the Indo-Grecian coins, see WZKM. 8, 198 f.; regarding the script of the Śaka and Kuṣāna inscriptions, see J. RAS. 1868, 289, pl. 4 (where, however, in I. 1 the second *ch* must be deleted, in 1. 2 *sa* must be substituted for *si*, and *ṭha* for *ṭṭ* and in 1. 8 *rya* for *rs*, and the signs for *sy* in 1. 4 are doubtful), and O. Franke, ZDMG. 50, 602 ff.

119. O. Franke, *op. cit.*, 604, proposes to read this *ssa*; but cf. 85, XIII, which can be only *ṣya*.

120. C. ASR. 1, XII.

121. C. ASR. 1, VIII-XI; J. ASB. 6, 460 ff.

122. J. ASB. 6, 228; P. IA. 2, 40 (pl. 89).

123. B. IS. III. 2, 81.

124. C. IA (CII. 1), pl. 27.

125. S. IP. 1, 86.

126. J. ASB. 56, 74.

127. EI. 2, 868.

128. J. BBRAS. 10 xxiii.

129. See above § 2, B (end).

130. B. IS. III. 2, 40-48.

131. See above § 7.

132. According to an impression and a photograph kindly sent by Mr. L. Rice.

133. B. ASRWI. 4, pl. 45 and 52; 5, pl. 51.

134. EI. 2, 242; B. ASRWI. 4, pl. 52 and 54.

135. EI. 1, 871 ff.; 2, 195 ff

136. B. ASRWI. 2, pl. 14; 5, pl. 51.

137. B. IS. III, 2, 48, note 8.

138. C. IA (CII. 1), pl. 14.

139. C. IA (CII. 1) pl. 15.

140. B. ASRSI. 1, 128, note 45; 129, note 88.

141, S. IP. 1, 88 ff; B. ESIP. 2. note 1.

142. *Preparation of the Plates :*

PLATE II

Col. I.: drawn according to a cast of the Eraṇ coin; cf. C. CAI. pl. II, No. 18; *A* from Patnā seal, C. ASR. 15, pl. 2.

Cols II, III: cuttings from facsimile of Kālsi, EI. 2, 447 ff.

Cols. IV, V: cuttings from facsimile of Delhi-Sivālik, IA. 18, 806 ff.

Cols. VI, VII: cuttings from facsimiles of Jaugada. B. ASRSI. 1, pl. 67, 68, 69; 20, VI, from Radhia, EI. 2, 245 ff.; and 44, VII, drawn according to impression of Sahsarām.

Cols. VIII-X: cuttings from facsimiles of Girnār, EI. 2, 447 ff.; 84, *ra*, between VII, VIII, from Rūpnāth, IA. 6, 156.

Cols. XI, XII: cuttings from facsimiles of Śiddāpura, EI. 8, 184 ff.; 44, XII, drawn according to impression of Bairāt, No. I; 45, XI, according to facsimile of Bharahut, ZDMG. 40. 58 ff.

Cols. XIII-XV: cuttings from facsimiles in EI. 2, 828 ff.

Col. XVI : traced from the facsimile in J.ASB. 56, 77, pl. 5 *a*.

Col. XVII : cuttings from facsimile in IA. 20, 361 ff.

Col. XVIII : traced from the facsimile in IA. 14, 139 ; 6 from facsimile of Bharahut, No. 98, ZDMG. 40, 58 ; and 41 from impression of Sāñcī Stupa I, No. 199.

Col. XIX : cuttings from facsimile in EI. 2, 240 ff.

Col. XX : cuttings from facsimiles in EI. 1, 396, No. 33, and EI. 2, 195, No. 1.

Cols. XXI, XXII : drawn according to Cunningham's photographs of the Hāthigumphā inscription of Khāravela.

Cols. XXIII, XXIV : cuttings from facsimiles in B. ASRWI. 5, pl. 51, Nos. 1, 2.

PLATE III

Cols. I, II : cuttings from facsimiles in EI. 2, 199, Nos. 2 & 5, and Cunningham's photograph of the era well inscription ; cf C. ASR. 20, pl. 5, No. 4.

Cols. III, V : cuttings from facsimiles of dated Kuṣāna inscriptions in EI. 1, 371 ff., and 2, 195 ff.

Col. VI : drawn according to facsimile in B. ASRWI. 2, 128, pl. 14.

Cols. VII-XVI : cuttings from facsimiles in B. ASRWI. 4, pl. 51, No. 19 ; pl. 52, Nos. 5, 9, 10, 18, 19 ; pl. 53, Nos. 13, 14 ; pl. 55, No. 22 ; pl. 48, No. 3 ; and tracings for Col. XV, from pl. 45, Nos. 5, 6, 11.

Cols. XVII, XVIII : cuttings from facsimiles in B. ASRWI. 1, pl. 62, 63.

Cols. XIX, XX : cuttings from facsimile in EI. 1, 1ff.

The background of all the cuttings and indistinct strokes have been touched up.

Scale of Plate II = 0·5 of the cuttings, except 13, II, and the signs in cols. VI, VII, XXIII, XXIV, which have the same size as in the facsimiles. Scale of Plate III = 0 7.

143. Cf. the following trustworthy facsimiles of Aśoka edicts not mentioned in Note 142 above :—B. ASRWI. 2, 98ff, Girnār ; IA. 13, 306 ff , Allahabad ; IA. 19, 122 ff., Delhi-Mirat, Allahabad Queen's edict, Allahabad Kosāmbī edict ; IA. 20, 361, Barābar caves ; IA. 22, 299, Sahsarām and Rupnāth ; EI 2, 245 ff. Mathiā and Rāmpurvā ; EI. 2, 366, Sāñcī ; JA. 1887, I, 498, Bairāt No I ; and the table of letters in B. ASRWI. 4, pl. 5.

144. J. RAS. 1895, 865 (pl).

145. C. CAI. pl. 2, 3 ; pl. 8, No. 1 ; pl. 10, No. 20.

146. C. MG. pl. 10, Nos. 2, 3.

147. Facsimiles in EI. 2, 366 ff.

148. C. ASR. 20, pl. 6.

149. Proc. ASB. May-June ,1894, pl. 1.

150. P. Gardner, *Cat., of Ind. Coins Br. Mus.*, pls.3,4.

151. Pt. in ZDMG. 40, 58 ff. ; EI. 2, 366 (facsimiles of Stupa I, Nos. 288, 377, 378).

152. Cf. plate in *Sixth Oriental Congress*, 3, 2, 142.

153. IA. 9, 121.

154. Cf. C. CAI. pl.4, Nos. 8-15 ; pl. 5 ; pl.8, No. 2 ff ; pl.9, Nos. 1-5 ; C. MG. pl. 10, No.4 ; B.ASRWI. 4,pl.44, Bhājā Nos. 1-6, Kondāne.

155. B.ASRWI. 4, pl.44, Pitalkhorā, Nos. 1-7 ; pl. 51, Nāsik, No.1.

156. Cf. B.IS. III,2,49ff.

157. E.Müller, *Anc. Inscrs. from Ceylon*, pl. 1.

158. Cf. M. De Zilva Wickramasinghe in J.RAS. 1895, 895 ff.

159. L.IA. II,2, 257 ff.

160. Von. Sallet, *Nachfolger Alex. d. Gr.*, 31 ; P. Gardner, *Cat. of Ind. Coins Br. Mus.*, XXVI.

161. Cf. B.IS. III, 2, 86ff.

162. The bracketed Arabic figures of section C correspond with those of plate II ; for § 16, C to E, cf. also B. IS. III, 2, 58 ff.

163. O. Franke *Gurupujākaumudī* 26, thinks that these groups should be read *tsā, tsī*, as they are written.

164. *Sixth Oriental Congress*, 3,2,149 ; cf. *Ostreichiesche Monatsschr für d. Or.*, 1884,231 ff.

165. *Sixth Oriental Congress*, 3,2,146 ; differently Bhāṇḍārkar, *Early Hist. of the Dekkan*, 2,84, who assigns Sātakaṇi to the period B.C. 40 to A.D. 16.

166. Cf. above § 16. (note 159).

167. *Sixth Oriental Congress*, 3,2, 179, Udayagiri inscription Nos. 3,4.

168. *Buddhist Cave Temples*, 246.

169. See above, § 10.

170. Cf. also facsimiles in C.ASR. 3, pl. 13, No.1 ; EI. 1,392, No.17 ; C.CAI. pl.3, No. 14 ; pl.6 ; pl.8, No.2 ff.

171. EI. 2, 201, No.12 ; 207, No.32 ; hollow wedges are found also in the facsimiles in C.ASR. 10, pl. 23, No.1 ; F.GI (CII.3), No.23.

172. In [illegible], C.ASR. 20, pl. 5, line 2.

173. IA. 10,213 ; C.CIS. 51 ff., 57 ; Bhāṇḍārkar, *Early Hist. of Dekkan*, 2,26, note 1, thinks that Kaniṣka ruled later ; but S. Lévi J.A. 1897, I,5ff. places even Vāsudeva in the first century A.D. ; the years 4 and 5 of this era occurs in EI. 2, 201, Nos. 11, 12 ; Kaniṣka, the year 7, EI. 1,391, No.19.

174. See facsimile, EI. 2,369.

175. Cf. my remarks, EI. 1,371 ff. ; 2,197.

176. Cf. the *tu* of plate II, 43, III.

177. EI.1, 339, No. 13.

178. Cf., for instance, *nah*, EI. 1, 382, No.3.

179. Bhāṇḍārkar, *Early Hist. of the Dekkan*, 2, 26ff; C.CMI. 3-5; Bhagvānlāl, J.RAS. 1890, 642; Bühler, *Die ind. Inschr. u.das. Altr. d. ind. Kunstpoesie*, 46ff.

180. C.CMI. pl.1; J.RAS. 1890, pl. at p. 688; B.ASRWI.2, pl.7.

181. *Cf.* facsimiles in B.ASRWI. 2, pl. 20; J.BBRAS. 8,231; *Sanskr. and Prākṛ. Inscrs. Bhaunagar*, pl.17-16 (unreliable).

182. See the plate cited in note 180 above.

183. Usabhadāta only in Kārle No. 19, B.ASRWI. 4, pl.51.

184. Thus Bhāṇḍārkar, *Early Hist. of the Dekkan*, 2,26, and Bhagvānlāl, J.RAS, 1890, 642; see also Bühler, *Die ind. Inschr. u. das. Alter der ind. Kunstpoesie*, 57 f.; while Cunningham CMI. 3f., refers Nahapāna's dates to the Mālva era of B.C. 57-56, and Oldenberg, IA. 10,227, places Nahapāna between A.D. 55 and 100.

185. Kārle, Nos. 1-14, B.ASRWI. 4, pl. 47, 48: Nāsik, No.4, *op.cit.*, pl. 51.

186. See the works quoted in note 184 above.

187. According to Bhagvānlāl's estimate, J.RAS. 1894, 657, "somewhat later than Nahapāna".

188. *Cf.* facsimiles in B.ASRWI. Vol. 4, pl.45, Kuḍā Nos. 12-18; pl. 46, Kuḍā Nos. 22-28; Mahād Nos. 1-4; Kol Nos. 3,5; pl.47, Bedsā Nos. 1-3; pl.48, Kārle Nos. 15-18; Śailarvāḍī No.19; Junnar No.1, 2; pl. 49-51, Junnar Nos. 4-34; pl. 52, Nāsik No. 6a; pl. 54, Junnar No. 32; Kānle No. 20; pl. 55, Nāsik Nos. 17-19, 21-24; and vol. 5, pl. 51, Kaṇheri Nos. 2-5, 10, 12-14.

189. B.ASRSI. 1, pl. 56, 57; pl. 58, Nos. 23-34, 37; pl. 59, Nos. 39, 43; pl.60, Nos. 44, 45, 47-50; pl. 61, Nos. 51-53, 55, 56; and the autotypes of the Andhra coins, C.CAI. pl. 12, and J.BBRAS. 13, pl.3.

190. B.ASRSI. 1, pl. 58, Nos. 35, 36; pl. 59, Nos. 38, 40-42; pl.60, No.46; pl. 61, No.54; pl.62.

191. *Cf.* facsimiles in IA. 9,100; EI. 1, 1ff.

192. *Preparation of Plates IV. V and VI*:—

PLATE IV

Cutting from facsimiles.

Cols. I, II, III: from F.GI (CII.3), pl.1.
Col. IV: from F.GI (CII.3), pl. 5.
Cols. V, VI: from F.GI (CII. 3), pl. 9,A.
Col. VII: from F.GI (CII.3). pl. 9, B.
Col. VIII: from plate at EI. 1, 288.
Col. IX; from F.GI. (CII.3), pl. 16.
Col. X: from F.GI (CII.3), pl. 22.
Cols. XI, XII: from F.GI (CII.3), pl. 30,B, and 31, A.B.
Cols. XIII, XIV: from F.GI (CII.3), pl. 41,A.
Cols. XV, XVI: from plate at EI. 1, 10.
Col. XVII: from plate at IA. 9, 172. Nos. 7, 8, 9.
Cols. XVIII, XIX: from F. GI (CII.3), pl. 28.
Col. XX: from plate at IA. 18, 284.
Col. XXI: from plate at IA. 15, 112.
Col. XXII: from plate at IA. 11, 108.
Col. XXIII: from plate at IA. 15, 140.

PLATE V

Col. I: from photolithograph of impressions of EI. 1, 97.

The other columns cut from facsimiles.

Col. II: from plate at EI. 1, 160.
Col. III: from plate at EI. 1, 242.
Col. IV: from plates at IA. 6, 65, and 11, 158.
Col. V: from unpublished facsimiles of IA. 18, 104.
Col. VI: from plate at IA. 17, 310.
Col. VII: from unpublishedf acsimiles of EI. 1, 162.
Col. VIII: from plate at EI. 1, 77.
Col. IX: from plate at EI. 2, 120.
Col. X: from plate at IA. 6, 50.
Col. XI: from plate at IA. 6, 192.
Col. XII: from plate at IA. 13, 11.
Col. XIII: from plate at EI. 1, 284.
Col. XIV: from plate at IA. 16, 205.
Col. XV: from plate at EI. 2, 297.
Col. XVI: from *Bhaunagar Sankr. and Prākṛ. Inscriptions*, pls. 40, 41.
Col. XVII; from plate at IA. 16, 22.
Col. XVIII: from plate at EI. 1, 308.
Col. XIX: from plate at EI. 2, 350.
Col. XX: from plate at IA. 18, 180.
Col. XXI: from plate at IA. 11, 71, 337.
Col. XXII: from plate at IA. 16, 254.
Col. XXIII: from plate at EI. 1, 81.

PLAET VI

Cuttings from facsimiles.

Cols. I, II, III, IV: from plates in Hoernle's Bower MS., parts 1, 2,

Cols. V, VI, VII, IX: from *Anecd. Oxon., Ar. Ser.*, 1, 3, pl. 6, cols. 1, 2, 3.

Col. VIII: from plate at *Vienna Oriental Congress, Aryan Section*, 127ff.

Col. IX; see above with cols. V, VI, and VII.

Col. X : from Bendall, *Cat. Buddh. MSS.*, pl. 2, 4, and *Berlin Oriental Congress, Indian Section*, pl. 2, 1.

Col. XI : from Bendall, *op. cit.*, pl. 3, 1.

Col. XII : from *Berlin Oriental Congress, Indian Section*, pl. 2, 2, 3.

Col. XIII : from Bendall, *op. cit.*, pl. 1. 3.

Col. XIV : from *Anecd. Oxon.*, *Ar. Series*, 1, 1, pl. 4.

Cols. XV, XVI, XVII : from Leumann, photogr. of Deccan College Collection, 1880-81, No. 57 : 7, XV, XVI ; 14 and 16, XV ; 18, XV, XVI, XVII ; 19 and 23, XV, XVI ; 24, XV ; 27, XV, XVI ; 35, 37 and 41, XVII, added from Leumann's *Viśeṣāvaśyaka*, pl. 35 ; 7, XVII, and 8, 9, 10, XV, and 12, 14, 16, XVI, added from photogr. of the Royal Asiatic Society's *Gaṇaratnamahodadhi*.

Cols. XVIII, XIX : from plates at *Vienna Oriental Congress, Aryan Section*, 111 ff.

Scale of the three plates = two-thirds of the facsimiles.

193. F. GI (CII. 3), 8f., and passim.

194. J. ASB. 60, 80 ff ; and IA. 21, 29 ff.

195. Fragments of inscriptions with northern characters of this period, from Valabhī, are preserved in the Museums of Bombay (the Branch of the Royal Asiatic Society) and Rājkot. *Cf.* also the sign-manuals on the Gurjara land-grants, J. RAS. 1865, 247 ff.

196. B. ESIP. 53, and plate 22 *a* ; IA. 18, 161, 172.

197. I agree with Hoernle, who considers certain portions of the new Godfrey Collection from Kashgar to be older than the Bower MS. ; J. ASB. 66, 258.

198. Kielhorn, *Report on Sanskrit MSS.*, 1880-81, 1ff. ; Peterson, *Second Report*, Appendix I, and *Third Report*, Appendix I.

199. J. RAS. 1895, 217.

200. *Cf.* B. ESIP. 20, 53 ff. ; Fleet in EI. 3, 2.

201. *Cf.* Hoernle, J.ASB. 60, 81, who mentions *ṣa* alone, because his remarks refer also to the type discussed below in § 23.

202. SB. WA. 122, XI, 32 ff.

203. IA. 9, 168 ff. ; in my opinion the era is not, as Fleet holds in *Gupta Inscriptions* (CII. 3), Introduction, 95, 177 ff., that of A. D. 318-19, but one peculiar to the Nepalese, the exact beginning of which has still to be determined.

204. C.MG. pl. 25 ; the era may be that of the Guptas.

205. IA. 18, 225.

206. According to Fleet, IA. 19, 227 f., the kings of Uccakalpa probably dated according to the Cedi or Kalacuri era of A. D. 249.

207. EI. 2, 210.

208. J. ASB. 58, pl. 2-4 ; J. RAS. 1889, pl. 1-4, and p. 84 ff., and 1898, pl. 2.

209. Haug, *Wedischer Accent*, 64.

210. *Cf.* facsimile in F. GI (CII. 3), No, 61.

211. J. ASB. 60, 88 ff.

212. J. ASB. 60, 92 f ; WZKM. 5, 104 f. The discovery of an inscription of the 7th. century with mostly tripartite *ya*, EI. 4, 29, makes a modification of Hoernle's argumentation necessary, but does not invalidate his final result

213. *Anecd. Oxon.*, *Aryan Series*, 1, 3, 76.

214. *Cf.* also the facsimiles in F. GI (CII. 3), Nos. 20, 24, 33, 34, 36, 37, 47, 51, 70 75, and of the seal of Kumāragupta II, J. ASB. 58, 84.

215. *Cf.* also the facsimiles in F. GI (CII. 3), Nos. 72, 76, 78, 79, 80.

216. See, e.g., Tod, *Annals of Rājasthan*, 1, 700 ff., Madras edition.

217. F. GI (CII. 3), 274.

218. *India*, 1, 173 (Sachau).

219. *Anecd. Oxon.*, *Ar. Series*, 1, 3, 64.

220. *Cf.* also the facsimiles in IA. 9, 168 ff., Nos. 4-10, 12 ; Bendall, *Journey in Nepāl*, 72, Nos. 1, 2 ; and Hoernle's remarks in J.ASB. 60, 85.

221. F. GI CII. 3), 201, 284 ; EI. 3, 323, note 1.

222. J. ASB. 6, 778, pl. 41.

223. EI. 1, 76. In confirmation of my explanation of the phrase, *kuṭilānyakṣarāṇi viduṣā*, "by him who knows crooked letters", i.e., letters difficult to read, I would point to Vikramāṅkacarita, 18, 42, where we have the statement that queen Sūryamatī did not allow herself to be cheated, *kāyasthaiḥ kuṭila-lipibhiḥ*, "by writers using crooked alphabets".

224. *Cf.* his remarks on inscriptions of this class, IA. 17, 308 ; 19, 55 ; 20, 123 ; 21, 169 ; EI. 1, 179 ; 2, 117, 160.

225. *Cf.* for this and the preceding varieties, the facsimiles at IA. 2, 258 ; 5, 180 ; 9, 174 ff., Nos. 11, 13, 14, 15 ; 10, 81 ; 17, 310 ; 19 58 ; Bendall *Journey in Nepāl*, pl. 10, 11, 13 ; EI. 1, 179 ; 4, 29 ; C.ASR. 17, pl. 9 ; and the autotypes of coins in C. CMI. pl. 3, Nos. 7-14 ; pl. 6, No. 20 ; and pl. 7.

226. According to Fleet, IA. 18, 231, "transitional type from which the North-Indian Nāgarī alphabet was soon after developed".

227. According to Fleet, IA. 15, 106, "North-Indian Nāgarī".

228. *Cf.* IA. 17, 308.

229. Bendall, *Cat. Cambr. Buddh. MSS. from Nepāl*, XLI ff. ; *Anec. Oxon.*, *Ar. Series*, 3, 71 ff.

230. S. Lévi, JA. 1894, II, 55 ff.

231. EI. 1, 76; IA. 6, 48.

232. IA. 6, 59; 11, 158; cf. also facsimiles in EI. 8, 108, and IA. 14, 200.

233. Cf. also facsimile, IA. 16, 174.

234. The genuineness of the earlier Umetā and Bagumrā plates (IA. 7, 68; 17, 199) is disputed (IA. 18, 91 ff.); their Nāgarī letters have been given in *Anec. Oxon., Ar. Series*, 1, 8, pl. 6.

235. See facsimiles, J. RAS. 1865, 247 ff.; EI. 5, 40; IA. 5, 118; 18, 78; and the remarks in SB. WA. 135, 8, 2.

236. IA. 11, 105.

237. IA. 18, 285; 20, 421.

238. Cf., e.g., the Ambarnāth inscription, J.BBRAS. 9, 219; 12, 384; IA. 19, 242.

239. IA. 16, 15 ff.

240. Cf. also the facsimiles, IA. 7, 304; 9, 32; 14, 141; 17, 122; J.BBRAS. 18, 1; 15, 386; EI. 8, 272, 800 f., 806 f.

241. Cf. the facsimiles, EI. 8, 88 f., 152 ff.; B. ESIP. pl. 30, and the alphabet, pl. 20

242. B. ESIP. 52 (where the Nandināgarī is derived erroneously from the Siddhamātṛkā), and pl. 21.

243. IA. 15, 140.

244. See the facsimile. IA. 18, 64.

245. See above, § 21, note 192; cf. also the facsimiles at IA. 12, 250, 268; 16,202: EI. 1, 122; J.BBRAS. 18, 289.

246. See above § 21, note 192; Cf. also the facsimiles at IA. 6, 58, 54; 8, 40; 12, 126, 202; 15, 86; 16, 208; 18, 84; EI. 1, 216, 316; 8, 50.

247. See above § 21, note 192; cf., e.g., the facsimiles at IA. 11, 72; 17, 226; 18, 180.

248. Kielhorn, *Report on Sanskrit MSS. for 1880-81*, pp. vii, 87; J.RAS. 1895, 247, 504; cf. also the facsimiles, *Pal. Soc., Or. Series*, pl. 1, 2, 8, 58; *Cat. Berlin Sansk. und Prākṛ. Hdschft.*, Band 2, 8, pl. 1. In the marginal glosses of the *Viśeṣāvaśyaka* and other MSS. frequently appear other cursive alphabets; see Leumann's edition, pl. 85.

249. Bendall, *Cat. Buddh. Sanskrit MSS. from Nepāl*, pp. xxiv f., 1 f.; cf. also the facsimile, *Pal. Soc., Or. Series*, pl. 16. According to Oldenberg (letter of 7th April, 1897), the alphabet of these Nepalese MSS. is the so-called Lañjā script, in which is written a complete MS. of the *Saddharmapuṇḍarīka*, preserved in St. Petersburg.

250. Cf. for this paragraph, Bendall, *Cat. Cambridge Buddhist MSS. from Nepāl*, xliii-li; *Anec. Oxon., Aryan Series*, 1, 8, 78-87.

251. *Anec. Oxon., Aryan Series*, 1, 8, 70.

252 See above § 28, p. 69.

253. See above § 16, D, 1, 2; and pl. II, 2, II-X.

254. Communication by letter.

255. An exception is, e. g., the Jhālrāpāṭan inscription, IA. 5, 180, which shows throughout the old dagger-shaped form.

256. EI. 2, 297.

257. See above § 19, B, 12.

258. J. ASB. 60, 87.

259. J. ASB. 60, 85.

260. Cf. the facsimile of the Jhālrāpāṭan inscription, IA. 5, 180; See also IA. 18, 162.

261. This is the regular form since the 9th. century.

262. *Anec. Oxon, Ar. Series*, 1, 8, 87.

263. F. GI (CII. 8), 202; Kielhorn, EI. 1, 179 f.

264. Cf. for this paragraph, *Kashmir Report* (J. BBRAS. 12), 31; J. ASB. 60, 88.

265. C. CMI. pl. 4, 5.

266. *Seventh Oriental Congress, Ar. Section*, 188; IA. 17, 83, 275.

267. SB. WA. cvii.

268. A good facsimile from a Śāradā MS. of the same period is found in the *Catalogue of the Berlin Sanskrit and Prākṛt MSS.*, Vol. 2, 8, pl. 2; an inferior one, from the India Office MS. 8176, together with a table of the letters and ligatures, in *Pal. Soc., Or. Ser.*, pl. 44.

269. SB. WA. cxvi, 584.

270. *Kashmir Report* (J.BBRAS. 12), 32; for the alphabet, see J.RAS. 1891, 362.

271. See above, § 24, C, 8.

272. EI. 1, 305 f.

273. EI. 2, 347.

274. Cf. Bendall, who slightly differs in *Cat. Sanskr. Buddhist MSS. from Nepāl*, xxxvi, and letter-press of *Pal. Soc., Or., Series*, pl. 81.

275 Both the triangle and the hook are found in the Gayā inscription, IA. 10, 342.

276. J.ASB. 41, pl. 1, 2.

277. Cf. the Gayā inscriptions in C.ASR. 8, pl. 37, No. 12; pl. 38, No. 13.

278. See the Mahoba inscription, C.ASR. 21, pl. 21.

279. Cf. the facsimiles of Bengālī MSS. in *Pal. Soc., Or. Series*, pl. 38, 82, 69; Rājendralāl Mitra, *Notices of Sanskrit MSS.*, Vol. 8, pl. 5, 6; Vols. 5 & 6; and the proto-Bengālī inscription, J.ASB. 48, 818, pl. 18.

280. Bendall, *Cat. Sanskr. Buddhist MSS. from Nepāl*, xxii ff.

281. *Op. cit.*, xxxv, xxxvii.

282. *Op. Cit.*, pl. 8, 4 ; *Berlin Oriental Congress, Indian Section*, pl. 2, 1.

283. *Pal. Soc., Or. Series* pl., 82 ; *Berlin Oriental Congress, Indian Section*, pl. 2, 2, 8.

284. For facsimiles of MSS. with Nepalese "hooked characters", See Bendall, *Cat. Sanskr. Buddhist MSS. from Nepāl*, pl. 8 ; *Pal. Soc., Or. Series*, pl. 43, 57 ; Cowell & Eggeling, *Cat. Buddhist MSS. of the Royal Asiatic Society*, J.RAS. 1876, 1 ff. ; for the alphabet, see Bendall, *op. cit.*, pl. 4 ; J. Klatt. de CCC Cāṇakyae sententiis.

285. *Cf.* also Fleet's remarks on ornamental characters, IA. 15, 864.

286. *Seventh Oriental Congress, Aryan Section*, 111 ff. ; and *Tenth Oriental Congress*, Part II, 151 ff.

287. Preparation of Plates VII and VIII :—

PLATE VII

Cuttings from facsimiles

Col. I : from F.GI (CII. 8), No. 5, pl. 8 B ; with *E* from No. 62, pl. 88, B.

Cols. II & III : from F. GI (CII. 8), No. 18, pl. 11.

Col. IV : from plate at IA. 7, 66.

Col. V : from plate at IA. 5, 205 ; with *A, Ā, U, ghā, dhau, hā, kṣa, ttā,* from plate at IA. 6, 9, and *nta* from plate at IA. 7, 68.

Col. VI : from F. GI (CII. 8), No. 88, pl. 24.

Col. VII : from F. GI (CII. 8) No. 89, pl. 25.

Col. VIII : from plate at EI. 2, 20, No. 1 ; with *I, na, ba, ñca, brā, lya,* from No. 8, at p. 22.

Col. IX : from plate at IA. 18, 78.

Col. X : from F.GI (CII. 8), No. 55, pl. 34 ; with *U* and *AU* from No. 41, pl. 27, and *Ū* from Ajaṇṭā No. 8, B. ASRWI. 4, pl. 57.

Col. XI : from F. GI (CII. 3), No. 56, pl. 85.

Col. XII : from plate at IA. 7, 85.

Col. XIII : from plate at IA. 7, 87 ; with *I, ṅśa, jye, ṇām, tsā,* from plate at IA. 6, 24.

Col. XIV : from plate at IA. 10, 58 ; with *Ā, U,* and *ccha* from plates at IA. 7, 161, and *kḷ* from plate at IA. 6, 72, and *lı* from plate at IA. 8, 44.

Col. XV : from plate at IA. 10, 104, Fleet's No. 94 ; with *Ī* (8, XV, *b*), *ṅge, śi,* and *li* from Fleet's Nos. 99, 100, plate at IA. 10, 164, and *lla* from Fleet's No. 95, plate at IA. 10, 104.

Col. XVI : from plates at IA. 8, 24 ff.

Col. XVII : from plate at IA. 18, 187.

Col. XVIII : from plates at IA. 8, 820.

Col. XIX : from plate at IA. 18, 128.

Col. XX : from plates at IA. 5, 50ff.

Col. XXI : from plates at IA. 5, 154 ff.

Col. XXII : from Hultzsch's SII. 2, pl. 10.

Col. XXIII : from Hultzsch's SII. 2, pl. 9.

Col. XXIV : from Hultzsch's SII. 2, pl. 11.

PLATE VIII

Cuttings from facsimiles.

Col. I : from plates at IA. 12, 158 ff.

Col. II : from plate at IA. 11, 126, Fleet's No. 128.

Col. III : from plates at IA. 12, 14.

Col. IV : from plates at IA. 18, 186 ff.

Col. V : from plates at IA. 7, 16.

Col. VI : from plates at IA. 14, 50 ff.

Col. VII : from plate at IA. 6, 188 ; with *A, U, cā,* and *ṭṭa* from plate at IA. 9, 75.

Col. VIII : from plates at IA. 11, 12ff.

Col. IX : from plate at EI. 8, 62.

Col. X : from plate at IA. 18, 275.

Col. XI : from plate at IA. 18, 144.

Col. XII : from plate at EI. 8, 18.

Col. XIII : from Hultzsch's SII. 2, pl. 18.

Col. XIV : from plate at EI. 8, 76.

Col. XV : from plate at EI. 8, 14.

Col. XVI : from Hultzsch's SII. 2, pl. 12.

Cols. XVII : XVIII : from Hultzsch's SII. 2, pl. 4.

Cols. XIX, XX : from plate at EI. 8, 72, the lower part.

Cols. XXI, XXII : from plate at EI. 8, 72, the upper part.

288. *Cf.* B. ESIP. 14.

289. IA. 20, 286.

290. B. ESIP. 48.

291 *Cf.* the facsimiles in F. GI (CII. 8), Nos. 5, 14, and 62, plates 8 B, 8, 38 B, and Fleet's remarks.

292. *Cf.* the facsimiles in F. GI (CII. 8), Nos. 88, 89, plates 24, 25 ; IA. 1, 17 ; 5, 204 ff. ; 6, 14 ff. ; 7, 66 ff. ; 8, 802 ; 9, 288 ; 14, 828 ; J. BBRAS. 11, 868 ; EI. 8, 820.

293. *Cf.* the facsimiles at J. RAS. 1865, 247 ; IA. 18, 78 ; (7, 62 ; 13, 116 ; 17, 200 ; disputed) ; EI. 2, 19ff.

294. *Cf.* the facsimiles at EI. 8, 52 ; IA. 7, 164 ; 8, 46 ; 9, 124 ; J. BBRAS. 16, 1 ; *Seventh Oriental Congress, Ar. Section*, 288 ; IA. 19, 810.

295. *Cf.* the facsimiles at B. ASRWI. No. 10, 58.

296. *Cf.* the facsimile at IA. 16, 98.

297. *Cf.* the facsimiles at IA. 12, 158 ; J. BBRAS. 16, 105 ; EI. 8, 56.

298. *Cf.* the facsimiles at B. ASRWI 4, pl. 55, 9 ; pl 58, 5 and 9 ; plates 59, 60 ; Vol. 5, pl. 51, 6 9.

299. Cf. the facsimiles in F. GI (CII. 3), No. 6, 17, 61, plates 4 A, 10, 38 A.

300. Cf. above § 21 end.

301. Cf., for instance, *likhitam*, facsimile at IA. 7, 72.

302 Transitional forms occur in the Calukya inscriptions.

303. Cf. facsimile at IA. 9, 124.

304. Cf. IA. 6, 10, and facsimile at 14, 328.

305. Cf. facsimile at J. ASB. 64, 1, plate 9, No. 2.

306. See also my remarks in IA. 6, 110, and below, §28, B.

307. F. GI(CII. 3), Nos. 2, 3, pl. 2, A. B.

308. *Op. cit.*, Nos. 40, 41, plates 26, 27.

309. *Op. cit.*, Nos. 53-56, plates 33, A. to 35; IA. 12, 239; B. ASRWI. 4, pl 56, No. 4; pl. 57, No. 3; EI. 3, 260; the earliest of them belong in Bhagvānlāl Indrāji's and my opinion to the 5th., according to Fleet to the 7th., century

310. F.GI (CII. 3), No. 81, pl. 45; according to Fleet from the 8th. or 9th. century; according to Kielhorn, EI. 4, 258, undoubtedly from the 8th.

311. See Fleet, IA. 21, 93; of the some type is, according to an impression presented to me by L. Rice, the Tāḷgund (Sthānakundura) Praśasti of Kubja from the reign of Śāntivarman, Ep. Carn. 7, Sk. 176 (and EI. 8).

312. Bergaigne-Barth, *Inscriptions Sanskrit du Campā et du Cambodge*, 2, 23; the Campā inscriptions show the northern *ka* and *ra* without curves at the end.

313. Fleet and Kielhorn assume that the writers by mistake put *na* for *ta* and vice versa.

314. Cf. facsimiles of Śālaṅkāyana inscriptions at B.ESIP. pl. 24; IA 5, 176; EI. 4, 144; at Kadamba inscriptions at IA. 6, 23ff.; 7, 33ff.; J. BBRAS. 12,300; of Western Calukya inscriptions at IA, 6, 72, 75; 8, 44, 237; 9, 100; 10, 58; 19, 68; and of Eastern Calukya inscriptions at B. ESIP. pl. 27.

315. B. ESIP. 16, pl. 1.

316. Fleet, IA. 20, 94.

317. *Academy*, 1895, 229.

318. See Fleet's dates of the Calukyas, EI. 3, table at p 2; IA. 20, 95 ff.

319. B. ESIP. pl. 1.

320. Cf. also the facsimile at IA. 6, 72, and B.ESIP. pl. 27.

321. IA. 6, 72.

322. IA. 8, 44.

323. See the plates at IA. 8, 241; EI. 6, 6.

324. Cf. the facsimiles at IA. 6, 86, 88; 7, 300; J. BBRAS. 16, 223 ff.

325. Cf. the facsimiles at IA. 10, 61 ff., 104, 166, 170; 11, 126; 20, 70; Ep. Carn. 3, 80, 87, 92 (for the last of these See also EI. 6, 54).

326. See the facsimile at IA. 14, 200.

327. Cf. the facsimiles at IA. 12, 92; 13, 214, 248; EI. 3,194.

328. EI. 3,162 f.

329. EI. 3,163.

330. Burgess and Fleet, Pāli, Sanskrt. and Old-Canarese inscriptions, Nos. 271, 214; see also for the Ganga record, IA. 6,102.

331. Cf. also the facsimiles at IA. 9, 74; 14, 56; EI. 3, 26, 88, 194, 228; Ep. Carn. 3, 116, 121; B. ASRWI. No. 10, 100; and J. RAS. 1891, 135 (the original of Prinsep's Kistna alphabet, which is archaic and retrograde: *A*, *ka*, *ra*, *la*).

332. IA. 8, 241; EI. 6,6.

333. Cf. this paragraph B. ESIP. 15 ff.

334. IA. 13,274; 16,133.

335. EI. 3,128.

336. IA. 13, 120; Cf. 16,131 f.

337. EI. 3,132.

338. The words *śita-dvaya* probably have been left out by mistake after *saṃvatsara*.

339. IA. 14, 10 f.; Hultzsch's undoubtedly correct reading of the date has been adopted by Fleet in his *Dynasties of the Kanarese Districts, Bombay Gazetteer*, Vol. I, Part II, p. 297, note 3, the printed sheets of which I owe to the author's courtesy. Fleet declares this inscription, as well as those represented in plate VIII, Cols. X, XII to be suspicious,—in my opinion without sufficient reasons.

340. EI. 3, 220.

341. The use of northern characters is proved by the Buguḍa plates, EI. 3, 41; cf. also B.ESIP. 58, and plate 22 *b*.

342. IA. 5, 50, 154; cf. B.ESIP. 86, note 2.

343. I owe the facsimiles of this inscription and of those used for pl. VII, Col. XXIV, and pl. VIII, Col XII to Hultzsch's kindness; see now his SII, 2, part 3.

344. IA. 9, 100, No. 32, 102, No. 35; 13, 48; EI. 1, 397.

345. *Dynasties of the Kanarese Districts, Bombay Gazetteer*, Vol. I, Part II, p. 328.

346. Hultzsch, SII. 1, 144 ff.; Fleet *op. cit.* (preceding note), 322 f.

347. Fleet, *op. cit.*, 329 f.

348. Fleet, *op. cit.*, 323 ff.

349. EI. 3, 75.

350. EI. 3, 3.

851. Cf. facsimiles at IA. 6, 142; 8, 274; 9, 46 (EI. 8, 79 f.); EI. 3, 228; Ep. Carn. 3, 166; II. 2, pl. 2; the last inscription and the last but two are older than the 11th. century.

852. B. ESIP. pl. 18.

853. Caldwell, *Comparative Grammar of the Dravidian Languages*, 21-27.

854. Differently Burnell, ESIP. 44, 47 ff., who considers the Vaṭṭeḻuttu as independent of the Brāhmī, but likewise of Semitic origin, and declares the Tamil alphabet to be the result of a Brahmanical adaptation of the Grantha letters to the phonetical system of the Vaṭṭeḻuttu. This view has already been characterised "as hardly in accordance with the facts" by Caldwell, *op. cit.*, 9.

855. SII. 1, 147; cf. 2, pl. 12; the characters of the Vallam Cave inscription, *op. cit.*, 2, pl. 10, fully agree.

856. SII. 2, pls. 14, 15.

857. Cf. the facsimiles of 10th. and 11th. centuries at EI. 3, 284; SII. 2, pls. 2-4; of the 15th. century at SII. 2, pl. 5; uncertain at SII. 2, pl. 8; IA. 6, 142; alphabet, B. ESIP. pls. 18, 19.

858. Cf. Veṅkayya, EI 3, 278 ff.

859. *Madras Journ Lit. Soc.* 13, 2, 1; IA. 3, 333; B.ESIP. pl. 32 *a*; EI. 3, 72; alphabet, IA. 1, 229; B. ESIP. pl. 17.

860. IA. 20, 292.

861. IA. 1, 229; B. ESIP. 49; disputed by Hultzsch, IA. 20, 289.

862. EI. 3, 67.

863. Cf. above, § 25, note 270.

864. Cf. E. C. Bayley, *The Genealogy of the Modern Numerals*, J. ASB (n. s.), 14, 335 ff.; 15, 1 ff.

865. The signs of col. XIV have been drawn according to S. NEI, 8, pl. 1 (JA. 1890, I, pl. 15); J.ASB. 58, pl. 10; Fleet's photograph of the Taxila copperplate (EI. 4, 56); and a gelatine copy of the Wardak vase, kindly presented by Oldenberg.

866. J. RAS. 20, 228.

867. Thus Cunningham, Senart, *op. cit.*, 17, reads 84, doubting the existence of 200 (which, however, is plain in the autotype of J.ASB. 58, pl. 10), while Barth reads 284. There is at least one unpublished inscription with 200, and, according to a communication from Bloch, also one with 300.

868. Drawn according to Burgess' impression of Shāhbāzgarhi edicts I-III, XIII.

869. B. ESIP. 64; J. ASB 32, 150.

870. *Nabatäische Inschriften*, 96 f.

871. *Corp. Inscr. Sem. P. Aram.*, 145 A (pointed out by Euting).

872. *Palaeographical Society, Or. Ser.*, pl. 68.

873. Cf. Bhagvānlāl, IA. 6, 42 ff.; B. ESIP. 59 ff., and pl. 23; E. C. Bayley, *On the Genealogy of the Modern Numerals*, J. ASB (n. s.), 14, 335 ff.; 15, 1 ff.

874. J. BBRAS. 5, 85, and pl. 18; P. IA. 2, 60 ff.; C. ASR. 1, XLII, and J. ASB. 33, 38; J. BBRAS. 8, 225 ff; the results of the last article belong chiefly to Bhagvānlāl Indrāji, though his name is not mentioned.

875. Cf. below, §34, B. The latest epigraphic date in letter-numerals is probably the Nevār year 259 in Bendall's *Journey in Nepāl*, 81, No. 6; cf. also F. GI (CII. 3), 209, note 1.

876. See Hoernle, *The Bower MS.*; WZKM, 7,260 ff. The Bower MS. occasionally has the decimal 8.

877. Cf. Bhagvānlāl's table, IA. 6, 42 f.; Kielhorn, *Report on the Search for Sanskrit MSS.*, *1880-81*, VIII. ff.; Peterson, *First Report*, 57 f., and *Third Report*, App. I, passim; Leumann, Śīlāṅka's *Commentary on the Viśeṣāvaśyaka* (especially table 35); Cowell and Eggeling, *Cat. Sanskr. Buddhist MSS.*, 52 (J.RAS. 1876); Bendall, *Cat. Cambridg Sanskrit Buddhist MSS*, LII. ff., and table of numerals In Bendall's Nos. 1049 and 1161, the letter-numerals are also used for dates. The latest date in letter-numerals from Nepāl (Bendall's table of numerals) is A. D. 1583. Letter-numerals are usually only found in Jaina palm-leaf MSS. up to about A. D. 1450; but the Berlin paper MS. No. 1709 (*Weber Verzeichniss d. Skt. und Prāk. Hdschrft.*, 2, 1,268; cf. D. WA. 87, 250) shows some traces of them.

878. Bendall, J.RAS. 1896, 789 ff.

879. Cf. J.RAS. 1889, 128.

880. IA. 6, 44; Kielhorn, *Report for 1880-81*, X; Peterson, *First Report*, 57.

881. Kielhorn, loc. cit.; Bendall, *Catalogue*, LIII.

882. Cf. facsimile in EI. 3. 133 and see the Additions and Corrections of that volume; the signs have been given in pl. IX, col. XV, under 2, 8, 8 *b*, 100 *a*. For other cases of mixtures, see F.GI (CII.3), 292, and IA. 14, 351, where the date is, however, 800 4 9 = 849.

883. Oral information.

884. IA. 6, 47.

885. *Preparation of Plate IX*, A. Cols. XIX-XXVI :—

Col. XIX : from facsimiles in Hoernle's *The Bower MS.*

Cols. XX-XXIII, and XXVI : cuttings from Bendall's table of Numerals, Nos. 1049, 1702, 866, 1648, 1683.

Col. XXIV : drawn according to the tables of Bhagvānlāl, Kielhorn, and Leumann.

Col. XXV : drawn from the same sources ; but 8, 9, 100 are cuttings from Zachariae's photograph of the Sāhasāṅkacarita of the *Royal Asiatic Society*.

886. For this *pha*, cf. plate VI, 86, V.

887. Common also in the Bower MS. Peterson's *gha* is due to a misreading of the old *tha*.

888. Peterson's *rghu* is a misreading.

889. *Preparation of Plate IX, A, Cols. I-XVIII* :—

Col. I : the 4, cutting from Burgess's facsimile of the Kālsī edict XIII, EI. 2, 465 ; the 6, 50, 200 drawn according to facsimiles of the Sāhsārām and Rūpnāth edicts, IA. 6, 155 ff.

Col. II : cuttings from facsimile of the Śiddāpura edict, EI. 3, 138.

Col. III : cuttings from facsimiles of Nānāghāṭ inscriptions, B. ASRWI. 5, pl. 51.

Col. IV : cuttings from facsimiles of Nāsik inscriptions, B. ASRWI. 4, pl. 52, Nos. 5, 9, 18, 19 ; pl. 53, Nos. 12-14 : the 70 drawn according to the Girnār Praśasti, B. ASRWI. 2, pl. 14.

Col. V : drawn according to the facsimiles of Kṣatrapa coins, J. RAS. 1890, pl. at 639.

Cols. VI, VII : cuttings from facsimiles at EI. 1, 381 ff. ; 2, 201 ff.

Col. VIII : cuttings from facsimiles at B.ASRSI. 1, pl. 62, and EI. 1, 2 ff.

Cols. IX, X : cuttings from facsimiles at F. GI(CII.3), Nos. 2, 3, 5, 7 9, 11, 19, 28, 26, 59, 63, 70, 71.

Col. XI : cuttings from facsimiles at F.GI (CII. 3), Nos. 38, 39 ; IA. 6, 9 ff., and other Valabhi inscriptions.

Col. XII : drawn according to facsimile at J.BBRAS. 16, 108.

Cols. XIII, XIV : drawn according to facsimiles at IA. 9, 164 ff.

Col. XV : drawn according to facsimiles at IA. 18, 120 ff. ; EI. 3, 127 ff.

Col. XVI : cuttings from facsimiles at F.GI (CII. 3), Nos. 40, 41, 55, 56, 81.

Col. XVII : cuttings from facsimiles at IA. 15, 112, 141.

Col. XVIII : drawn according to facsimile at J.ASB. 40, pl. 2.

Cuttings reduced by one-third.

390. Probably to be read thus ; not as a modification of *phra* or *phu*.

391. Thus Bayley doubtfully ; for the ū of the sign in IV, B, cf. *nū*, pl. III, 25, 6.

392. Earliest instance in the inscription of Mahānāman, F.GII (CII.3), No. 71 ; 200 in col. X.

393. Cf. also the date of the Gujarāt Calukya inscription, *Seventh Oriental Congress*, *Aryan Section*, 211 ff. ; and the facsimile at J.BBRAS. 16, 1 ff. and the Valabhi form at EI. 3, 320, 1, 14, where a *śa* of the period mutilated on the left is used ; and the date of the Koṭa inscription IA. 14, 351, with a distinct *śa* of the 9th. century. The form *su* occurs in a Western inscription lately found at Udepur by G. H. Ojha, in the numeral *sū-u* or *sū-ā*, =800.

394. IA. 6, 143.

395. B.ESIP. 65, Note 1.

396. Cf. Hoernle's explanation, *Seventh Oriental Congress*, *Aryan Section*, 132 ; IA. 17, 35.

397. IA. 17, 36.

398. *Vāsavadattā* (ed F. E. Hall), p. 182.

399. Cf. facsimiles at EI. 2, 19 ff. ; and see F.GI (CII. 3), 209, note 1.

400. The apparent difference in 6 is due to a fault of the impression.

401. Preparation of Plate IX, B, Cols. III-XIII (for cols. I, II, see the text above) : all hand drawn :—

Col. III : from facsimiles of Rāṣṭrakūṭa inscriptions at Kanheri, Nos. 15, 43 A, B.

Col. IV : from facsimiles of Rāṣṭrakūṭa copper-plate from Torkhede, EI. 3, 56.

Col. V : the 3 and 6 from an impression of the Haḍḍālā copper-plate (IA. 12, 190) ; the 4, 7, 9, 0 from facsimile of the Asnī inscription, IA. 16, 174 ; the 5 and 8 from facsimile of the Morbī copper-plate, IA. 2, 257.

Col. VI : from facsimile of the Sāvantvāḍī copper-plate, IA. 12, 266.

Col. VII : from facsimile of the Calukya copper-plate, IA. 12, 202.

Col VIII : the 1, 3, 8, from the Gayā inscription, IA. 10, 342 ; the 5 from CMG plates 28, A.

Cols. IX, X : Hoernle's Bakhshālī figures.

Cols. XI, XII : from Bendall's table of numeral in *Cat. Cambridge Sanskr. Buddhist MSS.*

Col. XIII : from B. ESIP. pl. 23, Telugu and Kanarese numerals, 11th. century.

402. W. IS. 8, 166 f.

403. The abbreviations mark the sources from which the words have been collected as follows :—

Bakh.—the *Bakhshālī MS.*, Hoernle, 180.

Ber.—Berunī's *India*, Sachau, 1, 178.

Bro.—C. P. Brown's list, as quoted by Burnell, ESIP. 77 f.

Bur.—Burnell's additions, ESIP. 77 f.